MODE **CHESS STRATEGY**

MODERN
CHESS STRATEGY

BY

EDWARD LASKER

DAVID McKAY COMPANY, INC.
New York

First published 1951

19 18

ISBN: 0-679-14022-0
Manufactured in the United States of America

PREFACE TO FIRST EDITION

THIS volume is a modern version of *Chess Strategy*, my first-born book, on which I laboured almost forty years ago. Although that book had a success which transcended my most optimistic expectations, it has long been to me the source of conflicting emotions. On the one hand I was flattered by its popularity. On the other, I grew more and more perturbed at some of my statements, as the years separated me from that brash youngster who wrote the book.

I am glad to have an opportunity of correcting those statements and bringing up to date my attempt at a scientific exposition of the laws governing the manoeuvres on the chess board. There is no doubt in my mind that the developments of the past twenty-five years have more or less outmoded that attempt.

The first impetus to write *Chess Strategy* I received while studying engineering at the Institute of Technology in Berlin and simultaneously studying chess at the Café Kaiserhof and Café Bauer, where at one time or another every illustrious chess master of that period was to be found. They were certainly a colourful lot, and I much preferred them to some of my college professors. There was one-eyed Teichmann who—Polyphemus-like—reigned over the daily assembly of chess fans, seeing more with his one eye than most chess masters did with two; there were Emanuel and Berthold Lasker, who—while never playing a game themselves—would often engage in a fascinating analysis of tournament games which occupied the interest of the day; and tall, bearded, multi-lingual Ossip Bernstein, who seemed to commute between Petersburg and Paris and who would drop in frequently and tell of strange developments in Russia, where two schoolboys, Alekhine and Niemzovich, whom no one ought to take lightly because they were so young, had started what appeared to be an entirely new school of chess.

In absorbed attention at the feet of these masters, I learned things I had never read in a book. In those days most chess books were mere collections of countless opening variations which had been tried in master tournaments. As I found out much later, many of these variations were faulty, and an attempt to memorize them was usually waste of time.

I became aware even more strongly of the sorry inadequacy of these books as I compared them with textbooks accessible to me at the University on my favourite subjects, mathematics and physics. Thus, gradually I conceived the plan for a book in which I would develop general laws governing the manoeuvres on the chess board, just as there were general laws governing the behaviour of elements in physics and engineering.

The analogy between chess and physics fascinated me from the start. The chessmen were obviously distinguished from each other in value only on account of their ability to contribute more or less fighting force toward achieving the object of the game; and this fighting force varied according to the 'potential energy' stored in each piece by the player, to be released at the right moment into 'kinetic energy.'

Six months of enforced rest after an accident gave me leisure to develop these ideas on 'chess kinetics', and I wrote *Chess Strategy*.

Whatever its demerits—obvious to masters of the game—the phenomenal sale of the book showed that it filled a definite need. Apparently students of the game quite generally shared my dislike of that time-honoured teaching method which offers analysed variations for memorization, and preferred the appeal to their understanding; by an explanation of the motives behind these variations, and the demonstration that they all stem from a few fundamental principles, the reader was freed from reliance upon memory.

A grasp of these principles, as applied to the chess board, I still consider necessary and sufficient for the intelligent conduct of a game of chess. It will bring easy victory to the beginner competing against other beginners who do not have that grasp; and likewise it will assure the advanced player of marked superiority over others of comparable experience, who have not yet learned to judge every move from the standpoint of these strategic generalities.

Of course, a textbook on chess must not confine itself to the derivation of general principles, but must explicitly illustrate the proper method of their application to the three phases of the battle—the opening, the middle-game and the end-game. In *Chess Strategy* I did this only within the limits of what is to-day called 'classical chess'; for no one then dreamed that an entirely 'modern' note could be introduced into the conduct of the game.

Modern chess—or, as the jocular Tartakower calls it, 'hyper-modern chess'—reared its head shortly after the First World War, at about the same time that modern art and modern music appeared on the scene. That such a thing as modern chess should be possible was perhaps somewhat of a surprise even to those who were quite aware of a certain parallelism between the creative activity of a chess master and that of an artist or scientist.

As in art, the new school was first considered a mere grotesque aberration—an affectation, dictated by a desire to be different, that one might smile at and then forget. But soon even the most prejudiced had to admit that the ideas behind the bizarre-looking new openings could not be disposed of with a smile of condescension.

Naturally, I toyed for quite some time with the thought of rewriting *Chess Strategy* so as to embrace modern chess. When I discussed the idea with Reti, one of its fathers, he surprised me by contending that those general principles, which were acknowledged as governing classical chess, would not hold for the modern developments of the game. He felt that these developments were the creations of chess artists rather than chess scientists and, as such, could not be subject to the restrictions general strategic laws would impose. I disagreed with Reti's view then, and I still disagree with it to-day. I consider it a logical necessity that a general strategic principle which has proved valid in classical chess must hold in modern chess as well. All that Reti might have claimed was that the classical *interpretation* of the strategic laws did not hold in modern chess.

That interpretation had indeed been too rigid, particularly in its definitions concerning the control of centre-squares, and in its evaluation of the time element during the opening stage of the game. However, I felt certain that a more subtle interpretation would include even the most modern methods of play, and would help a player to find his way in *any* position.

In rewriting *Chess Strategy* I have again thought especially of the player who has little or no opportunity to pit himself against masters, but who wants to understand the reasoning behind the master's moves and learn to apply it to his own games.

I believe the reader of this book will rapidly improve his prowess over the board, no matter what his present playing strength. I hope he will also carry with him that sense of enjoyment which any person of artistic or scientific sensitivity experiences when he sees the power of a simple general law manifest itself in an almost effortless solution of difficulties which had seemed unsurmountable.

EDWARD LASKER

NEW YORK, 1950

PREFACE TO THIRD EDITION

AFTER the last war chess activity increased tremendously, in Europe as well as in North and South America. International masters' tournaments followed each other in close succession, and new opening variations made their appearance which became the study of intense analyses by experts everywhere. These innovations did not really offer anything basically new, but represented merely tactical refinements of lines of play introduced some fifty years ago by the great masters of the game—particularly Niemzovich, Alekhine, Reti, and Tartakower—who are generally referred to by the collective name, 'The Modern School'. None of the older masters had ever questioned that early occupation of centre squares with Pawns was the most important thing to strive for in any opening, because this will secure superior mobility for the pieces. The moderns argued that Pawns in the centre are often apt to prove excellent targets to shoot at, and they actually tried to provoke their early advance. They won their argument in a good many cases.

In this revised edition of *Modern Chess Strategy* I have included some of the most important new opening lines in discussing recent master games. As in the earlier editions, these games are intended merely as examples of the proper application of the general chess-strategic principles, the subject with which this book is mainly concerned. A detailed knowledge of openings is of value only for players competing in serious tournaments. It requires the study of books comprising a thousand or more pages, and for an amateur this is just a waste of time. What he needs is the proper guidance to the understanding of the principles of chess strategy which govern good play in *any* opening, middle-game or ending.

I am sure that the unhurried reader of this book will come away with the realization that these general principles, to which I constantly refer, form a sound basis on which he can build when left to his own devices. I cannot urge him too strongly to accept these principles as his guides, rather than trying to remember what he has seen others play, masters included. He will neither completely understand the motives behind the moves of the master nor equal his virtuosity in extricating himself from situations which may have merely been the unwelcome result of an improvisation.

The student will naturally lose many a game, even when trying to let general principles guide his every move. But each game he loses will help him clarify his interpretation of those principles and thus improve his playing strength. Finding himself in a hopeless position after unthinkingly adopting an opening he has seen in a master-game would merely leave him puzzled.   In chess as in life, to rise above the average one must have the courage of his own convictions, and one must shun uncomprehending imitation—even though he be imitating the great!

EDWARD LASKER

NEW YORK, 1967

CONTENTS

CONTENTS

PART II

PRINCIPLES OF CHESS STRATEGY

CONTENTS

ILLUSTRATIVE GAMES

CONTENTS

MODERN
CHESS STRATEGY

INTRODUCTION

THE beginner who thinks he can play a game of chess after learning how the men move is like a soldier who believes he can lead an army after he has learned how to shoot. No matter how great his strategic gift, he cannot exploit it as long as he is not thoroughly familiar with the tasks of the various branches of the armed forces, and with the tactical possibilities arising from their proper co-operation.

Likewise, a chess player cannot form an idea as to what he may expect from his men until he has acquainted himself thoroughly with the tasks each of them is capable of performing, and with the ways in which several of them can co-operate toward winning the game.

Since checkmating the King is the final object, the logical manner in which to conduct this investigation is to ascertain first what minimum superiority of fighting forces is required to compel a checkmate against the lone King, then to examine checkmating procedures against a King who still has defensive forces at his disposal, and finally to study the circumstances and the methods which enable a player to obtain a winning superiority.

In trying to gain this knowledge in a purely empirical manner, the beginner would prolong unduly what might be called his chess adolescence—that period of evolution from wild, chaotic play to mature, reasoned restraint, through which every chess player has to find his way. The length of time required for such development naturally depends upon the special gifts of the student, but it is greatly influenced by the manner in which he pursues his study. Most beginners do not trouble very much about any particular plan, but rush into the turmoil of actual play without a vestige of preparation.

It is obvious that this method cannot produce satisfactory results. The play of a beginner is planless, because he has too many plans. He lacks the capacity for subordinating all his combinations to one leading idea. Most beginners seem to be guided—or rather misguided —by a strange thought, which apparently comes to them quite naturally. At first they storm forward with their Pawns, showing no appreciation of the fighting power of the pieces. Conscious of the inferiority of the Pawns, the beginner does not conclude that it must be advantageous to play with his own pieces, but he is chiefly concerned with attacking the opposing pieces with his Pawns in the hope of capturing them. His aim is not to utilize his own strength, but to weaken that of the other player. Moreover, most of his combinations are made with the thought that his opponent will not see through them; nor does he stop to scrutinize his adversary's intentions. Only after most of his

Pawns are gone, do his pieces get their chance. He has a great liking for the Queen and the Knight, the former because of her tremendous mobility, the latter, on account of its peculiar step which seems particularly adapted to take the enemy by surprise. That is why in beginners' games we can frequently see numberless moves by the Queen, and reckless excursions by a Knight into the opponent's camp; and when the other pieces join in the fray, fantastic combinations follow each other in bewildering sequence. Captures of pieces are planned which can easily retreat to safe positions, or mating attacks undertaken with totally inadequate forces against a strongly protected King, with serene indifference to the opponent's threats.

Naturally, the beginner is much surprised by the outcome of these disjointed combinations, which is always so different from what he had planned; but such surprises afford him great enjoyment as long as he keeps his sense of humour—the result of the adventure being a lost game in almost every case—and a few dozen games of this type represent an experience which is not altogether without value.

After certain dispositions of the pieces have proved his undoing time and again, the beginner develops the perception of *threats*. He sees dangers one or two moves ahead and thus reaches the second stage of his development, characterized by the greater accuracy of his combinations and better evaluation of his forces. In this second stage he will husband with greater care not only his pieces but even his Pawns, and his playing strength will increase steadily. However—and this is the drawback—only his power of *combination* will improve. Unless a player be exceptionally gifted, he will learn only after years of practice—if at all—what is usually termed *positional play*. By this term is meant the conduct of the opening in such a way as to lay the foundation for a favourable middle-game, and the treatment of the middle-game so that the exigencies of the end-game are constantly kept in mind. Such play does not comprise a series of incoherent combinations, but concerns itself with the more lasting characteristics of a position, which result from the skeletal structure of the Pawn formation and guide all combinative efforts in the right direction.

This brings me to the substance of my subject. It is mainly the understanding of *sound positional play* which I seek to convey to the reader. This understanding distinguishes the player who may become a master from him who will never reach that stage, no matter what his combinative virtuosity may be.

Naturally, the benefit the reader will derive from the contents of this book will increase as his playing strength develops. That is why in rereading some of the chapters the student will find much, the full import of which has previously escaped him.

Anyone intending to compete in chess tournaments will naturally have to devote some time to the study of more detailed analyses of openings and endings than could have been incorporated in this book without exceeding its scope. For this purpose I believe *Modern Chess Openings* and *Basic Chess Endings* by Reuben Fine will serve better than any other textbooks.

Collections of master games, annotated by masters, will also prove of great help, particularly when the games are discussed by the players themselves. Outstanding in this field are Tarrasch's and Alekhine's collections of their best games. Very interesting and instructive, though less accurate in many details, are the books containing the games of the various Master Tournaments played during the last twenty-five years. Their study, particularly in so far as middle-game problems are concerned, will be much facilitated by a perusal of Niemzovich's *My System* and Emanuel Lasker's *A Manual of Chess*.

It should be understood that no amount of reading will make a chess master of any player unless he has the opportunity of competing with masters in match or tournament play. Considerable experience of this type is needed to develop the 'positional instinct' which enables a player to make the proper selection when two or more moves seem to be equally good from the point of view of general strategic laws, or to decide which strategic principle is the most important to follow in positions in which several of them appear to be applicable, pointing to different continuations.

Even the strongest player in the world will not always make the best choice, and he will therefore lose a game here and there. This does not make the winner of the game a better player. The class of a player is shown only by the record he makes against masters over a period of years.

The modern master's equipment for tournament and match play must necessarily include a thorough knowledge of contemporary analyses of opening play, because the time limitation imposed on the players would place too great a handicap on anyone attempting to find his way through a variation familiar to his opponent but unknown to himself.

The amount of memorizing involved in this type of preparation is something the average chess player can dispense with altogether. As long as he has grasped the meaning of the all-important principles of chess strategy, he will easily outplay any opponent who lacks this understanding, no matter what his 'book knowledge' may be.

1. THE RULES OF THE GAME

EQUIPMENT AND OBJECT OF THE GAME

A GAME of chess is played by two opponents called 'White' and 'Black', on a square board comprising sixty-four squares alternately light and dark in colour, and commonly referred to as 'white' and 'black'. The forces on each side consist of sixteen men, namely a King, a Queen, two Rooks, two Bishops, two Knights and eight Pawns. The board is so placed that the players have a white square at their right-hand corner. The position taken up by the forces at the beginning of the game is shown in Diagram 1.

The 'pieces' occupy the first 'rank', the Pawns the second. King and Queen are placed in the centre, the Queen occupying the square of her own colour, so that the two Queens and the two Kings oppose each other in the same 'file'. The Rooks take up their positions at the corner-squares, and next to them the Knights. The Bishops occupy the remaining two squares.

From this initial position the players move alternately one man at a time, with one exception—explained

Diagram 1

later—which is called 'castling'. White always makes the first move.

The object of the game is the capture of the opposing King. To understand what is meant by this it is necessary to consider the rules of the game in full.

HOW THE PIECES MOVE

The different men move and capture in different ways: *The Rook* can move to any square which it can reach in a straight line, either horizontally or vertically, unless its path is blocked by another man. If it is a friendly man, the Rook can move only as far as the square adjoining that man. If it is a hostile one, the Rook can capture it by placing itself on the square occupied by the enemy and removing it from the board.

The Bishop may move to any square located on a diagonal with the square on which it stands, provided again that its path is not obstructed by a man of its own colour. If a hostile man is in its way, it can capture it by occupying its place. It is obvious that from a white square a Bishop can never reach a black one and vice versa. Thus, only thirty-two of the sixty-four squares of the board are accessible to a Bishop. In Diagram 2 the arrows show which squares are accessible to the Rook and the Bishop. Either of them could capture the black Pawn, while the white Pawn stops them.

The Queen unites the power of both Rook and Bishop, being free to

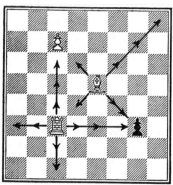

Diagram 2

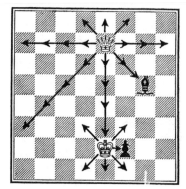

Diagram 3

move to any square she can reach in a straight line or diagonal from the square on which she stands. The same rules apply to obstructions of her path as in the case of the Rook and the Bishop. Accordingly, the Queen in Diagram 3 can reach only the squares marked by arrows. She can capture the Bishop, but cannot go beyond the square in front of the King.

The King moves like the Queen, but only one square at a time. As in real life, His Majesty's freedom of movement is curtailed—perhaps with the thought of guarding him against the dangers entailed in excursions to distant parts. The King cannot move to a square on which he could be captured by a hostile man. According to the definition of the object of the game, this would immediately end the battle, and it would do so in a manner which would reflect no credit upon the victor. Thus, in Diagram 3, two of the eight squares surrounding the King are not accessible to him. The other pieces are not restricted in this manner and they can sacrifice themselves if they want to—in fact, they often do, in order to save the life of their King.

The Knight moves in a way which often puzzles the beginner: From a square on which it stands it goes to any square of opposite colour not directly adjoining, which it can reach in two steps of one square each, as indicated in Diagram 4. Obviously, it matters not whether the Knight's jump is conceived as composed of one straight step first, followed by a diagonal one, or of a diagonal step first, followed by a straight one. Some people like to think of it as one straight step followed by two straight ones at right angles to the first. I have always preferred to consider the Knight's move a jump to the nearest but one square of opposite colour, without regarding the squares directly adjoining it as lying in its path.

In the Diagram the Knight could capture the Rook. The white

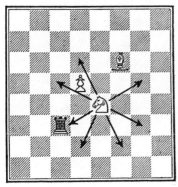

Diagram 4

Diagram 5

Bishop makes the square on which it stands inaccessible to the Knight, while the Pawn does not obstruct it.

Knight and Bishop are called 'minor pieces' in contrast to the more mobile Rook and Queen, the 'major pieces'.

The Pawn is the only man who does not capture, in the same way in which it moves. It marches only *straight forward*, one square at a time, except on its first move, when it has the option of moving two squares. On the other hand, it is permitted to capture only *diagonally*, and never more than one square at a time.

If a Pawn—taking advantage of its right to make two steps on its first move—traverses a square on which a hostile Pawn could capture it, the latter may capture it as if it had moved only one square. This is called *capturing en passant*, a privilege the enemy can exercise only on the move immediately following the double step of a Pawn.

When a Pawn reaches the eighth rank it is 'promoted' into any piece of its own colour which its player chooses, except a King. Thus it may happen that players have three or more Rooks, Bishops, Knights or Queens. Since the Queen is the most powerful piece, a player usually selects a Queen to take the place of the Pawn. For this reason, the process of Pawn promotion is generally referred to as 'queening'. In Diagram 5, the white Pawn on the second rank could move either one or two squares ahead. In either case, the black Pawn in the adjoining file could capture it by placing itself on the square indicated by the arrow. The Pawn on the third rank could not move forward because it is blocked by the Pawn in front of him. However, he could capture the Pawn on the adjoining file, and, vice-versa, the latter could capture him if it were Black's move. The Pawn on the seventh rank could either move forward to the eighth rank in his own file or he could capture the Rook, and in either case White would exchange the Pawn for a Queen or any other piece except a King.

The one exception to the rule that a player may move only one man at a time, is a double step which the King is permitted to take in conjunction with a Rook's move, and which is termed *castling*. In castling, the King moves two squares sideways in either direction, and the Rook toward which he moves is placed on the square the King has skipped. Castling is allowed only if neither the King nor the Rook concerned have moved before, if there is no piece between Rook and King, and if the square skipped by the King, or the square on which he lands, does not lie in the path of a hostile man.

Diagram 6

Diagram 6 shows the white King castled on the King's side and the black King on the Queen's side. White could not have castled on the Queen's side because his Knight obstructs the Rook, and also because his King would have landed on a square in the path of Black's Bishop. Black cannot castle on the King's side because his King would have to pass over a square controlled by the white Knight. On the Queen's side a white Knight controls a square passed by Black's Rook in castling, but this is not forbidden by the rules.

CHECK AND CHECKMATE

A man placed so that he could capture another man if it were his move, is said to 'attack' the latter. Thus, in Diagram 7, Black's Queen is attacking White's black Bishop and the Pawn in front of White's white Bishop. White's Knight is said to 'protect' the Bishop, because it could recapture any man who captured the Bishop. If a player makes a move which attacks the opposing King, the latter is said to be in 'check'. This is the only case in which a player is not free to make any move he pleases. When in check, a player must meet the attack by either moving his King out of check, or interposing a man in the path of the attacker, unless he happens to be in a position to capture the latter. In Diagram 7, White would be checking Black's King by capturing the Knight with

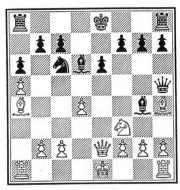

his Bishop. Black can defend himself by recapturing the Bishop with his Pawn. Otherwise he would be forced to move his King, since he has no man whom he could interpose between the Bishop and the King. If Black captured the Pawn in the same rank with his Queen, the latter would be checking White's King. White could defend this check by interposing either his Queen or his Knight or one of his Pawns, who can move into the path of the Queen, or he could move his King. Castling

Diagram 7

is not permitted when in check. If there is no move with which to get a King out of check, the King is 'checkmate' and the game is lost.

DRAWN GAME

In some rare cases it happens that a player cannot make any move which would not place his King in check, though he is not in check at the time it is his turn to move. Such a position is called a 'stalemate' and the game is considered 'drawn', that is, it counts as a win for neither player. A game is also drawn when a player is able to check the opponent incessantly by a repetition of a series of moves. Check or no check, if the same position recurs three times with the same player on the move, that player may claim a draw. Finally, a game is considered a draw when 50 moves have been made without accomplishing a checkmate, provided no man has been captured and no Pawn has moved. Excepted from this rule are positions in which it can be proved that a mate would require more than 50 moves.

ILLEGAL MOVES

It is customary, though not obligatory, to call 'check' when attacking the King. Should the opponent overlook the check and make a move which does not defend it, he must take back the move and make another which protects the King, if possible with the same man.

Thus, it can never happen in a game that a King is actually taken. A move must also be taken back if one of the contestants notices that it is not in accordance with the rules of the game. Again, the offending player must make a move with the same piece with which he has made the illegal move, provided this is possible. After castling illegally, a player must move his King instead, if this can be done without placing it in check.

If a player having the move touches one of his men he is under compulsion to move it; if he touches a hostile man he must capture it, provided in either case that the man can be properly moved or captured. So long as the hand has not been withdrawn from the man to be moved, the latter can be placed on any accessible square. If a player touches a man with the sole object of adjusting its position, he must apprise his opponent of his intention by saying 'j'adoube' (I adjust) *before touching the man*. When castling, one is supposed to touch the King first and then the Rook. If the Rook is moved first, a doubt might arise whether castling or only a Rook's move was intended.

THE DESCRIPTION OF THE MOVES

To simplify the description of the moves a special set of symbols has been adopted, and it is necessary for students of the game to become thoroughly conversant with it, in order to follow readily the discussion of a position.

Thus, White. Black.

The earliest method of recording moves with symbols is still in use in English, French and Spanish speaking countries, while in the rest of the world a more modern method has been adopted. The original notation was derived from the position which the pieces occupy at the start of the game, the files taking their names from the pieces which stand on them. The names of the men are abbreviated by giving merely their first letter. To distinguish the symbol for the Knight from that for the King, the former is designated as Kt. The Rook, Knight and Bishop which originally stand on the Queen's wing of the board are called *Queen's Rook*, *Queen's Knight* and *Queen's Bishop* and described as QR, QKt and QB throughout the game. In this way confusion with the *King's Rook* (KR), *King's Knight* (KKt) and *King's Bishop* (KB) is avoided where the description of a move might otherwise be misinterpreted. The Pawns are distinguished from each other as QRP, QKtP, QBP, QP, KP, KBP, KKtP and KRP, unless the symbol P suffices to give the description of a move a unique meaning.

In this notation, which is called the descriptive notation, the ranks are numbered from 1 to 8 by each player, beginning with the rank on which his pieces stand. As a result, there are two names for each square, depending upon whether a move of White or Black is described. Thus, White's left-hand corner becomes QR1 when describing a white move, and QR8 when describing a black move. The adjoining square in the same rank would be QKt1 for White and QKt8 for Black, and so on.

In describing a move, only the symbol for the man moved and for the square to which he moves are given, and in describing a capture, only the symbols for the men involved are quoted.

A dash (—) stands for 'moves to', a multiplication sign (×) for 'captures', ch for check, e.p. for en passant, (Q) for 'queens'. A question-mark is sometimes placed after a move by an annotator to denote its weakness, and an exclamation mark to denote its strength.

In the modern (algebraic) notation the files are lettered from a to h beginning at White's left, and the ranks are numbered from 1 to 8, starting always from White's side. Thus each square has always the same symbol. White's QB2, which is Black's QB7 in the descriptive notation, becomes c2, while Black's QB2 (White's QB7) is always c7. A colon after the description of a move signifies that a man has been captured; + means 'check'; O—O signifies 'Castles KR'; and O—O—O 'Castles QR'.

Obviously, this notation is more concise, simpler and unmistakably clear. But it has shared the fate of the decimal system of measurements which has never been adopted in English-speaking countries because a large number of textbooks would have to be rewritten.

All moves possible for White and Black in the position of Diagram 7 would look as follows in the descriptive notation:

White: P—QKt3, P—QKt4, P—B3, P—B4, P—Q5, P—KKt3, P—R3, R—R2, R—R3, R—QKt1, R—QB1, R—Q1, R—KKt1, R—KB1, Castles QR, Castles KR, Q—Q1, Q—Q2, Q—B1, Q—K3, Q—K4, Q—K5, Q×P ch, Q—Q3, Q—B4, Q—Kt5, Q×RP, B—QKt5, B×Kt ch, B—KKt5, B—KB6, B—K7, B—Q8, Kt—Q2, Kt—K5, Kt—Kt5, Kt—Kt1, K—Q1, K—Q2, K—B1.

Black: P—QKt3, P—QKt4, P—K4, P—B3, P—B4, P—KKt3, P—KKt4, P—R3, R—R2, R—QKt1, R—QB1, R—Q1, R—KB1, R—KKt1, Castles KR, Q—R3, Q—Kt3, Q×B, Q—KKt4, Q—KB4, Q—K4, Q—Q4, Q—QB4, Q—QKt4, Q×P ch, B×P, B—Kt6, B—B5, B—K4, B—QR6, B—Kt5, B—QB4, B—K2, B—KB1, B—KR6, B—KB4, B×Kt, K—Q2, K—Q1, K—B1.

Black cannot castle on the Queen's side, because on his way to QB1 the King would have to traverse the square Q1 which lies in the path of White's Queen's Bishop.

Naturally, only very few of the possible moves cited would be *sensible* in the position of the Diagram. Which ones these are, however, we have as yet no means of telling. The moves which were actually made by two players of rather unequal experience in the game from which the position is taken are the following, recorded in both the descriptive and the algebraic notation:

1. Castles KR	P—QKt4?	1. O—O	b5?
2. P×P e.p.	K—Q2	2. ab:	Kd7
3. B×Kt ch	K×B	3. Bc6:+	Kc6:
4. P—Kt7	K×P	4. b7	Kb7:
5. Q—K4 ch	K—R2?	5. Qe4+	Ka7?
6. R×P ch!	K×R	6. Ra6:+!	Ka6:
7. Q—B6 ch	K—R2	7. Qc6+	Ka7
8. R—R1 ch	K—Kt1	8. Ra1+	Kb8
9. R×R mate		9. Ra8: mate	

2. ELEMENTARY END-GAMES

THE first problem which confronts the student is to acquire an understanding of the relative value of the various chess pieces. He will want to measure their value by the contribution they can make toward achieving the final goal of the game, the checkmating of the opponent's King. But how can a beginner judge the greater or lesser importance of that contribution?

A clue is likely to be found while investigating which pieces can force a mate and which pieces cannot. We may find that the value of the pieces cannot be fixed at a definite level but varies during the different phases of the game. At any rate, we must know what minimum force is needed to arrive at a checkmate, first against the lone King and then against a King who is defended by one or more men.

We can conclude almost *a priori* that the Queen is the strongest piece, because from any given square she can reach more squares on the board than any of the other pieces. The Rook is obviously more powerful than the Bishop, as the latter has access to only thirty-two of the sixty-four squares which constitute the battlefield. And the Bishop is very likely stronger than the Knight, because the latter cannot travel as fast and cannot reach as many squares from a given spot as the Bishop, though this deficiency seems compensated to some extent by its ability to reach all sixty-four squares of the board.

This deduction is indeed borne out by the following investigation of the capabilities of the different pieces in their assault on the lone King.

MATING THE LONE KING

In trying to avoid being checkmated, the King will keep away as long as possible from the edge of the board where his mobility is curtailed. In a corner the King has only three flight squares, on the edge of the board five, and in any other position eight. Even in a corner he could not be checkmated by one of the opponent's pieces alone, because none of them can take away from him all three of his flight squares and at the same time place him in check. The

Diagram 8

opposing King or another man must always aid the checkmating piece. Diagram 8 shows how he can do so by approaching as closely as possible.

In two of the examples he guards two of the flight squares, while Queen or Rook deprive the King of the third and at the same time attack the square on which he stands. In the other two the King enables the Queen to approach so closely that she can check the King and simultaneously cover all flight squares.

Similar mating positions result when the lone King stands on any other square on the edge of the board, as shown in Diagram 9.

The question is how he can be *forced* into such a mating position when he is in the middle of the board. Checking him is obviously ineffective as long as it does not compel him to flee toward the edge of the board. This will be the case only when the King of the checking piece bars the escape of the defending King toward other

Diagram 9

Diagram 10

central squares. Thus, in the position of Diagram 10, White will first approach with his King. After 1. **K—Kt2, K—Q4** White can use his Queen to deprive Black's King of a retreat to the King's file by 2. **Q—K7.** Black has the choice between B3, B5 and Q5. The method of forcing the mate is similar in all cases. **K—Q5; 3. Q—K6.** Again limiting the King's field of action. **K—Q6; 4. Q—K5, K—B5; 5. K— B2.** From now on Black's King has no more choice. 5. Q—Q6 would be equally effective, because K—Kt4; 6. K—B3, K—R4; 7. K—B5 (not Q—B6, which would produce a stalemate), K—R5 leads to mate on the 8th move either on Kt4 or R6. 5. .... **K—Kt5; 6. Q—Q5, K—R5.** If K—R6, 7. Q—Kt3 mates. 7. **K—B3!** Again Q—B5 would be incorrect, as Black would be stalemate. **K—R6; 8. Q—Kt3** or **Q—R5** mate.

The beginner should note that White has not given a single check except on the last move. An examination of the position will show that at almost any stage, a check with the Queen would have opened an avenue of escape to Black's King. On the other hand, the moves of the Queen which did not check him prevented his escape.

With a Rook instead of the Queen, as shown in Diagram 11, the mate can also be forced, though it takes a few moves longer. The method consists in approaching the King until an opportunity arises to check the opponent in such a way that he must retreat toward the edge of the board. For example: 1. **K—Kt2, K—K5;** 2. **K—B3, K—K4;** 3. **K—B4.** If now K—K5, White checks on K8, driving Black into the Bishop's file, and the same play is repeated until finally the King lands on the Rook's file from which there is no retreat: 4. .... K—B4; 5. K—Q4, K—B5; 6. R—B8 ch, K—Kt5; 7. K—K5, K—Kt6; 8. K—K4, K—Kt5; 9. R—Kt8 ch, K—R4; 10. K—B4, K—R3; 11. K— B5, K—R2; 12. R—Kt6, K—R1; 13. K—B6, K—Kt2; 14. K—B7, K—R1; 15. R—R6 mate. 3. ....

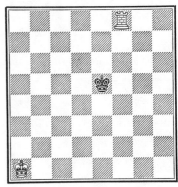

Diagram 11

K—K3; 4. **K—Q4.** K—B5, K—K4; 5. **R—K8 ch** would lead to a similar line as just illustrated. **K—K2;** 5. **R—B1, K—K3;** 6. **R—B2.** White is waiting for Black to go 'into opposition' on Q3 to check him back into the seventh rank. If Black now plays K—K2; 7. K—Q5, K—Q2; 8. R—B7 ch, K—K1; 9. K—K6, K—Q1; 10. K—Q6, K—B1; 11. R—KR7, K—Kt1; 12. K—B6, K—R1; 13. K—Kt6, and mate on the next move. 6. .... **K—Q3;** 7. **R—B6 ch, K—K2;** 8. **K—K5, K—Q2;** 9. **K—Q5, K—K2;** 10. **R—B1!, K—Q2;** 11. **R—B7 ch,** etc., as above. The student should note that again very few checks are given during the checkmating drive. There is no sense in checking if the result is not a limitation of Black's mobility.

There are two stalemate positions to look out for in this ending. These occur when Black's King is in the corner and White's Rook stands in the adjoining Knight's file.

With a Bishop or Knight alone it is not possible to checkmate the lone King, as a rather simple consideration will show. The most unfavourable position for the King would again be one of the corners where only four squares are accessible to him. But since only two of these can be guarded by the opposing King there will always be two more left which the Bishop or the Knight would have to control. As these two squares would be adjoining each other on a straight line so that one would have to be white and the other black, neither Bishop nor Knight could cover them both.

One extraordinary position exists in which King and Knight alone can bring about a mate if the opponent still has a Rook's Pawn left which he is forced to move so as to block one of the flight squares of his King. This can happen only when the Pawn has reached the sixth rank, with the King in front of it and the opposing King blocking the way to the Knight's file, as in Diagram 12.

After 1. **Kt—B5, K—R8;** 2. **Kt—K4,** Black would be mated with 3. Kt—Kt3 if he advanced his Pawn. He will therefore try 2. .... **K—R7.** But White forces the advance of the Pawn by 3. **Kt—Q2** (not Kt—Kt3, which would be stalemate), **K—R8;** 4. **Kt—B1.** Now the King can no longer move. Black must play **P—R7,** and 5. **Kt—Kt3** is mate.

Diagram 12

Diagram 13

This mate could also have been enforced if the Knight had been placed on any other white square on the board instead of QR6, with the exception of QR8 and KR1. From a black square, however, the Knight could never arrive at KB1 at a moment when it is Black's turn to move, with his King in the corner, and as a result the game would end in a draw either by stalemate or by repetition of moves.

Let us assume, for argument's sake, that White's Knight stands on Q4 in Diagram 12. After Kt—K2, K—R8; 2. Kt—Kt3 ch, K—R7; 3. Kt—B1 ch, K—R8, it is White's move, and if he goes to any other square but Kt3 with his Knight, Black plays P—R7 and is stalemate unless White's King moves so as to permit Black to go to Kt8. But then the black Pawn would proceed to eighth rank and queen, whereupon White would even lose the game.

With two Bishops it is an easy matter to checkmate the lone King, but it is again necessary for the attacking King to support his forces and to approach the opponent as closely as possible. The mate can be forced only in a corner, and various forms of stalemate have to be guarded against, as illustrated in the play which may arise from the position of Diagram 13.

After 1. **K—Kt2, K—B5;** 2. **K—B3, K—K4;** 3. **B—K3, K—B4,** White proceeds to limit the territory at Black's disposal in such a way as to take possession of the centre squares of the board with his King or his Bishops. He could now play 4. B—Q5, for example, and answer K—K4 with 5. K—B4, K—B4; 6. K—Q4, K—B3; 7. K—K4, pushing Black into the second rank or the seventh file. The continuation would then be similar to the play I am giving as the main line. 4. **K—Q4, K—K3;** 5. **K—K4, K—Q3;** 6. **K—B5, K—Q2.** Black tries to stay away from his KR corner where White tries to drive him. Note how the Bishops, placed in adjoining diagonals, keep Black from crossing these diagonals. 7. **B—B5, K—Q1;** 8. **K—K6, K—K1;** 9. **B—Kt6.** B—K7 would stalemate Black. **K—B1;** 10. **K—B6, K—K1;** 11. **B—B6 ch, K—B1;** 12. **B—B5 ch, K—Kt1;** 13. **K—Kt6, K—R1.** There would be no sense in checking the King now because after K—Kt1 the escape to B1 would again have to be prevented. If the white Bishop were so placed that Black has no access to Kt1, B—Q4 would now be mate. But B—Q5 in this position would stalemate Black. Therefore White makes a 'waiting move' so that he takes the square Kt1 from Black with a check. 14. **B—R1, K—Kt1;** 15. **B—Q5 ch, K—R1;** 16. **B—Q4** mate.

To checkmate with Bishop and Knight is more difficult. The mate can be forced only in a corner controlled by the Bishop, as the following argument will prove. Diagram 14 shows a check-

mate with Knight in a corner which is not of the colour of the Bishop.

On the move preceding the checkmate White must have checked the King with the Bishop. Black must then have had the choice between going to R1 or R3, because the Knight must have stood on a black square so that it could not have controlled Black's R3. Therefore Black was mated only because he made the wrong move.

Similarly, in the other mating position shown in Diagram 14, the

Diagram 14

black King must have had the choice between several squares on the previous move, when he elected to go to R5. Again he was checkmated only because he failed to make the best move.

The method of forcing the black King into the corner of the colour of the Bishop consists in first driving him to the edge of the board. Bishop and Knight co-operate in limiting the black King's mobility, the Knight cutting him off from squares of the colour which the Bishop does not control. In other words, the Knight is best placed on squares of the same colour as the Bishop, as illustrated in the following play:

1. **K—Kt2, K—Kt2**; 2. **K—B3, K—B3**; 3. **K—Q4, K—K3**; 4. **Kt—Kt3, K—B3**; 5. **B—B5, K—Kt4**; 6. **K—K5, K—R5**; 7. **Kt—K4.** *Not* K—B4, as this would stalemate Black. White aims with the Knight at KKt4 in order to cut the King off from his R3. **K—R4**; 8. **K—B6, K—R3**; 9. **Kt—B2, K—R4**; 10. **Kt—Kt4, K—R5**; 11. **K—K5, K—Kt4**; 12. **K—K4, K—R4**; 13. **K—B4, K—R5**; 14. **B—Kt6!, K—R6**; 15. **Kt—K3, K—R7**; 16. **K—B3, K—R6**; 17. **Kt—Kt2, K—R7**; 18. **K—B2, K—R6**; 19. **B—B5 ch, K—R7.** At last the King is confined to the proper corner and one neighbouring square, and the Knight will drive him from the latter. 20. **Kt—K3, K—R8**; 21. **B—B8.** A waiting move.

Diagram 15

Diagram 16

Kt—B1 at this moment would stalemate Black. **K—R7**; 22. **Kt—B1 ch, K—R8**; 23. **B—Kt7** mate.

The King and two Knights cannot force a mate against the lone King. For similar reasons, as explained when discussing the positions given in Diagram 14, a mate is reached only if the opponent makes a bad move. However, if the defending King has a Pawn left which prevents him from being stalemated, the Knights can accomplish the checkmate, as shown in the play arising from the position of Diagram 16. 1. **Kt—K6, K—R1**; 2. **Kt—K7, P—B4**; 3. **Kt—Kt5,** and 4. **Kt—B7** mate. If the lone King is not confined near a corner, as in this example, but must first be driven to the edge of the board, the mating procedure is usually so difficult and lengthy that a player is not required to force the mate within 50 moves to avoid a draw.

Now that we know what minimum force is required to win against the lone King, let us turn our attention to simple types of endings in which the defending King has a Pawn or a piece left with which he tries to hold the game against a superior force.

THE QUEEN *v*. OTHER PIECES

The Queen wins against any other piece; the opportunity almost always offers itself after a very few moves to check the King and at the same time attack the piece. If the latter stays close to the King for protection, the attacking King approaches and forces the piece away, to a square on which the Queen can be brought to bear while checking the King.

The ending Queen against Rook will suffice to illustrate this method. In Diagram 17 the direct attack on the Rook by 1. Q—R6 fails, because

Black replies R—B2 ch. If the King goes to Kt6 Black forces the draw by R—B3 ch, for after K × R he would be stalemate. If, instead, White plays 2. K—K6, Black checks again on K2, and once more Black would be stalemate if White takes the Rook. Thus, the King would be forced to go away to the Queen's wing, and White would have to embark on a lengthy manœuvre to enable the King's approach again.

The position of the Diagram is favourable for White, because Black cannot drive the King away with a

Diagram 17

check. If it were Black's move he would have to take the Rook away from the King to an unprotected square and he would soon lose it. For example, if the Rook moved to Q2 it would be lost through a check on Kt4. If it moved to Kt2 the check on Q5 would get it. Equally unfavourable would be the white square Kt7, where the Rook would be won by the check on Q5. But even on a black square the Rook would not last long. After R—QB2 White would play Q—Q5 ch and the King would then have to leave the first rank because there the Queen could check it on Q8 and attack the Rook at the same time. On the second rank, too, it is safe only for a moment. K—R2 is answered by Q—Q3 ch, and unless the King goes back to the first rank, permitting the check on Q8, it is mated by Q—R3.

If in the position of the Diagram Black starts with R—QR2, all White has to do is to aim at a check on QKt8. He accomplishes this with 2. Q—Kt4 ch, K—R1 or R2 (not B1 on account of Q—B8 mate); 3. Q—R3 ch, K—Kt1; 4. Q—Kt3 ch, K—R2; 5. Q—R2 ch, K—Kt1; 6. Q—Kt8 ch, etc.

Similarly, in reply to 1. R—Kt8, White would proceed as follows: 2. Q—Q5 ch, K—R2; 3. Q—K4 ch, K—R1; 4. Q—R8 ch, K—R2 (if R—Kt1, Q—KR1 mates); 5. Q—R7 ch, winning the Rook.

It takes only four moves to win the Rook if it goes to Kt6; 2. Q—K8 ch, K—R2; 3. Q—K4 ch, K—Kt1; 4. Q—B4 ch, K—R1; 5. Q—R4 ch.

Neither can Black escape his fate by playing 1. K—B1, as Q—R6 would win the Rook immediately. Therefore, all White has to do, if it is his move in the position of the Diagram, is to gain a 'tempo', i.e. transfer the onus of moving to the other side. He does so by playing 1. **Q—Q5 ch, K—R1; 2. Q—R1 ch, K—Kt1; 3. Q—R5,** and Black is left without a defence.

After studying this example, the beginner will find it easy to win with the Queen against a Bishop or a Knight. A Pawn will offer hardly any difficulty, but there are two exceptional positions in which a Pawn can draw against a Queen, and these positions occur quite frequently in actual end-games. They are both shown in Diagram 18.

In one case the Rook's Pawn and in the other the Bishop's Pawn threatens to queen, and the only way for White to stop this is to check on Kt3. In both cases the King goes into the corner. The Queen cannot capture the Bishop's Pawn without stalemating the King. And in the case of the Rook's Pawn, Black is also stalemated unless the Queen leaves the Kt file again, whereupon the King returns to Kt8 and threatens to queen the Pawn once more.

Diagram 18

The only exceptions are positions in which the attacking King can reach the square Kt3 immediately after the Rook's Pawn queens. If in Diagram 18 White's King were on Q5, for example, White would win with 1. Q—KB1 ch, K—Kt7; 2. Q—K2 ch, K—Kt1; 3. K—B4, P—R8 (Q); 4. K—Kt3. Now checkmate is threatened on White's B2 or any square on the first rank, and all Black can do is prolong the agony one move by sacrificing the Queen.

Any other Pawn always loses against the Queen, because whenever it threatens to advance to the eighth rank, the Queen forces the King to block the advance, and in that way gains time for her own King to approach. Thus, in Diagram 19, White would proceed as follows:

1. Q—QB2, K—R8; 2. Q—R4 ch, K—Kt8; 3. K—Q4, K—B8; 4. Q—R3, K—B7. If the King goes to Kt8 instead, White wins the Pawn through **K—B3. 5. Q—B3 ch, K—Kt8; 6. K—Q3, K—R7; 7. Q—B2, K—R8; 8. Q—R4 ch, K—Kt8; 9. K—B3,** and checkmate on the next move.

Diagram 19

Diagram 20

ROOK v. BISHOP

The Rook can win against a minor piece in exceptional cases only. If the defending piece is a Bishop, the weaker King must take refuge in a corner square of different colour from that of the Bishop, as in Diagram 20, with the Bishop prepared to interpose when the Rook checks. Unless the Rook releases the resulting 'pin' of the Bishop, Black is stalemate. **1. R—Q4, B—R7; 2. R—Q1 ch, B—Kt8.** If the Bishop is not placed so that it can readily take its place next to the King, it is liable to be lost. For instance, with the Bishop on KB3, 1. R—KB4 would win. Likewise, with the Bishop on QB6, 1. R—QB4 decides, with the Bishop on QKt7, 1. R—QKt4, with the Bishop on QR8 or QB8, 1. R—K4. The latter move also wins against the Bishop on KKt2 or KKt4, because after Black relieves the mating threat with K—Kt8 White checks on KKt4.

A tricky win is possible with the Bishop on KB1. White plays 1. K—Kt3 discovered check, and after K—Kt8 threatens mate again on Q4, at the same time preventing Black from checking on Q3. The only way to avoid mate is K—B8, and then the Bishop is lost through check on KB4.

Dangerous for the defending player are also King positions on the edge of the board which are not of the colour of the Bishop. In Diagram 21, for example, White wins with 1. R—QKt5, B—K2; 2. R—Kt8 ch, B—Q1; 3. R—R8 or B8. The King must move and the Rook takes the Bishop.

This combination is rarely possible with the King on a square of the colour of the Bishop, because usually the Bishop can check the attacking King out of the opposition.

Diagram 21

Diagram 22

ROOK v. KNIGHT

The Rook wins against the Knight where the latter is cut off from his King. In Diagram 22 the winning move would be 1. **R—K5!** This 'oblique opposition' takes four squares away from the Knight, and it is unable to establish communication with its King. 1. .... **Kt—Q8; 2. K—B5, Kt—B7; 3. K—Q4, Kt—R6.** If the Knight goes to Kt5 he is lost through the check on Kt5. Such a fatal check is almost always possible in this type of ending, so that the position of the Diagram is not in any way a chance-win. **4. K—K3, K—B2; 5. R—KR5, Kt—Kt8; 6. R—R1,** *and wins.*

Diagram 23

Against a Knight protected by his King the Rook cannot win, even when the King is already forced to the edge of the board.

It is important, however, that the King avoid the corner. In Diagram 23 White wins through 1. R—Q5, Kt—Kt1 ch; 2. K—Kt6.

The same position moved one or more squares to the right is a draw, as the Knight then has another square to go to on which it is defended by its King.

PAWN-ENDINGS

In the majority of end-games, Pawns are left on the board, and the knowledge of Pawn-endings is therefore most important. The simplest type of these is found in positions in which there are Pawns on both sides, but one of the players is a Pawn ahead. Let the play arising from the position of Diagram 24 illustrate the winning method. The Pawns on one side of the board block each other. On the other, White has a 'passed Pawn', i.e. a Pawn the advance of which is not hindered by a hostile Pawn either in the same file or in a neighbouring file. This passed Pawn curtails the mobility of Black's King, for the latter must always be prepared to stop it from queening, i.e. he must be able to reach the queening square in as few moves as the Pawn can do it. This handicap suggests the proper proceeding for White. He will attack the black Pawn. If the King tries to defend it, White will advance his passed Pawn and force Black to capture it, thereby relinquishing the defence of his own Pawn. 1. **K—Q3, K—Q4**; 2. **P—Kt5, K—B4**; 3. **K—K4, K×P**; 4. **K—Q5, K—Kt3**; 5. **K—K6, K—B3**; 6. **K×P, K—Q2**; 7. **K—Kt7**, and the Pawn marches on.

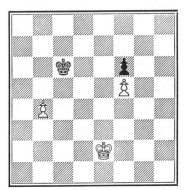

Diagram 24

Diagram 25

Very similar in type is the position of Diagram 25. Though both players have the same number of Pawns, White wins because he has the 'distant' passed Pawn, i.e. his passed Pawn is farther away from the blocked Pawns on the other wing.

He will force Black's King into the QR file with the Rook's Pawn, and thus gain access to Black's Bishop's Pawn. Then he will be closer to the Pawns on the King's wing than Black, so that he will capture Black's Pawns and queen one of his own. The technique of this procedure would be: 1. **K—Kt3, K—Kt3**; 2. **K—Kt4, K—B3**; 3. **P—QR4, K—Kt3**; 4. **P—R5ch, K—R3**; 5. **K—B5!** (Not K—R4, in answer to which Black would win with P—B4, forcing White to give up his Rook's Pawn without getting the Bishop's Pawn for it.) **K×P; 6. K— B6, K—Kt5; 7. K×P, K—B5; 8. K—Q6, K—Q5; 9. K—K6, K—K5; 10. K—B6, K—B5; 11. K—Kt6, K—Kt6; 12. K×P, K×P; 13. K×P,** and the Knight's Pawn queens in six moves.

Let us now turn our attention to a few types of endings in which the Pawns of the players are equal in number and placed so that no passed Pawn can be produced by advancing them. Everything, then, depends upon the relative position of the Kings. A deciding factor in evaluating the King's position is whether Pawn-moves are possible or whether they are already exhausted so that only manœuvres with the Kings can be undertaken.

If the Pawns are blocked, the player whose King can go into 'opposition' wins the game in many cases, because he is enabled to invade the opponent's camp after the latter retreats or moves to one side. In Diagram 26, for example, either player, on the move, wins by K—

Diagram 26

Diagram 27

Q4, followed by either K—B5 or K—K5, depending upon the opponent's reply. After the fall of one of the Pawns the position is reduced to the type illustrated by Diagram 24.

In Diagram 27 White's Pawn-position is better because Black cannot attack White's Pawns even if he has the move and gains access to the fifth rank by going into opposition. White on the move forces his way to QB5, and Black's Bishop's Pawn is then lost: 1. **K—K4, K— Q3; 2. K—B5, K—Q2; 3. K—K5, K—B3; 4. K—K6, K—B2; 5. K— Q5, K—Kt3; 6. K—Q6,** and Black cannot keep the Bishop's Pawn protected. The Knight's Pawn then is also lost, and White easily queens one of his Pawns.

With Black on the move, the play would be this: 1. .... **K—K4; 2. K—Q3, K—B5; 3. K—Q2!** (not K—K2, because Black would then be able to resume the opposition and force his way to K6 with K—K5; 4. K—Q2, K—Q5; 5. K—B2, K—K6; 6. K—B1, K—Q6; 7. K—Kt2, K—Q7; 8. K—Kt1, K—B6; 9. K—R2, K—B7, and White's Pawns fall), **K—K5; 4. K—K2.** White has now gained the opposition, and Black cannot force access to the sixth rank. Had Black played 3. .... K—B6, White would have gone into opposition on Q3.

In positions in which the Pawns are not blocked, the value of gaining the opposition lies in the fact that the opponent must make a Pawn-move in order to maintain the opposition, or, giving it up, must permit the advance of the hostile King. In either case the attacking King is likely to obtain access to an opposing Pawn that cannot be defended.

In Pawn-endings of this type, two factors are of paramount importance. One is the ability of a player to reach the centre of the board with his King before the opponent can do so, and the other is his ability to place his Pawns in such a way as to prevent the approach of the opposing King if the latter has gained the opposition, so that the player's own King cannot stop that approach.

In Diagram 28 White, on the move, has two different winning manœuvres at his disposal, both of them deriving from his ability to reach the centre of the board first. He can either force Black's King into the KR corner by attacking the King's side Pawns and then win the Queen's side Pawns by changing the course of his King toward that side, or he can approach the Queen's

Diagram 28

side Pawns immediately by obtaining the opposition of the King's, and in that way forcing Black to yield a square from which one of his Pawns can be attacked.

In the first case White will proceed as follows: 1. **K—B4, K—K2;** 2. **K—Kt5, K—B2;** Black would here also consider K—Q3, in order to capture White's QR Pawn and queen his own. But the very simple method of counting the moves which both would need to queen their passed Pawns would show him the futility of this plan. White would capture the two black Pawns in three more moves and then have to make five moves with his KR Pawn to obtain a Queen. Black would capture White's QR Pawn in three moves. Then he would have to move the King out of the way of his own Pawn and make four more moves to queen the Pawn, also eight moves. But since White moves first, the white Queen on KR8 would control Black's QR8 just as Black is ready to queen, so that the Pawn cannot reach the queening square alive. Thus Black is forced to defend his King's side Pawns instead.

3. **K—R6, K—Kt1.** It looks as if Black were safe, as he can go back and forth from Kt1 to R1 and hold his Rook's Pawn in that manner. However, White can gain control of the square KB5 by advancing his KB Pawn, and from there he can attack the Queen's side Pawns successfully. 4. **P—KB4, K—R1;** 5. **P—B5!, P×P.** Unless Black captures, White will play 6. P×P, P×P; 7. K×P, gaining a Pawn. 6. **K—Kt5, K—Kt2;** 7. **K×P, K—B2.** Again counting separately the number of moves required by White and Black to obtain a passed Pawn and queen, quickly shows that Black cannot play K—R3. White would need five moves to capture the QR Pawn, one more to move his King out of the Rook's file, and four to queen his Pawn, that is ten moves altogether. Black would capture White's Pawn in four moves, then play K—Kt8 and queen his Pawn in five more moves. In other words, he would also have a Queen in ten moves. But again White's Queen would be so placed that she could capture Black's, and though Black would recapture with his King, White would win because he would take Black's QB Pawn and queen his own before the Black King can stop him.

After 8. **K—K5, K—K2;** 9. **K—Q5, K—Q2;** 10. **K—B5,** there is no way for Black to defend his Rook's Pawn, and White wins as explained in connection with the position of Diagram 24.

Diagram 29 shows the position which would ensue if White, instead of playing 1. K—B4 in the previous Diagram, attacked Black's Queen's wing immediately. Here Black can prevent White's approach to the Rook's Pawn with **P—B3,** and after 2. **K—B5** assume the opposition with **K—B2,** so that White's King cannot advance any further. However, in positions of this type, in which success or failure depends upon the ability to maintain the opposition of

Diagram 29

the Kings, the player whose King has reached the fifth or even only the fourth rank, very frequently wins because he has more spare moves with his Pawns, so that the opponent is finally forced to move his King out of the opposition. In the present case, all that White has to do is to block Black's King's side Pawns which still have some moves to spare, and then make a move with the QB Pawn so that

Black must move his King and yield either the square QKt3 or Q3 to White's King. The position is then reduced to one of the winning positions discussed in previous examples. *After* 3. **P—KB4, P—R3;** 4. **P—R4, P—R4;** 5. **P—B3,** Black must give up the King opposition. **K—Kt2;** 6. **K—Q6, K—Kt3;** 7. **P—B4, P—B4;** 8. **K—Q5** (7. .... K—Kt2; 8. P—QB5), then settles his fate quickly, and so would have 5. .... K—Q2; 6. K—Kt6, K—Q3; 7. K×P, K—B4; 8. K—R6, followed by K—Kt7 and P—R5, etc.

The play in this example should be studied very carefully by every beginner, as similar manœuvres must be considered in the majority of all endings in which only King and Pawns are left on the board.

Of equal importance is the knowledge of the ending *King and one Pawn against King*, as typified by the position of Diagram 30. Without this knowledge, a player who is a Pawn ahead in an ending cannot

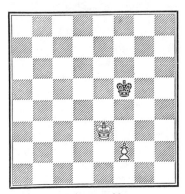

Diagram 30

Diagram 31

decide whether to permit or to avoid exchange which the opponent might offer and which would leave only the Kings and one Pawn on the board.

It is amazing how few players, even among those of quite considerable experience, know that the game is drawn if the Pawn moves, and that 1. **K—B3** is the only move with which White can win.

To understand why this is so, we must first investigate the position of Diagram 31. If it is White's move, he wins by advancing his Pawn because the only move Black has then left is K—Kt2 and White plays K—K7, enabling his Pawn to queen on the next move.

However, if it is Black's turn to play in the position of the Diagram, he goes into opposition with K—K1, and now the Pawn cannot queen because after P—B7 ch, K—B1, White must either play K—B6, stalemating Black, or he must relinquish the protection of his Pawn by moving his King elsewhere.

From this we gather that in order to draw against a Pawn advanced to the sixth rank, the defending King must be so placed as to be able to go into opposition, when the King of the adversary advances to the sixth rank. As long as the defending King controls the queening square, he can always accomplish this by occupying that square when forced to the edge of the board. In the position of Diagram 32, for instance, which might have preceded that of Diagram 31, Black on the move would go to B1, because now White cannot go into opposition. If Black went to K1 or Kt1, White would go into opposition of K6 or

Diagram 32

Kt6, and after Black's King has returned to B1, the position of Diagram 31 would be reached with White to move, so that Black is lost.

Returning now to Diagram 30, we can readily see that if White advances his Pawn, Black can always play so as to arrive at the position of Diagram 32 so that the game is drawn. For example: 1. P—B3, K—K4; 2. P—B4 ch, K—B4; 3. K—B3, K—B3; 4. K—K4, K—K3; 5. P—B5 ch, K—B3; 6. K—B4, K—B2; 7. K—K5, K—K2; 8. P—B6 ch, K—B2, etc.

However, after 1. K—B3 White can force the position of Diagram 31 with himself to move, *by going into opposition whenever Black's King occupies a square in the file of the Pawn.* The procedure will be this: **K—K4; 2. K—Kt4, K—B3.** If, instead, K—K5, White simply advances the Pawn: 3. P—B4, K—Q4; 4. K—Kt5, K—K3; 5. K—Kt6, K—K2; 6. P—B5, K—B1; 7. K—B6! as in the main variation. 3. **K—B4!, K—Kt3; 4. K—K5, K—B2; 5. K—B5!, K—K2; 6. K—Kt6, K—K3; 7. P—B4, K—K2; 8. P—B5, K—B1; 9. K—B6!** Not P—B6, because this would produce the position of Diagram 31 with Black to move into opposition. **K—Kt1; 10. K—K7,** and the Pawn marches in.

A simple way in which to remember the crucial point in this ending is this: With the attacking King on the sixth rank and the defending King in opposition on the first rank, the game is drawn if the Pawn advances to the seventh rank with a check, but it is won if the Pawn advances to the seventh without check. The only exception is the Rook's Pawn ending. This is always drawn, even when the Pawn advances to R7 without check. The defending King is stalemated, since the edge of the board cuts off the escape available to him when other than Rook's Pawns are attacking.

The important knowledge we gain from the investigation of

Diagram 30 is that King and Pawn against the lone King in control of the queening square win if the attacking King can go into opposition *in front* of his Pawn, provided the latter is not a Rook's Pawn.

If the defending King is the one who goes into opposition he draws even against a King one rank in front of his Pawn, unless the latter has already reached the sixth rank, in which case the position of Diagram 31 would result, with White to move. In Diagram 30 Black, on the move, would draw with K—K4. In Diagram 33, however, where

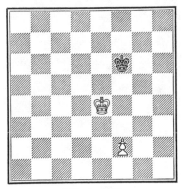

Diagram 33

Diagram 34

White's King is two ranks in front of his Pawn, Black cannot draw even though he can go into opposition on K3, for White has the spare move P—B3! which forces Black's King again out of the opposition.

If the defending King does *not* control the queening square, he can draw only if he can reach it in as many moves as the Pawn requires and if the attacking King cannot go into opposition in front of the Pawn. In Diagram 34, for example, White could not win with 1. P—B5 because he needs four moves to queen the Pawn, and in four moves Black's King can reach the queening square. However, White can keep going into opposition with 1. K—Kt6, following the black King as far as the Queen's file. Then he wins by advancing the Pawn as in Diagram 31.

Diagram 35 shows the only case in which the lone King can draw against a passed Pawn whose queening square he does not control. If it is White's move, Black keeps the White King in front of the Pawn so that the latter cannot pass. 1. K—R8, K—B1; 2. K—R7, K—B2, etc. 2. P—R7, K—B2, would stalemate White. Black could accomplish the same end with 1. .... K—Kt3; 2. P—R7, K—B2. If it is Black's move in the position of the Diagram and White leaves the

Rook's file after K—B1, Black reaches the corner where the advance of the Pawn would stalemate him.

Before turning to endings with pieces and Pawns, the type most frequently reached in actual games, I want to call attention to a manœuvre for which an opportunity often presents itself in pure Pawn endings—a temporary Pawn sacrifice which changes an apparently lost

Diagram 35

Diagram 36

position into a draw or an apparent draw into a won game. In Diagram 36, it looks as if White could rather easily force a win by going into opposition: 1. K—Q4, K—Q2; 2. K—K5, K—K2; 3. P—B5, K—Q2; 4. K—B6, etc., as shown in the play arising from the position of Diagram 27. However, Black plays

Diagram 37

1. .... **P—B4 ch!**; 2. **P×P ch, K—B3.** Now White must relinquish the protection of his Pawn on B5 and Black thus turns the position into the draw discussed in connection with Diagram 32.

A variation of the same theme is shown in Diagram 37. It is White's turn to play. He is a Pawn ahead, but Black has the opposition, and White cannot wrest it from him with 1. K—B2 because Black replies K—B3! (distant opposition), which places his King in readiness to assume

opposition on the fourth rank again as soon as White returns to the third rank. However, 1. **P—Kt4 ch!** wins for White, as **P×P ch**; 2. **K—Kt3, K—Kt3**; 3. **K×P**, reduces the position to the ending illustrated in Diagram 24.

PIECES v. PAWNS

When it comes to evaluating Pawns against pieces, the most important question is how close the Pawns are to their queening squares. Two connected Passed Pawns on the seventh rank will win in all but exceptional cases against Knight, Bishop or Rook, while the Queen usually wins against any number of Pawns because there are so many possibilities for it to check the King and attack a Pawn at the same time.

In Diagram 38, White has a hair-breadth escape through 1. **Kt—K4 ch, K—R5**; 2. **Kt×P**, because, now Black's other Pawn cannot queen without getting caught by Kt—B3 ch, an eventuality always to look out for when playing against a Knight. If, instead, 2. .... **K—Kt6**, White saves himself with 3. **Kt—B3,** because after **K×Kt** he catches the Pawn through 4. **B—R5 ch.**

Diagram 39 shows another miraculous escape, one which I had

Diagram 38

Diagram 39

myself in the first game I ever played with Capablanca, in 1911, when he visited Berlin after his victory in the San Sebastian tournament that laid the foundation for his world fame. I played 1. **K—B6,** threatening mate on R8. After **K—R2,** 2. **R—B7 ch, K—Kt1;** 3. **R—B8 ch, K—R2;** 4. **R—B7 ch, K—R3;** 5. **R—B8, K—R4;** 6. **K—B5, K—R5,** I could not continue with K—B4 because the King's Pawn would queen and on 8. R—R8 ch the Queen would interpose. However, 7. **R—B4 ch, K—Kt6;** 8. **R—B3 ch** saved the day, for if Black goes to the seventh rank 9. R×P draws, since the King's Pawn is now pinned and will be captured on the next move. Or Black goes back to R5 and the game is drawn through repetition of moves. I could have made things much easier for myself by simply playing 5. R×P. For after P—K8(Q); 6. R—R2 ch, Black would have had to interpose his Queen.

Without the aid of its King a Rook ordinarily cannot hold the game against two connected passed Pawns if they have reached the sixth rank, because one of them will queen while the Rook is preventing the other from doing so.

Against two connected Pawns on the fifth rank the Rook will win if it can attack from the rear and the opposing King is not close enough to support one of its Pawns while the Rook is capturing the other. Thus, in Diagram 40, White can win one of the Pawns with 1. R—

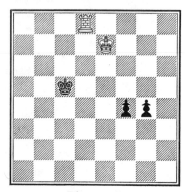

Diagram 40

Diagram 41

KB8, P—B6; 2. R—B4, but after K—Q4; 3. R×KtP, K—K4, the Rook will finally have to sacrifice itself for the queening Pawn.

The Rook will win against the two Pawns even when they have reached the sixth rank, if its King is in front of the Pawns. The proper procedure is to force the advance of one of the Pawns by attacking it from the rear. In Diagram 41, White would play 1. **R—R8, K—B5** (K—R6?; 2. R—

Diagram 42

R4!, P—B7 ch; 3. K—B1, and Black loses both Pawns as he cannot move the King due to the threat R—R4 mate); 2. **R—KKt8, P—Kt7** (if P—B7 ch, the consequence would be 3. K—Kt2 and 4. R×P); 3. **K—B2, K—K5**; 4. **R—Kt4 ch** and **K×P.** If Black plays 1. .... K—R5, White wins quite similarly through 2. R—KB8, K—Kt5; 3. R—B7, P—B7 ch; 4. K—Kt2, K—R5; 5. R—B4, etc.

Against a single passed Pawn supported by its King, the Rook wins only if its own King can reach the scene and cover the queening square when the opposing King arrives on the seventh rank. Diagram 42 shows such a case.

Black needs five moves to get both his Pawn and King to the seventh rank and threaten to queen the Pawn. If it is White's move he can just make the grade. 1. **K—Kt7, P—Kt5; 2. K—B6, P—Kt6; 3. K—Q5, P—Kt7; 4. K—K4, K—Kt6; 5. K—K3, K—R7; 6. K—B2,** and the Pawn is lost.

ROOK-ENDINGS WITH ONE OR MORE PAWNS

The most frequent endings are those in which both players are left with a Rook and Pawns. The possession of an extra Pawn is here seldom sufficient to win, unless the stronger side also has an advantage in the greater mobility of the Rook. Diagram 43 is typical of such

cases. White wins by reducing the mobility of the black Rook through the following manœuvre: 1. **R—Q2, R—K2; 2. R—R2, R—R2.** Now Black's Rook has only one move left while White's Rook has the freedom of the Rook's file. He could post the Rook at R5, for example, and prevent the black King from attacking White's Queen's side Pawns whilst the white King makes for the Rook at R7 and effects its capture. If, on the other hand, Black's King obstructs the way to the King's side, White penetrates into the black Pawn

Diagram 43

position. Black cannot prevent this by maintaining the opposition of the Kings because the white Rook has spare moves, the black Rook has none. For example: 3. **K—B3, K—Kt3; 4. R—R5, K—B3; 5. K—Q4, K—Q3; 6. R—R4, P—Kt3; 7. R—R5, K—K3; 8. K—K4, K—B3; 9. K—Q5,** and wins the Pawns.

Having the move, Black would draw the game by 1. .... **R—K7 ch; 2. K—R3, R—KR7.** In placing his Rook *behind* the passed Pawn, he condemns the opposing Rook to inactivity, while his own is free to move in the Rook's file. It is true that the white King can again come up and in the end force the black Rook to sacrifice himself for the passed Pawn, but meanwhile the black King captures the remaining white Pawns, and the connected black passed Pawns might then even offer winning chances.

Generally speaking, a Rook is placed best on the seventh rank, because often two or more Pawns are on their original square so that they are endangered by the Rook. Moreover, from the rear, the Rook can attack advanced Pawns more effectively, and for this purpose the seventh rank is very convenient. Of course, sometimes the eighth or sixth rank will do just as well.

So great is the advantage conferred upon a player who controls the seventh rank, that sometimes it is worth sacrificing a Pawn in order to open a file for the Rook through which it can invade the opponent's Pawn base.

In Diagram 44 White will obtain very good winning chances with 1. **P—Q5, P×P; 2. R—B7.** Although Black can defend the Knight's Pawn with **R—Kt1,** this passive defence would soon get him into serious

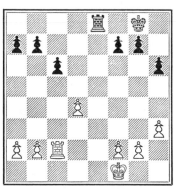

Diagram 44

trouble. An attempt to regain the mobility of his Rook with P—R3 followed by the advance of the QKt Pawn would fail, because the Rook's Pawn still remains weak and requires the protection of the Rook, and, after advancing, the Pawns are more easily attacked by White's King. Similarly, advancing the King's side Pawns in order to march the King to the Queen's side will not do, because the Rook would attack the King's side Pawns from the back.

Since none of these possibilities looks rosy for Black, he would resort to an entirely different line of play. He would give up his QKt Pawn right away and answer 2. R—B7 with R—K3!; 3. R×KtP, R—QB3, in order to free the Rook for attacking activity. Then 4. R×RP, R—B8 ch; 5. K—K2, R—B7 ch would lead to a draw. 3. .... R—QKt3? would have lost the game for Black immediately, as after 4. R×R, P×R, White obtains the 'outside passed Pawn'. Black's King would have to cross over to the Queen's Rook's file to stop the Pawn and meanwhile White would capture the Queen's Pawn and then raze Black's King's side.

I recommend the student to analyse this ending thoroughly. It will bring home to him the important realization that Rooks belong in open files and that in Pawn-endings, whenever possible, they should be used for attack rather than for defensive play.

When there is only one Pawn left in addition to the Rooks, the weaker side can force a draw, provided his King commands the queening square of the Pawn. Diagram 45 shows a position which is favourable to the stronger side which can usually be obtained in this ending, unless the defending Rook has succeeded at an early stage in getting behind the Pawn and King of the opponent. Even here Black forces a draw with a pretty manœuvre: 1. .... R—B2; 2. R—QR2, R—K2 ch; 3. P×R, and Black is stalemate.

A Rook and two connected Pawns against a Rook will almost always win, unless the defending King can block the Pawns and the other King cannot get in front of them. Even in the latter case, the stronger side will sometimes find an opportunity to keep the opposing King or Rook —or both—busy stopping one of the Pawns while the other advances under cover of its King. The same idea points the way in endings with a Rook and two separated Pawns against a Rook. One of the

Diagram 45

Diagram 46

Pawns is used to reduce the mobility of the opponent whilst the other pushes forward toward the queening square.

BISHOP v. KNIGHT

Endings with one minor piece on either side in addition to several Pawns, equal in number, are generally drawn whilst in most cases even one extra Pawn will win, by forcing the sacrifice of the opposing piece to prevent the queening of that Pawn. There are a few typical exceptions to this rule which I will illustrate.

In Diagram 46 White must give up his Knight for Black's passed Pawn, but he draws the game all the same because Black, whilst going after White's Pawn with his King, must give White's King access to the corner in which the remaining black Pawn would have to queen in order to force a win.

From that corner he can never drive White out again, because his Bishop is 'of the wrong colour'. White will finally be stalemated, just as in the ending with the Rook's Pawn alone. In other words, Bishop and Rook's Pawn can win against the lone King only if the Bishop is of the colour of the queening square. Play would proceed as follows:
1. Kt—K2, P—B7; 2. Kt—Q4 ch, K—Kt7; 3. Kt×P, K×Kt; 4. K—K2, K—Kt6; 5. K—Q2, etc.

BISHOP v. BISHOP

In end-games of Bishop versus Bishop, in which both players have several Pawns left, a passed Pawn on the wing at a distance from the Kings usually wins when the Bishops are of the same colour, because then the gradual advance of the Pawn can be forced with the aid of the Bishop. If the opposing King blocks the Pawn, the attacking King can make for the adversary's Pawns on the other wing. The stronger side must, however, avoid Pawn exchanges as much as possible, because when only one Pawn is left there is always a good chance that the opposing Bishop will be able to sacrifice itself for the Pawn, thus drawing the game.

The player whose Pawns are on squares of the colour of the Bishops is at a disadvantage if one or more of them are attackable by the opposing King, even if the latter has no passed Pawn with which to

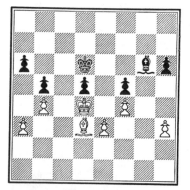

Diagram 47

limit the mobility of his adversary's King or Bishop. Diagram 47 furnishes an example.

Black's Pawn position is weaker because he has two isolated Pawns on white squares whilst White's Pawns cannot be attacked by Black's Bishop. The latter has less mobility than White's Bishop, and Black's King is tied to his Q3, to prevent White's entry at B5 or K5. These drawbacks decide the issue, though it takes a rather tricky manœuvre to take advantage of the situation. White starts with 1. **P—KR4.** Now Black must reply **P—KR4,** because if he retreats with the Bishop to R2 White plays P—R5 and Black's Bishop's Pawn is lost. White's plan will be to place his Bishop on B3, attacking both the Q Pawn and the R Pawn, at a time when Black's Bishop is on B2 defending them. Then Black can move only his Bishop, and there is no other square from which it can keep both Pawns protected. White could accomplish this end if his Bishop were at B1, for he could then force Black's Bishop to B2 by playing B—Kt2, after which he would occupy B3. However, if White played B—B1 now, Black would reply B—B2 and then retreat to either K1 or Kt1, depending upon whether White continues with B—K2 or Kt2. Thus Black would be in a position to foil White's plan by occupying B2 *after* White goes to B3.

Black would not have this defence if it were his move at this moment. For he would have to play B—R2, and then White would win with

B—B1. Whether Black continues with B—Kt1 or B—Kt3, White would force B2 with either B—K2 or Kt2, so that he could occupy B3 at the right moment.

White's problem therefore resolves itself into the question how to maintain the present position but make it Black's turn to move. Due to the greater mobility of his Bishop, White can accomplish this task. He plays 2. **B—B2, B—R2;** 3. **B—Kt1!, B—Kt3;** 4. **B—Q3.** After **B—R2;** 5. **B—B1,** he wins a Pawn as explained above, and the rest is simple. If Black gives up the KR Pawn, White's KR Pawn becomes free to advance. If he gives up the Q Pawn, White's Bishop gains access to QKt7 and gets another Pawn.

In end-games in which both players have a Knight and Pawns, or one has a Bishop and the other a Knight, it is also usually the strength or weakness of the Pawn position which decides the issue. Where the Pawns are blocked, the Knight is ordinarily stronger than the Bishop because the latter can attack only Pawns on squares of his own colour.

A Bishop fighting against a Bishop of opposite colour and a Pawn, can almost always draw because it can rarely be stopped from sacrificing itself for the Pawn. A Bishop of the same colour, however, can sometimes block the defending Bishop's access to the Pawn.

In Diagram 48, the winning procedure would be 1. **B—B6, B—K8;** 2. **B—Kt5, B—B3;** 3. **B—B4, K—Kt6;** 4. **B—K5, B—Q7;** 5. **P—B6, K—B5;** 6. **P—B7, B—R3;** 7. **B—Q6, B—Kt2;** 8. **K—B5, K—Q4;** 9. **K—Kt6,** etc.

Diagram 48   Diagram 49

When a player has two connected passed Pawns and a Bishop against a Bishop of opposite colour, *it is important that he place the Pawns on squares of the colour of the opposing Bishop*, because otherwise the Pawns may be blocked. In Diagram 49 White cannot win although he is three Pawns ahead. All Black has to do is move his Bishop backwards and forwards and play K—B3 to keep White from KKt5.

In Diagram 50, White will play 1. **P—K6,** and not P—Q6, because in the latter case Black would again block the Pawns for ever with K—K3.   After **B—K1; 2. B—R4 ch, K—B1; 3. P—Q6,** White is free to push his Q Pawn into the Queen.   Had Black played 1. .... K—Q1, White would again have won through 2. B—R5 ch, K—B1;

Diagram 50   Diagram 51

3. P—Q6.   Black has no chance to sacrifice his Bishop on Q2 and to get both Pawns in return, because White first plays his King to K7.

ROOK v. MINOR PIECE, AND PAWNS

A Rook will almost always win against a Bishop or Knight with an even number of Pawns on both sides, unless the player of the minor piece has an advanced passed Pawn and his King nearby, so that the opposing King and Rook are immobilized by the necessity of stopping the Pawn.   Ordinarily, two extra Pawns are needed for the minor piece to draw against the Rook.   That is one reason why the value of a Rook is usually considered equal to a minor piece and two Pawns.

The way for White to win in the position of Diagram 51 is to sacrifice his Rook for Bishop and Pawn and then win Black's Knight's Pawn in the manner explained in the discussion of Diagram 27.   For example: 1. **R—Kt4, B—B7; 2. R—Kt8, B—K5; 3. R—Kt8 ch, K—B3; 4. R×P!, P×R; 5. K×B, K—Kt4; 6. K—K5,** etc.

3. FUNDAMENTAL MIDDLE-GAME COMBINATIONS

FROM the study of the end-games investigated in the preceding pages, the beginner will arrive at two important conclusions. One is that even if he loses a mere Pawn he will very likely be checkmated in the ending, because the extra-Pawn of his opponent is a potential Queen. The other is that the rough guess at the relative value of the men which we made on the basis of their greater or lesser mobility is actually correct, at least as far as the end-game is concerned. This comparative evaluation the student will now be in a position to set down in a more concrete form. He will appreciate that—apart from positions in which a Pawn is far advanced and cannot be stopped from queening —a Rook is worth as much as a minor piece and two Pawns, two minor pieces as much as a Rook and one or two Pawns, and a Queen almost as much as two Rooks.

Usually a minor piece is considered equal to three Pawns, because in most endings a Bishop or a Knight can defend the game against three Pawns unless they are too far advanced. This would make a Rook worth five Pawns, but very few end-games occur in which this estimate can be tested.

There is one obvious exception, in which the relative value of the pieces involved in exchanges need not be considered. If it is possible to checkmate the King in a sudden assault, it does not matter in the least how much material is sacrificed for the purpose.

Positions harbouring the possibility of such mating assaults fall into certain types which we will now investigate. We shall learn from them a good deal about the methods of co-operation among the different pieces in 'combinations', i.e. in series of forcing moves calculated to bring about a checkmate or to gain an advantage in material against any defence. Such combinations may be relatively easy to visualize, if every move comprised by them represents a threat that can be met in only one way. They may be more complicated and require painstaking calculations, if one or more of the moves concerned permit the opponent a choice between several replies.

The ability to see through a combination correctly is not merely a matter of experience. It depends upon a certain gift of visualizing clearly the positions resulting after each move of that combination. Often players of comparatively little experience show remarkable combinative gifts. However, they usually waste a great deal of effort in labouring through combinations which have no chance of succeeding, because they fail to recognize certain general characteristics which indicate to a more advanced player that the object aimed at cannot be achieved.

To explain these characteristics is the principal aim of this chapter. The typical positions selected contain the elements of most combinations which occur in actual play. Their study will save the novice a great deal of the time he would ordinarily need to familiarize himself with them from his own experience.

Most frequently—and very naturally—the Queen, the most powerful piece, plays an important role in checkmating attacks in the middle-game. The characteristic distinction of these combinations from the type we encountered in end-game play is the absence of the attacking King.

For reasons which will be explained later, the players usually castle on the King's side, and most of the following illustrations are therefore chosen so as to show mating attacks against the King who has castled on that side.

In Diagram 52, White's Queen threatens checkmate on Kt7, where it would be protected by the Pawn on B6. Black can apparently defend

Diagram 52

Diagram 53

himself with R—KKt1. However, White would then checkmate in two moves through Q×RP ch, K×Q; R—R4. Playing R—R4 instead of sacrificing the Queen would not have accomplished anything, as Black would have protected his KR2 by Kt×P. Had he made this move instead of R—Kt1, White could have captured his Rook with the Queen.

In the position of Diagram 53, there is no way for Black to defend the mate threatened by White's Queen. He can move the Rook, so that after Q—R7 ch the King can go to B1, but the Queen blocks the King's flight to the second rank and White mates with Q—R8.

In Diagram 54, the white Queen again threatens mate on KR7, this time protected by its Knight, but after moving his Rook to Q1 Black will be able to escape with his King to K2 if White checks on R7 and then on R8, as in the previous example. White could then continue with Q×P, threatening mate on B7, but Black would defend himself with R—B1 and he might hold out for a long time.

White has a much stronger line of play. In reply to R—Q1 he would first take the Bishop's Pawn with check and after K—R1 he would return with the Queen to R5. The consequence would be K—Kt1; and now mate in four moves through Q—R7 ch, K—B1; Q—R8 ch, K—K2; Q×P ch, K—K1; Q—B7 mate.

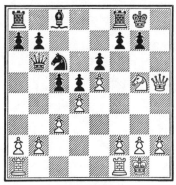

Diagram 54

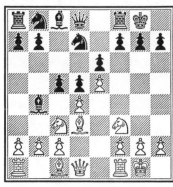

Diagram 55

Somewhat similar, though complicated by an additional variation, is the combination which is possible in the position of Diagram 55. Here White will start with 1. **B×P ch,** in order to continue, after **K×B,** with 2. **Kt—Kt5 ch,** so that K—Kt1; 3. Q—R5, would lead to a similar mate as shown in the previous example. Therefore, Black will have to play **K—Kt3.** However, that spot is no bed of roses either. White continues with 3. **Q—Q3 ch,** and the King cannot go to R4 on account of Q—R7 ch and mate on the following move. The only reply is therefore **P—B4.** Then White has the choice between Kt×KP and P×P e.p. After 4. **Kt×KP, Q—K1** (Q—R4?; 5. Q—KKt3 ch); 5. **Kt×QP!,** White wins at least one of the Rooks for a Knight and remains with a superiority of material, quite apart from the exposed position of Black's King, which invites a continuation of the mating attack. Black's Queen cannot capture the Knight, because White would check on B4 with the other Knight and win the Queen.

The other alternative, 4. **P×P e.p.,** affords White an even more devastating attack. After **K×P** he might continue with 5. **R—K1,** threatening mate through R×P and practically forcing **Kt—Kt3.** Then, by sacrificing more pieces, he would draw the King still farther forward, into a mating net. 6. **Kt×KP!** (threatening B—Kt5 ch, which would win the Queen), **B×Kt;** 7. **B—Kt5 ch!, K×B;** 8. **R×B** threatens mate through 9. Q—Kt6 ch, K—R5; 10. P—Kt3 ch, K—R6; 11. Q—R5 ch, etc., or 10. R—K5 followed by R—R5 or Q—Kt3. Black cannot defend with R—B3 because 9. R—K5 ch, K—R3; 10. Q—R3 ch leads to mate by the Queen on R5. His only move is **Q—B3,** offering his Queen for the Rook. White can take his time capturing the Queen. He can play with the exposed black King like a cat with a mouse. 9. **P—B4 ch, K—R4** (not Q×P on account of Q—Kt6 ch and P—Kt3 ch, winning the Queen for a Pawn); 10. **R×Q, R×R;** 11. **Q—R7 ch, K—Kt5** (R—R3; 12. Q—B5 ch, K—R5; 13. Q—R3 mate); 12. **R—KB1** (threatening Q—R3 mate), **R—R3;** 13. **P—R3 ch, K—R5;** 14 **Q×P,** and the mate cannot be prevented.

This example shows how easily the King may be caught in a mating net once it is forced out into the open where it lacks the protection of its Pawns. To make a breach in the protecting line of these Pawns is the first step in almost every mating attack. Where a Rook has an open file leading to the King's defences, such a breach is often accomplished without difficulty.

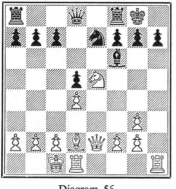

Diagram 56

In Diagram 56, 1. **R×P** offers a Rook sacrifice which Black cannot accept, as 2. Q—R5 ch and 3. R—R1 would lead to a mate on Black's R1 or R2. The threat after 1. R×P is 2. R—R8 ch, forcing K×R and the same mating procedure as just described. Black can temporarily defend himself with **Kt—Kt3,** but after 2. **Q—R5,** which threatens QR—R1 followed by the Rook sacrifice on R8 and mate with the Queen, he has no satisfactory continuation. He cannot provide for an escape of his King with **R—K1,** because after 3. **Kt×Kt, P×Kt;** 4. **Q×KtP, K—B1;** 5. **B—R6!, K—K2** (not P×B because of Q—B7 mate, nor Q—Q2 because of Q×B ch, nor R—K2 because of R—R8 mate); 6. **B×P,** he loses at least his Bishop. The threat is B×B double check, and if K—K3; 7. B×B, Q×B, White mates with 8. R—K1 ch and 9. Q×Q.

Since 1. .... Kt—Kt3 will not stem White's attack, Black's only defence is P—KKt3, which keeps White's Queen from R5.

White will then play 2. QR—R1, remaining at least a Pawn ahead, with many opportunities for further direct assaults on Black's King

in the opened Rook's file. Among other things he now threatens
3. Kt—Kt4. This could not be answered with B—Kt2, as White would
play 4. R×B ch, K×R; 5. B—R6 ch and mate through 6. Kt—B6
followed by a discovered check with the Bishop. Neither would the
reply 3. .... Kt—B4 be sufficient, for 4. Kt×B ch, Q×Kt; 5. Q—
K5, Q×Q; 6. P×Q would threaten mate through R—R8 ch and QR—
R7, and the only defence, P—KKt4, would not postpone the end very
long, as after 7. B×KtP the threat B—B6 and R—R8 mate would
force Black to continue with P—KB3. Then 8. B×P would compel
Black to give up his Rook for the Bishop in order to stop the threat
9. P—KKt4, since the Knight could not move without allowing mate
through R—Kt7 ch.

A Bishop placed on KB6, with a Rook and the Queen attacking in
the Rook's or Knight's file, very often leads to a mating attack, usually
after one of the Pawns in front of the King has been removed by means
of a sacrifice of a piece. Diagram 57 furnishes a typical example.

With 1. R—KKt4 White attacks
the Knight's Pawn. Black cannot
protect it by advancing to Kt3,
because he would be checkmated
through the Queen's sacrifice 2. Q×
P, K×Q; 3. R—R4 ch and 4. R—R8.
Protecting the Pawn by 1. ....,
B—B1 leads to an equally disastrous
finale: 2. **R×P ch!, B×R** (K—R1?;
3. Q×P mate); 3. **Q—Kt4, K—B1**;
4. **Q×B ch, K—K1**; 5. **Q—Kt8 ch,
K—Q2**; 6. **Q×BP ch, Kt—K2** (K—
Q3?; 7. Kt—K4 mate); 7. **Q×Kt ch,
K—B3**; 8. **Q—K6 ch, Q—Q3** (Black
must give up his Rook, as K—B4

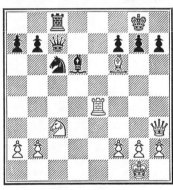

Diagram 57

would allow mate in two moves through Q—Q5 ch and Q—Kt5);
9. **Q×R ch, Q—B2** (if the King goes to Kt3, 10. B—Q8 ch wins
the Queen, since K—R3 would be answered by 11. Q—B4 ch and
12. Q×P mate); 10. **Q—K6 ch.** The exchange of Queens would, of
course, be sufficient; but White can actually win the Queen or force a
checkmate. **Q—Q3**; 11. **Q—K4 ch, K—Kt3**; 12. **B—Q4 ch,** and Black
loses the Queen through Kt—Kt5 ch if he goes to B2, or he is mated
by Q—Q3 ch or Q—B5 ch (depending upon where the King goes),
followed by Q—QKt5.

Let us now look at a few typical checkmates with Queen and Knight.
The following three positions are all taken from actual games. In
Diagram 58, White threatens mate with 1. R—R5, forcing the reply
P×R, and then 2. Q—B6 is mate.

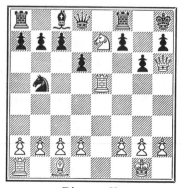

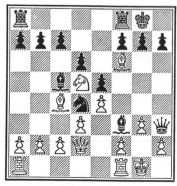

Diagram 58   Diagram 59

In Diagram 59, White apparently cannot defend the mate which the black Queen threatens on his Kt2. But a player who knows the mating position illustrated in Diagram 58 will turn the tables with 1. **Kt—K7 ch, K—R1**; 2. **B×P ch, K×B**; 3. **Q—Kt5 ch, K—R1**; 4. **Q—B6 mate.**

A checkmating combination in which Queen and Knight frequently co-operate in the middle-game, but of which not one in a million players would think unless it has been shown to him in a similar position, was first discovered by the French master André Philidor.

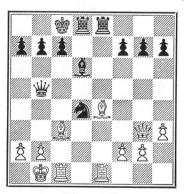

Diagram 60

Both players contesting the game from which the position of Diagram 60 is taken knew that combination, but White overlooked that after 1. **Q×P?** Black has the opportunity to lead into it with **R×B!**; 2. **R×R, Q—Q6 ch.** The Rook cannot interpose because the Queen would take it and then mate on B8. But after 3. **K—R1** follows **Kt—B7 ch**; 4. **K—Kt1, Kt—R6 double ch**; 5. **K—R1, Q—Kt8 ch!!,** forcing the Rook to capture the Queen, whereupon the Knight mates on B7.

Checkmates with Rook and Knight occur rather rarely in the middle of the game. Diagram 61 shows an example of the crude sort of combination with which these pieces accomplish the mate. 1. **Q—K8 ch** forces **R×Q** and 2. **R×R** checkmates. The same combination in a somewhat more veiled form would be possible in Diagram 58, if Black's KKt Pawn were on Kt2 instead of Kt3. In that case White could checkmate in two moves by **Q×RP ch.** The King must take and the Rook mates on R5.

The only other typical mating positions with Rook and Knight are illustrated in Diagrams 62 and 63. The former shows a position of a kind encountered not infrequently in games where a player has succeeded in getting an open Rook's file on the wing on which the

Diagram 61

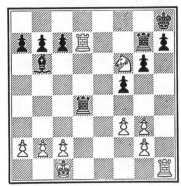

Diagram 62

opponent has castled. White checkmates through **R (R1)×P ch,** followed, after **R×R,** by **R×R.**

The mating position resulting from Diagram 63 is very similar, except that the Knight instead of the Rook gives the mate. In the game in

Diagram 63

Diagram 64

which this position occurred, Niemzovich played White against Hakansson (Kristianbad, 1922). He sacrificed the Queen on Q7 and after Kt×Q mated with Kt—K6.

With the Rook on the seventh rank and the Knight placed so that it can reach B6, it is sometimes possible to draw in the nick of time an ending which would otherwise be lost. Diagram 64 shows a typical example. White has no way of stopping Black's passed Pawn. But he saves himself through 1. **Kt—K4,** threatening to sacrifice the Knight for the Pawn, after which Black could no longer win. In answer to **P—B7** White continues with 2. **Kt—B6 ch.** The King cannot go into the corner on account of the mate illustrated in connection with Diagram 62. Therefore he must play **K—B1.** Then 3. **Kt—R7 ch** forces perpetual check, for if **K—K1** White plays again 4. **Kt—B6 ch** and Black cannot reply **K—Q1** because he would be mated with **R—Q7.** His King is restricted to the squares K1, B1 and Kt1.

Bishop and Knight once in a while succeed in checkmating the King in the middle-game, if he is surrounded by men of his own, with the exception of two diagonally adjacent squares controlled by the opposing Bishop. A Knight-check will then effect a mate.

The position of Diagram 65 occurred in a game which Niemzovich played at the age of eighteen, and in which he succeeded in bringing off a mate with Bishop and Knight after a most ingenious sacrifice.

Diagram 65

He probably saw that he could force a checkmate easily enough in a more brutal manner: 1. **Q—Kt4, P—Kt3;** 2. **Q×Kt, P—KR4;** 3. **Kt×KtP, P×Kt;** 4. **Q×P ch, R—B2;** 5. **B—K8, R×B;** 6. **Q×QR ch, R—B1;** 7. **Q×P mate.** But the temptation offered by the following line was too great: 1. **B—K8!!, QR×B;** 2. **Q—R6!!, P×Q;** 3. **Kt—Kt4,** and Black cannot guard against the mate because, due to the Bishop-sacrifice on the first move, the King's Rook cannot make room for the King.

Unfortunately, this beautiful combination has a hole. On the second move, Black can take the Bishop instead of the Queen. Naturally, Niemzovich had considered this possibility. Probably he intended 3. Kt—Kt4, Kt—Kt4 (to defend the square R2); 4. Kt×P ch, K—R1; 5. Kt—R5, R—KKt1; 6. Q—B6 ch, etc. But in reply to Kt—R5, Black has the remarkable excuse 5. .... **Kt—B6 ch!,** and either the Queen or the Knight has a perpetual check, depending upon whether White takes the Knight or goes to R3. He cannot go to Kt3, because R—Kt1 ch would win, and if K—R1, the Queen mates.

What is worse, Black can actually win the game by answering 3. **Kt—Kt4** with **Q×P!!.** After 4. **Kt×P ch, Q×Kt;** 5. **Q×Q,** Black escapes a perpetual check by **R—Kt1;** 6. **K×Kt, KR—B1,** and then one of the passed Pawns queens.

It happens very rarely that two Bishops execute a checkmate in the middle-game, though they are very often the accessories to a devastating attack in conjunction with Queen or Rook which leads to an early mate.

In Diagram 66, which shows a position that occurred in a game of mine against Englund (Scheveningen, 1913), play proceeded as follows:

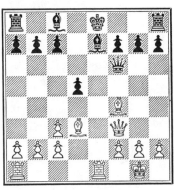

Diagram 66

1. **Q×P!** Black cannot capture the Bishop which this move leaves unguarded, because 2. B—Kt5 ch would lead either to mate through K—B1; 3. Q—Q8 ch!!, B×Q; and 4. R—K8, or, if Black plays 2. .... P—B3, White would obtain a Rook and three Pawns for two Bishops and still maintain his attack. The continuation would be 3. B×P ch, P×B; 4. Q×P ch, K—B1; 5. Q×R, etc.

For this reason Black played 1. .... **P—B3.** I replied 2. **Q—K4,** and Black had to safeguard his King's Bishop with **B—K3** before thinking of castling. Now I played 3. **QR—Q1,** and Black did not suspect that this innocent-looking move carried a load of deadly poison. He should have answered Q—R5 protecting his KR2, so that he could castle on the King's wing. Instead, he hastily castled on the Queen's wing and was checkmated: **Castles QR; 4. Q×P ch!!, P×Q; 5. B—R6 mate.**

The proportion of games in which the mating of the opponent's King is accomplished on a full board is comparatively small. In the normal, average game both sides employ their forces in executing manœuvres intended to gain a superiority of material which, after gradual exchange of most of the pieces left on the board, will lead to one of the typical winning endings discussed in the previous chapter.

Since we know from that discussion that, with some few exceptions, a single Pawn may suffice to win, we must always try to avoid losing material, be that only the shadow of a Pawn. It is a good habit to look upon every Pawn as a prospective Queen. This has a sobering influence on impetuous attacks the outcome of which is not clearly foreseen.

It is true that material is sometimes sacrificed, not with a checkmate in view, but merely to bring about a positional advantage. However, the considerations underlying such manœuvres are difficult for beginners to grasp before they have learned to appreciate how combinations are brought about which gain material. Therefore, let us first examine whether we cannot find certain characteristics that will tell us something about the likelihood of a combination turning out to be advantageous. This would be of immeasurable help when we are faced by a maze of variations, which would require us to see too far ahead to trust our calculations.

Fundamentally, all combinations resolve themselves into two classes. One, in which a man attacks two or more of the adversary's pieces simultaneously and there is no reply which defends them all. The other, in which only one man is attacked, but where this man cannot move away for one reason or another, and where more pieces can be accumulated against it than can be mustered for its defence.

A simple device, which amounts to a matter of elementary arithmetic, facilitates the calculation of combinations of the latter type. If the beginner neglects using this device, he will find it very difficult to cope even with rather simple combinations.

Diagram 67 shows a position from a game Capablanca-Blanco, played in 1913 at Havana. Black's King's Pawn is three times attacked

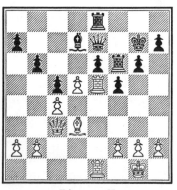

Diagram 67

—once by White's Queen's Pawn and twice by White's Rooks. The Rook on K1 must be included in this calculation although its path toward Black's Pawn is obstructed by the other Rook, because the obstruction is no longer present after 1. P×P, B×P; 2. R×B, Q×R.

Black's Pawn is apparently defended four times—by the Bishop, the Queen and the two Rooks. However, the Rook on B3 cannot be considered in the accounting procedure, because after White's Rook leaves K5, Black's Rook and King are in the diagonal controlled by White's Queen. Thus, after 1. P×P, B×P; 2. R×B, Black's Rook is pinned and cannot recapture, and if 1. .... R×P, White wins the Rook because R×R discovers a check by his Queen so that Black cannot recapture.

What actually happened in the game was 1. **P×P, B—B1;** 2. **B—K2.** Now Black can take the Pawn back, because he is attacking it three times, and only White's Rook defends it. The reason why White gives back the Pawn is that Black's Bishop remains pinned on K6, so that the white Bishop can be manœuvred to Q5, exerting more pressure on the hapless cardinal than he is likely to withstand.

Black did take the Pawn, and after **B×P;** 3. **B—B3** moved his King so as to unpin the Rook: **K—B2;** 4. **B—Q5.** Now the Bishop is four times defended and only three times attacked, but it is important for

Black to make sure that the value of the defending pieces which would be exchanged on K3 is not greater than that of the attacking pieces which disappear in that exchange. If it were White's move and he went through with the exchanges he would be getting a Bishop, a Rook and the Queen, and he would lose only a Bishop and two Rooks. Therefore, Black must take his Queen out of the King's file and get his Rook on K1 to take a hand in the defence immediately. He played **Q—Q3** and White replied 5. **Q—K3**, adding another piece to the attack on the Bishop. Although the latter is still protected as often as it is attacked, Black's game is extremely difficult to defend, if it can be saved at all. The reason is that his pieces are tied to the task of protecting the Bishop, cramping each other in the attempt, and cannot be shifted readily for the defence of another spot which White might attack with his more mobile forces.

This is a very important point to understand. It explains that the value of a piece in the middle-game cannot be measured exclusively with the yardstick we found suitable for this purpose in the end-game. In the middle-game, the mobility of a piece, its ability to shift quickly from one theatre of war to another, is a decisive factor. In the present case, Black's Rook on B3 has no move. His other Rook can only go back and forth on K1 and K2. The Queen has only Q2 and Q3 to choose from. White, on the other hand, has a great deal of mobility with his Queen. It is interesting to note that Black's game collapses within a few moves because he makes no attempt to restrict this mobility of White's Queen and confines himself to purely defensive moves. He might have tried P—B5 and P—KR4 in order to keep the Queen away from his KR3. He actually played **R—K2**. After 6. **Q—R6, K—Kt1**; 7. **P—KR4!** threatened to tear up the chain of Pawns protecting his King, and he had to look on helplessly. **P—R3**; 8. **P—R5, P—B5**; 9. **P×P, P×P**; 10. **R×B!** wins a piece, as R (K2)×R; 11. R×R, R×R leaves the Rook pinned, so that White can play 12. Q×P ch, at the same time attacking the Rook for the second time.

The pinning of a man, or the blocking of a Pawn, is the prerequisite basis for any combination conceived with a view to winning material by accumulating more attacking forces than the opponent can match. There is little sense in attacking a man who can save himself simply by going elsewhere, unless that man is driven from a favourable spot to a less favourable one and the attacking piece has not been taken from a good spot to a less desirable one, merely for the purpose of driving the opponent's man away.

A desirable spot for a piece is one from which it has many other squares to go to. Preferably it should be one which enables that piece to shift its activity from one wing to the other without too much difficulty, particularly if the opponent is in a position to shift his own forces readily for attack.   Generally speaking, this principle of mobility reigns supreme among the considerations influencing the decision where to place a piece.   Naturally, there is often a modifying factor, such as the location of other men with whom the piece moved is to co-operate, or the necessity to counter a specific manœuvre of the opponent.   But in nine out of ten cases the player who places his men on spots selected from the point of view of mobility, will get the better of an adversary who does not make this principle his guide; for if a good target offers itself, in the form of a blocked Pawn or a pinned piece, the player directing the more mobile pieces will be in a position to train more forces on the target.

The second class of combinations, which comprises simultaneous attacks on several targets, is comparatively simple to grasp.   It rarely takes a beginner long to learn from bitter experience that before making a move he must not merely investigate whether any of his men are exposed to immediate capture, but that he must guard against his opponent making a move which attacks more than one man at a time. In the latter case, he will be able to avoid loss only if he has a move which protects everything that is attacked, or if he can first withdraw one of the attacked pieces with a threat requiring a reply, thus gaining time for saving the other piece or pieces which had been attacked simultaneously.

In Diagram 68, White must move the Knight which is attacked by Black's Pawn.   To go to Kt5, attacking simultaneously Black's Queen,

Diagram 68

Rook's Pawn and Queen's Pawn, would be senseless because Black can reply Q—Kt3, protecting everything, and the Knight is badly placed because it cannot easily get to the King's wing for co-operation with Bishop and Queen.   The only moves worth while considering are Kt—Q5, Kt—K4 or Kt—K2, because from these spots the Knight can reach a good many others which are all within the field of activity of the other white pieces.

In a double attack the King is very frequently one of the two targets, not necessarily by way of a check but by the threat to checkmate him if the second target is protected.   Diagram 69 shows a typical example.   White wins through 1. **Kt×Kt ch, B×Kt**; 2. **Q—B3.**   The threat is now not only Q×R but also Q—B5, which would lead to mate with Q×RP ch and Q—R8 unless Black responds P—KKt3.

The latter, however, deprives the Bishop of its protection, so that White can capture it on the next move.

The most devastating double attacks usually result from discovered checks.   In the position of Diagram 70, which occurred in a game between Torre and Emanuel Lasker (Moscow, 1925), White won

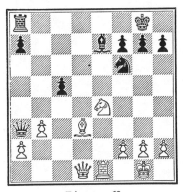

Diagram 69

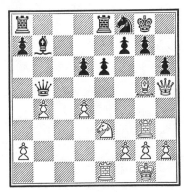

Diagram 70

through 1. **B—B6!**, **Q×Q**; 2. **R×P ch, K—R1**; and now the Rook razes everything in his path before recapturing the Queen: 3. **R×P ch, K—Kt1**; 4. **R—Kt7 ch, K—R1**; 5, **R×B ch, K—Kt1**; 6. **R—Kt7 ch, K—R1**; 7. **R—Kt5 ch, K—R2**; 8. **R×Q**; and though Black regains the lost piece with **K—Kt3**, the ending is hopeless for him as he is two Pawns down and loses a third one.

In Diagram 71, White could attack Black's Rook and Knight simultaneously by advancing the Queen's Pawn.   But the move would not be good, because Black can first play the Rook to R3, threatening mate on R8, and after White defends this threat, the Knight moves so that White has gained nothing from the advance of the Pawn.   The latter is weak on Q5, where it cannot be defended by another Pawn, while on Q4 it was perfectly safe.

Diagram 71

A slightly more complicated type of combination in a similar category to the one just illustrated might occur in the position of Diagram 72. Again White apparently wins a piece by 'forking' two black pieces with 1. **P—Q5**. Black can save the piece with **P—QR3**, which threatens to take the Bishop if White takes one of the Knights. White has the choice between either withdrawing the Bishop or exchanging it first against Black's Queen's Knight and then capturing the other Knight with the Pawn. However, after 2. **B×Kt, P×B; 3. P×Kt, P×KP,** Black regains his piece because White's Knight is pinned by

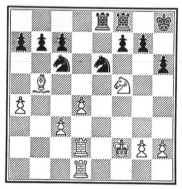

Diagram 72

Diagram 73

Black's Rook and Black will be in a position to capture it on the next move. Had White withdrawn his Bishop on the second move, Black would have withdrawn the Queen's Knight, and again White would not have gained a piece with P×Kt because his own Knight would be lost a move later.

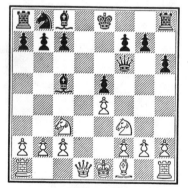

Diagram 74

There are two types of forks with the Knight which occur not infrequently and which I will especially illustrate because the beginner is not likely to see the combinations involved unless they have been shown to him. In Diagram 73 White wins a Pawn through Q×P, because if Black takes the Queen, White plays Kt—B7 ch, regaining her.

In Diagram 74, White plays 1. Kt—Q5, attacking the Queen and the Pawn on B7. Black must not defend the Pawn with Q—B3, because 2. B—Kt5, which pins the Queen, would actually win her although the Bishop is not protected, for after Q×B, 3. Kt×P ch attacks both King and Queen.

Sometimes a Rook has an opportunity to execute a pin of this type. In Diagram 75, White saves his game by 1. R×B, pinning Black's

Queen. After Q×R he wins the Queen by forking King and Queen with 2. B×P ch, which forces Q×B, 3. R×Q.

Most frequently the Rook has occasion to pin a hostile minor piece in the King's file, because there a player is often tempted to capture a Pawn before he has castled. Diagram 76 furnishes an example.

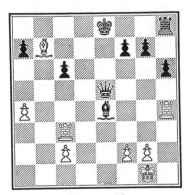

Diagram 75

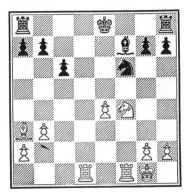

Diagram 76

Black must not capture White's King's Pawn with his Knight, although he can protect the latter with his Bishop from Q4 in case White pins the Knight with KR—K1. For White would sacrifice his Rook for the Knight and after B×R he would pin the Bishop with R—K1 and win it, thus getting two pieces for Rook and Pawn.

The Rooks' most desirable hunting ground, as already pointed out during the discussion of end-games, is the seventh rank. Not only is a simultaneous attack of several Pawns or pieces usually entailed in the occupation of that rank; if both Rooks, or Queen and Rook, succeed in doubling on the seventh rank, there is often a possibility for all sorts of checkmating combinations.

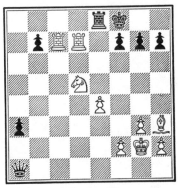

Diagram 77

In the position of Diagram 77, which is taken from a game I played against Frank Marshall, the Pawns on Black's second rank are the prey of White's Rooks. I played 1. R× BP ch, K—Kt1; and I could have continued with 2. R×QKtP (not R×KKtP ch, because after Q×R; 3. R×Q ch, K×R, the advanced Rook's Pawn would be very dangerous), P—R7; 3. Kt—Kt4, Q—Kt7; 4. Kt×P, Q×Kt; 5. R×P ch,

K—B1; 6. R×P, K—Kt1; 7. B—B5, followed by the advance of the Rook's Pawn to R6 with the threat R (QKt7)—Kt7 ch and R—R8 mate. There was not very much Black could have done to counter this plan. But I saw the opportunity for a speedier mate through 2. **Kt—B6 ch!** This blocks the path of Black's Queen which protects the King's Knight's Pawn, and subjects Black's King to the concerted attack of the two Rooks and the Bishop. **P×Kt; 3. R—Kt7 ch, K—Q1** (K—B1?; 4. R [QB7]—KB7 mate); 4. **R×P ch, K—Kt1; 5. R (R7)—Kt7 ch, K—R1;** 6. **B—B5!,** and there is no satisfactory defence against the threat 7. R—Kt4 and 8. R—R7 mate.

4. THE OPENING

THE reader who has followed me thus far will have equipped himself with the elementary knowledge indispensable to anyone who wants to have at least a vague idea on how to go about playing a game of chess. He will be aware of the comparative value which he should ascribe to the various men. He will also have observed a good many ways in which the pieces co-operate in executing combinations intended either to gain a superiority in material or to checkmate the King. However, he will still be completely in the dark as to how to open a game so that he has as good a chance as his opponent to arrive at a middle-game position which holds winning possibilities.

The considerations which point the way to an intelligent conduct of the opening are of a rather general nature. In playing through the combinations discussed in the preceding chapter, the observant reader will have noticed that the winning side almost always had a superior fighting force available at the spot where the actual fighting was in progress—something he would probably have expected even without seeing it demonstrated in examples. To be in a position to assemble such a superior force, it appears reasonable—again without specific illustrations—that a player should aim at securing as much mobility for his pieces as possible, so that, if necessary, they can be readily shifted from one part of the board to another. Moreover, it will be important to attain this mobility as rapidly as possible, for the player who first completes the 'development' of his forces will be ready first to gather them for an attack.

As White makes the initial move, he has the birthright of attack, whilst Black must be satisfied with a defensive role unless White plays indifferently. During the opening stage of the game, we would call a weak move one which does not appreciably increase the mobility of the pieces. The trouble is that often there seems to be a choice between two or more moves which apparently advance the development of the pieces equally well, and generalities no longer suffice to narrow that choice. However, such fine decisions are a concern only for masters. The beginner, and even the player who is considerably advanced, can make remarkable strides by letting the general principle of rapid development be almost his only guide.

RAPID DEVELOPMENT

This principle explains why it is generally advantageous to make *one* developing move with *every* piece before engaging in combinations involving a second move with a piece that is already developed—unless that second move is made to a square on which a player would like to place the piece in the early middle-game in any case.

If White wastes a 'tempo' by making an unnecessary second move with a piece during the development stage of the game, he will suffer no more than losing the advantage of the first move. Black, on the other hand, can rarely take that liberty without paying a severe penalty —provided, of course, his opponent knows how to exact it.

Since the Knights are the only pieces which can move at the beginning of the game, it is necessary to make Pawn-moves in order to open lines for the other pieces and thus to endow them with fighting power. When advancing either the King's Pawn or the Queen's Pawn, lines are opened for the Queen and a Bishop. Any other Pawn-move would open a line for one piece only. Therefore it should be dismissed from our consideration, unless it helps getting the Rooks into play or decreases the mobility of one of the opponent's pieces.

To create an open file for a Rook, a player must necessarily *remove* his Pawn from that file. In games starting with 1. P—K4, P—K4, the obvious method to accomplish this is to play P—Q4. White can always employ this method with ease, whilst Black has his difficulties with it, as we shall soon realize.

CONTROL OF TERRITORY

The attack on Black's K4 with P—Q4 serves another very important purpose which is also bound up with the principle of mobility. This is the attempt to secure more territory within which to shift one's pieces in accordance with the exigencies of the battle. Emanuel Lasker once made a rather nice observation to me as we were discussing this point. He said: 'The chess board has sixty-four squares. Therefore, the player who gains control of more than thirty-two squares has the better winning chance.' Naturally, this statement was not meant to be mathematically rigorous, as the importance of the different squares on the board will necessarily vary with the position of the Kings and with other factors. But other things being equal, we can make Lasker's remark a very helpful guide in judging a position. Take Diagram 78, for example. The position is symmetrical, except for the two Pawns in the King's and Queen's file. White's King's Pawn 'controls' two squares on Black's fourth rank, in that Black cannot occupy his Q4 or KB4 with a piece without being captured by White's Pawn. Black controls no squares in White's camp. This justifies the conclusion that White has the better game.

The advantage characterized by this Pawn position seems very insignificant to the inexperienced player. In reality, however, it is considerable. In the middle-game, it will express itself in the greater ease which White has in communicating between the King's and Queen's wing. White will be able to utilize the third rank to bring his Queen's Rook over to the King's side for an attack on Black's King. Black does not enjoy a comparable advantage. Furthermore, White's control of Black's Q4 and KB4 has the disagreeable consequence for Black that White may occupy either one of these squares with a piece, usually a Knight, carrying the fight deeper into Black's territory. We shall see that a piece posted in this

Diagram 78

aggressive manner tends to provoke a Pawn-move to drive it away and that such a Pawn-move often creates a serious weakness.

THE PRINCIPLE OF MOBILITY

Let us now examine, in a few openings selected at random, how the principle of securing the greatest possible mobility for the pieces, coupled with the thought of maintaining control over at least thirty-two squares, can guide us in the proper formation of our battle-front, so that we can face the hand-to-hand fight of the middle-game with confidence.

Let us assume that both contestants advance their King's Pawn to the fourth rank on the first move, and that on the second move White plays P—Q4, with the idea of provoking P × P and obtaining the advantage in the centre which we discussed in connection with Diagram 78.

In reply, Black's first thought will be to hold a Pawn on his K4 in order to maintain control over as many centre-squares as White. If he finds that he has nothing better than P × P he will try to avoid the Pawn-formation illustrated in Diagram 78 and, instead, he will play P—Q4 himself, to remove White's centre-Pawn in turn and thus re-establish the equilibrium of territorial control.

Black could maintain a Pawn on K4 only if he protected the King's Pawn with either P—Q3 or P—KB3. He will dismiss the latter move from his consideration because it would block the most favourable developing square for his King's Knight. From B3 this Knight would have more squares to go to than from either K2 or R3, and this is sufficient reason to presume that B3 is the best spot for the Knight. Additional arguments in favour of this post are that the Knight will be attacking White's centre-Pawn and that it will be defending the Rook's Pawn, which, after castling, would otherwise be protected by only the King.

Black will be dissatisfied with 2. .... P—Q3, because the mobility of his King's Bishop will be impaired. But, much worse, White could exchange first Pawns and then Queens. Thus he would gain a great advantage in development, because he would be able to castle and get his Rooks into action in the open Queen's file. Black, on the other hand, would have to lose much time by getting his King into safety behind the Pawns on one of the wings.

Defending the King's Pawn with 2. .... B—Q3 would not do because this move would block the Queen's Pawn and thus delay the development of the Queen's Bishop. 2. .... Q—K2 would block the King's Bishop, and 2. .... Q—B3 would block the Knight. The only reasonable-looking protection with a piece is 2. .... Kt—QB3, because this is a developing move which Black would want to make in any case sooner or later. But after 3. P×P, Kt×P, the Knight could be driven away from his desirable centre-post through 4. P—KB4, and White would remain in control of several squares in Black's camp while being unrestricted in his own.

For all these reasons, Black will conclude that he must play 2. ....

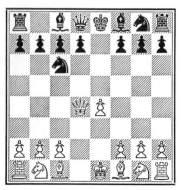

P×P, and upon closer investigation he will realize that this continuation is indeed very favourable for him if White recaptures the Pawn with the Queen, because after 3. Q×P, Kt—QB3 (Diagram 79) White's Queen must move again and Black can develop a second minor piece. This fact alone should be sufficient for White to dismiss 3. Q×P from his consideration, as he would be losing the advantage to which the first move entitles him.

Diagram 79

The beginner usually recognizes after a little practical experience that an advantage in development is desirable, and he appreciates why White would not invite a position like that of Diagram 79. However, he does not, as a rule, realize that getting two or three moves ahead in development is frequently sufficient to *win* the game *if a file in the centre is open for the Rooks.*

To illustrate this point I should like to cite a game between two fairly equal players who were not aware that they could judge every opening-move by the application of the principle of mobility. White continued from the position of Diagram 79 without scrupulous attention to speedy development, and within half a dozen moves his game was hopelessly lost. The score of the game follows:

1. P—K4	P—K4
2. P—Q4	P×P
3. Q×P	Kt—QB3
4. Q—K3	

Very likely this is not the best move, because it obstructs the Queen's Bishop. Probably Q—R4 or Q—Q1 is better, because it leaves free rein to White's minor pieces.

4.	Kt—B3
5. P—K5	

Again of doubtful value, because it does not increase the mobility of White's pieces. Besides, the attacked Knight can take up a menacing post.

5.	Kt—KKt5
6. Q—K4	

Apparently this is advantageous for White, as Black's Knight is attacked and cannot take the King's Pawn because it would then be pinned by the Queen, and 7. P—KB4 would win a piece. Neither does it seem possible, at first glance, for Black to protect the Knight with the developing move P—Q4, which unblocks the Queen's Bishop, as White can take the Pawn en passant with a discovered check. But in return for this Pawn Black again advances his development, and White's position becomes precarious.

6.	P—Q4!
7. P×P e.p. ch	B—K3
8. P×P	Q×P

Now Black is fully three moves ahead in development.

9. B—KB4	B—Q3
10. B×B	Q×B
11. Kt—QB3	Castles QR

This threatens mate on Q7. White defends the mate with the obvious R—Q1 and loses a piece in the transaction. However, there is no satisfactory reply available (Diagram 80).

12. Kt—B3, P—B4 would necessitate 13. Q—K2, as Q—R4 would permit Q—B4, threatening mate on B7, whereupon the only defence, 14. Kt—Q1, would lose a piece through R×Kt ch; 15. K×R, Kt×P ch, etc.   13. Q—K2 would simply be answered by KR—K1, developing the last black piece which is not yet in play, and White would again lose at least a piece.   For example: 14. R—Q1, Q—B4; 15. R×R ch, Kt×R; 16. Q—Q2, B—B5 ch; 17. B—K2, Q×P ch; 18. K—Q1, Q×P; 19. R—Kt1, B×B ch; 20. Kt×B, Q×Kt.

	12. **R—Q1**	**Q×R ch!**
	13. **Kt×Q**	**R×Kt ch**
	14. **K×R**	**Kt×P ch**
	15. **K—K1**	**Kt×Q, etc.**

The important thing for the beginner to realize is that combinations of this type are no accident in positions in which one of the contestants

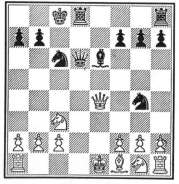

Diagram 80

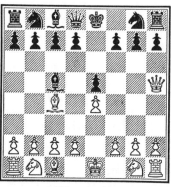

Diagram 81

is far behind in development.   The opponent quite naturally finds time for amassing superior forces against the King.   This almost always enables a mating attack which the defending player can stem only by giving up material, whereupon he remains with a lost ending.

PREMATURE ATTACKING MOVES

Premature excursions with the Queen are so often the cause of losing time for development that I should like to discuss another illustrative example of this type.

Diagram 81 shows the position which is reached if after 1. P—K4, P—K4; 2. B—B4, B—B4 White plays 3. Q—R5, attacking Black's King's Pawn and at the same time threatening mate on KB7.   A sortie of this kind may look very attractive to the beginner to whom our elementary strategic considerations have never been explained. But the student who understands the reason why rapid development of his pieces is the most important objective will be suspicious of any move which places a piece on a square from which it can be driven away by a developing move of his opponent. In our example, Q—R5 is such a move, although Black must first defend the mate before he can think of attacking the Queen with a developing move.

That the Queen's move must be futile should be obvious, without going into a detailed analysis, from the mere fact that Black's previous moves were just as good as White's. Chess would be a poor game indeed if it were possible to demonstrate an advantage over an adversary who has not done anything to deserve punishment. This is another very important point for the beginner to keep in mind. There is no sense in racking his brain for a winning combination in any opening in which his opponent has not violated the principle of mobility.

In the Diagram, Black defends White's threats very simply with Q—K2. On the grounds of our general considerations this must be better than Q—B3, which also defends both threats, and which in addition threatens check in turn on KB7. The reason is that KB3 should be kept open for the Knight, to take advantage of the exposed position of White's Queen. White could protect the check threatened by 3. .... Q—B3 with 4. Kt—KB3, which develops a piece at the same time, and on the next move he would play Kt—QB3, threatening Kt—Q5 with attack on Black's Queen and Queen's Bishop's Pawn. While Black can defend himself against these threats, he is kept busy doing so with moves which he could otherwise utilize to further his development.

After 3. .... Q—K2, Black will complete his development one move ahead of White no matter how White continues, because White will have to make another move with his Queen as soon as Black brings out his King's Knight. Thus the initiative will quite naturally pass over to Black.

From this example the student should not conclude that an early Q—R5 must be bad under all circumstances. If one of the players does not develop his men in a manner which gives them good mobility, the opponent may have an opportunity to make an early attack on the King for which the move Q—R5 is very useful.

To construct such a case, let us assume that after 1. P—K4, P—K4; 2. B—B4, Black plays Kt—K2. This move is not in accordance with the principle of rapid development because it obstructs the Bishop, so that another move with the Knight or a move with the King's Knight's Pawn is required to get the Bishop into play. Here the continuation 3. Q—R5 (Diagram 82) is good, for the only way in which Black can protect both of White's threats is Kt—Kt3, and then the white Queen remains menacingly posted and cannot be driven away for some time. In fact, White immediately wins at least a Pawn through 4. Kt—KB3, which threatens Kt—Kt5 with an attack on KB7, besides attacking the King's Pawn directly.

In this predicament, Black will try to gain at least some advantage in development, as compensation for the Pawn. He will play B—K2,

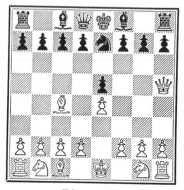

and after 5. Kt×P, Kt×Kt; 6. Q× Kt, he will castle. In that way he will gain two developing moves over White, for the white Queen will have to make another move as soon as Black develops his Queen's Knight.

If White plays carefully, he should no doubt emerge unscathed. But the slightest mis-step, perhaps a move which loses more valuable time during the remainder of the developing stage, might give Black a chance for a sudden, successful attack.

Diagram 82

Suppose White plays 7. Castles, Kt— B3; 8. Q—Kt3 and Black replies P—Q4, sacrificing another Pawn in order to arrest White's development further whilst advancing his own. It would be a mistake for White to capture with the Pawn rather than the Bishop, because in doing so he would relinquish control of KB5, thus increasing Black's mobility. Black could immediately take advantage of this error with Kt—Q5, when White cannot defend his QB2 with Q—Q3 on account of P—QB4 followed by B—KB4. If he plays B— Q3 instead, Black regains one of the Pawns with Q×P and White's Queen's wing remains undeveloped for quite some time.

AN ILLUSTRATIVE GAME

No discussion on the subject of rapid development can be considered complete without the inclusion of the following classic illustration, a famous game which Paul Morphy played against the Duke Karl of Brunswick and Count Isouard in the Royal box at the Opera House in Paris. Let us charitably assume that these gentlemen asked Morphy to play with them during an *intermission*.

1. P—K4		P—K4
2. Kt—KB3		P—Q3

According to the principles set forth, Kt—QB3 would have been the best way to protect the King's Pawn, because this move develops a piece. It is true that P—Q3 makes possible the development of

Black's Queen's Bishop. On the other hand, the King's Bishop is blocked by it, and it is reasonable to assume that it is better not to advance the Queen's Pawn until the King's Bishop has been developed.

3. P—Q4

Now Black's King's Pawn is attacked twice. To support it with Kt—QB3 at this stage would be bad, because after 4. P×P, P×P or 4. .... Kt×P; 5. Kt×Kt, P×Kt, White would exchange Queens, so that Black would forfeit his chance of castling and lose much time in getting his King into safety and developing his Rooks. We know that P—KB3 is not to be considered; it is not a developing move, and it blocks the natural developing square of the King's Knight. Protecting the Pawn with the Queen would also block other pieces. Kt—Q2 would block the Queen's Bishop and is therefore hardly to be recommended unless there is no other choice. A feasible alternative would be P×P, although after 4. Kt×P White has a piece placed on a centre-square, in a dominating position. Wishing to avoid this Black played

3. ......   B—Kt5

thus protecting his Pawn indirectly by pinning the Knight. This manœuvre, however, is ill-advised, as White, by exchanging on K5, forces Black to exchange his Bishop for the Knight. This loses a move, for the Bishop had moved twice and the Knight only once, and in recapturing the Knight with the Queen, White increases the mobility of the latter.

4. P×P   B×Kt

Black cannot recapture the Pawn immediately, because White would then exchange Queens, thus unpinning his Knight, and he would win Black's King's Pawn.

5. Q×B   P×P
6. B—QB4

White has two pieces in play and Black none. Incidentally, checkmate is threatened, and the obvious defence which Black chooses is no longer sufficient. The mobile white Queen threatens to go to QKt3, attacking both Black's King's Bishop's Pawn and Queen's Knight's Pawn. Had Black seen this threat, he would have played Q—B3 or Q—K2, protecting the Bishop's Pawn.

6. ......   Kt—KB3
7. Q—QKt3   Q—K2

The threat was B×P ch and Q—K6 mate.

8. Kt—B3!

A very instructive move! White does not take the Knight's Pawn, because Black could then force the exchange of Queens with Q—Kt5 ch, and though he would probably not be able to hold the game, a rather long drawn-out ending would result. Instead, White retains a strong initiative by bringing additional forces into play, and in view of Black's retarded development he has every right to expect that he will win the game very shortly in a violent attack on the King. The black Queen blocks the King's Bishop and thus indirectly also the King's Rook. The black King will therefore have to remain in the middle of the board for quite some time, exposed to the onslaught of White's men.

| 8. ...... | P—B3 |

Now Black's Knight's Pawn is protected, but only at the cost of another developing move.

| 9. B—KKt5 | P—Kt4 |

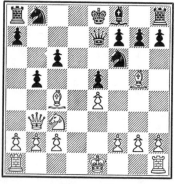

Diagram 83

Black could not play QKt—Q 2, as this would have interrupted the path of his Queen defending the Knight's Pawn. Thus, he had to make a preparatory move. Comparatively best would have been P—QKt3, though the advance to the fourth rank was tempting. Apparently the white Bishop must retreat; but in view of the fact that Black practically plays with several pieces down, Morphy sacrifices the Knight for two Pawns: he foresees the position which occurs a few moves later, when Black, hemmed in on all sides, is completely at his mercy.

10. Kt×P	P×Kt
11. B×KtP ch	QKt—Q2
12. Castles QR	R—Q1

The only move to protect the Knight. Black's position is truly pathetic. Apart from his Queen, every one of his pieces is tied up. He would need at least another three moves to regain the mobility of his Knights: a move with the Queen, one with the Bishop, and castling. White, on the other hand, has still another piece in reserve—his King's Rook. Bringing the latter forcefully into play after another sacrifice, White demolishes the Black game with a few strokes.

13. R × Kt!	R × R
14. R—Q1	

There is no way for Black to defend his Rook.

14.	Q—K3

Black would naturally like to exchange Queens, in order to arrest White's attack. But White could now win with ease by playing B × Kt, since Q × Q would be followed by B × R mate. Therefore Black would have to recapture the Knight, and B × R ch would then win the Queen. However, Morphy has prepared a checkmate by means of another surprising sacrifice.

15. B × R ch	Kt × B
16. Q—Kt8 ch!!	Kt × Q
17. R—Q8 mate	

The games just discussed typify the course of events in practically every contest in which one of the players obtains an advantage of several moves in development *and is able to open a line in the centre of the board.* Here his Rooks find an opportunity for invasion of the seventh or eighth rank. This either aids a direct mating assault in co-operation with other pieces, usually including the Queen, or leads to the gain of one or more Pawns, through an attack on their base line from the side or the rear.

We shall see later on that if no file can be opened which permits the Rooks to enter the battle at an early stage, the player who is behind in development can frequently catch up with his opponent and equalize the game. It is obvious, nevertheless, that keeping step with one's adversary by getting one piece after another into play as fast as possible must be a very good plan to follow in any opening.

SELECTING POSTS FOR THE PIECES

A question which presents itself quite naturally in this connection is whether certain squares of the board can be assigned to the different pieces as most favourable for their co-operation.

We conclude without difficulty that KB3 and QB3 are the most desirable developing squares for the Knights. A Knight would go to R3 on its first move only if forced to do so by an acute threat, for on the edge of the board the Knight's mobility is much restricted. The squares K2 and Q2 are also less desirable than B3, because from them a Knight needs another preparatory move to reach the enemy's territory and it exerts no pressure on his centre.

As far as the Rooks and the Queen are concerned, we can say quite generally that in the opening they should normally be confined to the first and second ranks, where they are not apt to be attacked by minor pieces or Pawns. We already know that Rooks aim at an invasion of the adversary's second or first rank, and that they are ideally placed when doubled in an open line. Specific squares, however, cannot be selected for them—and the same is true of the Bishops—without detailed consideration of the various types of Pawn-formation which are characteristic of the different openings, because it depends upon this Pawn-formation which lines can be readily opened. An invasion of the seventh rank by a Rook can rarely be envisaged during the opening or the early middle-game, because during the developing stage of the game the opponent's minor pieces normally occupy posts from which they cover the invasion squares. Nevertheless, as there is always the possibility that minor pieces will be exchanged, there is always the danger that a Rook which controls an open file will sooner or later realize its ambition and invade the seventh rank.

THE PAWN-SKELETON

It is in the nature of a game of chess that the formation of the Pawns is of a more permanent character than that of the pieces, in consequence of the latter's greater mobility. That is why the Pawn-formation must necessarily be the dominant consideration when selecting a line-up for our men. When we have made a rash move with a piece, tempted by an attacking disposition, we may still have a chance of retrieving the position by a timely retreat. Once a Pawn has moved it cannot turn back, and only after careful deliberation should we embark on changes in our Pawn-skeleton, lest we disturb the balance of this 'static element' of the game. In a good game, the Pawn-skeleton formed in the opening frequently weathers the storm of the middle-game and preserves its character up to the end-game. I will therefore make the Pawn-formation my starting-point in an attempt to show the way through *any* opening on the basis of general strategic principles.

Naturally, the formation of the Pawn-skeleton is not an independent factor but can be properly evolved only with a view to facilitating the favourable development of the pieces. If it is to promote the freedom of *all* pieces, we must consider from the very first in which way it will enable the Rooks to get into action after the minor pieces have been developed. We shall soon realize that we can unite these tendencies by making the *centre of the board* the main field of activity for all our forces. This means the squares K4 and Q4 for both sides, and to a lesser degree the squares KB4 and QB4. In the following we will consider such manœuvres as could apply either to White or Black, from the point of view of White to whom the initiative is a sort of birthright.

IMPORTANCE OF CENTRE-SQUARES

When a player advances either his King's Pawn or his Queen's Pawn to the fourth rank, he makes two central squares inaccessible to the opponent's pieces—his Q5 and KB5, or his K5 and QB5. At the same time he prepares the occupation of these desirable squares by his own men in case the opponent takes no measures to prevent such action. Ordinarily the adversary will also place a Pawn in the centre. It will then obviously be a good plan to lure this Pawn away. P—Q4 or P—KB4 will serve this purpose if the opponent has played P—K4. Against P—Q4, the corresponding manœuvre will be P—QB4 or P—K4.

This invitation to exchange his centre-Pawn will be accepted by a player only if maintaining the Pawn on its post entails serious difficulties. The only exception would be an instance where the exchange can be followed up with a manœuvre yielding an advantage which compensates for the disappearance of his centre-Pawn.

In discussing some of the commonly used openings we shall find that it is indeed often very difficult to avoid the exchange of the centre-Pawn. The question then arises: How can a player obtain adequate compensation for the loss of control of two centre-squares which the opponent can utilize for favourable development of his pieces?

Let us look at a few concrete examples.

Diagram 84 shows a position which occurred in a game I played against Alekhine in the tournament at Scheveningen, 1913. He had just played

Diagram 84

P—Q4, attacking my centre-Pawn for the second time. I replied P×P and thereby ruined my game, because I surrendered control of the squares Q5 and KB5 without any compensation. After Kt×P Black was able to advance his King's Bishop's Pawn to B4 and get his Rooks rapidly into play for a King's side attack. Confined to three ranks of the board due to Black's control of all centre-squares, I was unable to put up a satisfactory defence.

What I should have played in the position of the Diagram is Q—B2, maintaining my King's Pawn on K4. I do not remember why I did not make this reply, which should be obvious to anyone who appreciates the importance of centre-squares as part of what we might call the 'mobility syndrome'. Perhaps I did not want to move the Queen again, having developed her to Q2. But such a literal interpretation of a rule commendable for the conduct of openings in general is a mistake. When a player is forced to choose between moves which seem to violate one or the other principle of strategy, he must naturally select the one which entails the smallest of the evils he has to face. Surrendering the control of two centre-squares by exchanging a centre-Pawn is a *permanent* disadvantage. The Pawn cannot get back to the centre-square which it has left. On the other hand, making two moves with the same piece in the opening, while certainly not desirable, may give the opponent only a *temporary* advantage. As pointed out previously, the loss of a developing tempo on the part of *White* usually means merely the loss of the initiative which goes with the first move.

In contrast to this example, Diagram 85 shows a position in which a player cannot very well refuse the invitation to exchange the centre-Pawn. The considerations explaining the proper conduct in this

Diagram 85

position are important to understand because they apply to many similar situations which occur in games starting with 1. **P—K4, P—K4**; 2. **Kt—KB3, Kt—QB3,** whether White advances his Queen's Pawn on the third move or later. After 3. **P—Q4** Black cannot maintain a Pawn on K4, as explained in connection with the opening moves which led to Diagram 79.

3. .... **P×P**; 4. **Kt×P** is therefore the inevitable continuation. It leaves White in control of Q5 and KB5 while Black has lost the control of the corresponding squares. On the other hand, the Pawn-exchange has opened the Queen's file for White and the King's file for Black. Here Black has the better of the bargain. After placing a Rook in the open file, he will have the white King's Pawn as a target which is not protected by a Pawn, while a white Rook in the Queen's file would find no comparable target. Black could keep the Queen's file blocked by placing his Queen's Pawn on Q3.

Whether the play Black is liable to obtain against White's centre-Pawn is sufficient compensation for the superior mobility of White's pieces, resulting from the control of more centre-squares, is a question which cannot be answered axiomatically. Experience has shown that the greater mobility of the player controlling the centre usually leads to a successful King's side attack. In positions of this type, the tendency in master play has therefore been for Black to concentrate his efforts toward equalizing the game by also forcing the white centre-Pawn to leave its post.

He cannot imitate White's tactics by playing P—Q4 immediately, because 5. B—QKt5 would follow, attacking the Knight for the second time. 5. .... B—Q2 would then lose a Pawn through 6. P×P, and 5. .... Kt—K2 would block the King's Bishop. The preparatory move 4. .... **Kt—B3** would therefore be in order, continuing with 5. **Kt—QB3, B—Kt5.** Now White's King's Pawn is again attacked, and whether White defends it with 6. P—B3 or with 6. Kt×Kt, KtP×Kt; 7. B—Q3, Black would rid himself of White's centre-Pawn through P—Q4. In the following pages we shall have occasion to observe the execution of this equalizing manœuvre in various forms whilst investigating the application of our mobility principle to the different openings which are ordinarily employed.

KING'S PAWN OPENINGS

Before leaving the discussion of Diagram 85, however, I should like to point out a common error which beginners make, due to misinterpretation of the rule that it is bad to bring the Queen out into the open at an early stage of the game.

We saw that after 1. P—K4, P—K4 the immediate advance 2. P—Q4 allows Black to gain a developing tempo through P×P; 3. Q×P, Kt—QB3 which forces the Queen to move again. It would be a mistake for Black, in the position of Diagram 85, to bring White's Queen into the centre through exchange of the Pawns *and* the Knights, because

Diagram 86

then White's Queen would occupy a dominating position from which she could *not* be displaced by a move which develops a black piece. Chasing her with P—QB4 would be a very bad plan because it would make the Queen's Pawn 'backward'. This Pawn could never advance to Q4—the only move with which Black could hope to contest White's control of the centre—and the result would be an irremediable weakness. The natural development of the pieces on both sides would lead to a position such as that of Diagram 86, where White has piled up all of his pieces against Black's backward Pawn and Black's pieces are cramped in an attempt to hold the Pawn—an attempt which is sure to be futile. We have observed the type of play resulting from such positions in connection with Diagram 67.

CRAMPED POSITIONS

The important thing for the beginner to realize is that in permitting his adversary to reach a position such as the exchange of the Knights in Diagram 85 produces, he ruins his game from the start. Even if he does not play P—QB4 he will drift into a badly cramped position because the white centre-Pawn and the commanding post of the white Queen in the centre deprive his pieces of the degree of mobility which they would normally obtain in the opening stage. Play might proceed as follows: 3. .... P×P; 4. Kt×P, Kt×Kt; 5. Q×Kt, Kt—B3; 6. B—KKt5, B—K2; 7. Kt—B3, P—Q3; when the position of Diagram 87 is reached. Here we observe the Pawn-skeleton typical

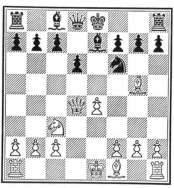

Diagram 87

of King's Pawn openings, in which White has succeeded in exchanging Black's centre-Pawn whilst Black has not accomplished the same laudable purpose. White has four or even five ranks at the disposal of his pieces. Black's pieces are confined to three ranks—just as we saw it in Diagram 84, with the roles of White and Black reversed.

In the Diagram, White might continue with 8. **Castles QR**, in order to complete his development with B—QB4 and KR—K1. Black, on the other hand, will have great difficulties in getting his Rooks into play. With his Queen in a file in which White has placed a Rook, he must always be on the alert against White opening this file with attack on the Queen, and with the threat of invasion by White's Rooks.

In such cramped positions the only hope of the defender to ease his game lies in exchanging as many pieces as possible. In the present case Black might try this strategy after 8. .... **Castles KR; 9. B—QB4** with Kt—Kt5 or B—K3. The latter does not look inviting, because it gives White the occasion for which he is lying in wait, to open the centre with P—K5. Then P×P; 11. Q×KP, Q—B1; 12. B×B, Q×B; 13. Q×Q, P×Q; 14. KR—K1 will yield at least a Pawn.

Instead of Q×KP, a tempting continuation would be the sacrifice 11. Q—R4, in order to institute a mating attack with 12. B—Q3 in case Black moves the Queen. But 11. Kt—Q4 forces the exchange of so much material that it is doubtful whether enough is left for

White to warrant the risk. The combination might wind up as follows:

12. Kt—K4, P—KR3; 13. B×B, Q×B; 14. Q×Q, Kt×Q; 15. B×B, P×B; 16. R—Q7. White has accomplished the invasion of the seventh rank, and he is sure to regain the Pawn he has sacrificed, but Black obtains counterplay due to the open Bishop's file. Kt—Q4; 17. P—QB4, Kt—B5!; 18. R×BP, QR—B!; 19. R×R, R×R; 20. P—QKt3, Kt×P; 21. R—Q1, R—KB1, with chances for both sides.

Black's other attempt at exchanging pieces, 9. .... **Kt—Kt5,** might lead to 10. **B×B, Q×B;** 11. **Kt—Q5, Q—Q1;** 12. **P—KR3, Kt—K4;** 13. **P—B4.** If then **Kt×B;** 14. **Q×Kt, P—QB3;** 15. **Kt—B3** will soon win the Queen's Pawn who has lost its protection through the advance of the Bishop's Pawn and cannot advance to Q4 on account of White's King's Pawn.

OPENING FILES FOR THE ROOKS

Both of these variations illustrate ways and means in which Rooks can be made effective in files opened for them at an early stage of the game. We shall encounter further examples of this type in almost every game; in fact, we shall see that every opening system is dominated by the desire of the players to obtain control of an open file for the Rooks before the opponent accomplishes the same aim.

This play for an open file is intimately connected with the provocation of the exchange of the opponent's centre-Pawn which we have already recognized as one of the major aims of all opening strategy.

When discussing the position of Diagram 85 we concluded that, after 3. .... P×P; 4. Kt×P, Kt—B3; 5. Kt—QB3, B—Kt5; 6. Kt×Kt, KtP×Kt; 7. B—Q3, Black forces the exchange of White's centre-Pawn through P—Q4. Diagram 88 shows the position reached at this point. To a beginner it looks tempting to advance the King's Pawn, driving Black's Knight, rather than exchanging Pawns. However, there are several objections to this move,

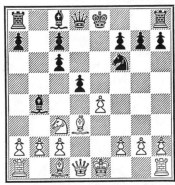

Diagram 88

which I will explain in detail because the problem involved in this advance is typical for similar situations frequently encountered in King's Pawn openings.

PREFERRED SQUARES FOR CENTRE-PAWNS

A good reason why we should be suspicious of the advance P—K5 in Diagram 88 is that the move does not add anything to White's development. It is true that White does not lose a developing tempo by this move because Black is forced to move for the second time a piece which is already developed. But on K5 the Pawn is weak. Black would play Kt—Kt5, attacking it immediately, and White cannot, in the long run, maintain it on his advanced post. He need not defend it immediately, because if he castles Black cannot take the Pawn without losing the Knight through the pin R—K1. But after Black has also castled, White has only undesirable moves to choose from to avoid losing the Pawn. He cannot play P—KB4 because Black would check on QB4 and then win the exchange through the check with the Knight on B7. Neither can B—KB4 be good, as it reduces the Bishop to the role of a Pawn. Besides, Black could continue attacking the Pawn with Q—K2 or with P—KB3. The latter move, though not winning the Pawn, would force its exchange in a manner which would give Black an open file for his Rook. The Queen, too, could add pressure on White's King's Bishop's Pawn in this file.

White could win Black's King's Rook's Pawn in exchange for the King's Pawn, rather than defending the latter. From the position of the Diagram, play would run as follows: 8. P—K5, Kt—Kt5; 9. Castles, Castles; 10. P—KR3, Kt×P; 11. B×P ch, K×B; 12. Q—R5 ch, K—Kt1; 13. Q×Kt. However, this combination would be distinctly in Black's favour, as he would emerge with two Bishops against Knight and Bishop, and with a majority of Pawns on the Queen's wing. These Pawns would commence to roll forward before long and resolve themselves into a passed Pawn.

Quite apart from the combinative objections to the advance of White's centre-Pawn to the fifth rank in the position of the Diagram, there are positional arguments which stamp it as a dubious procedure, and which apply quite generally to such an advance. On the fourth rank a centre-Pawn controls two important centre-squares. Advancing to the fifth rank, the Pawn gives up that control, shifting it to two squares on the opponent's third rank. These squares are rarely as important as centre-squares, except in cases where a piece is driven from them which is essential to the defence of the King's position. As a rule, such protection is needed only when the opponent is able to gather a superior force on the King's wing. We discussed instances of this type in connection with Diagrams 54 and 55. There Black had a Pawn on K3, blocking his Queen's Bishop's access to the King's wing, so that without a Knight on KB3 the Black King was almost denuded of defensive forces.

I should remind the reader here that the conclusions we are drawing as to preferred positions for centre-Pawns were reached in the course of considerations concerning *opening* strategy. These considerations need not hold in the middle-game, and they rarely hold in the end-game.

The value of a centre-Pawn on the fourth rank is greatly reduced when the minor pieces—particularly the Knights—have been exchanged, which might have utilized the Pawn to protect them on an advanced post in the fifth rank. Again, the value of a centre-Pawn is enhanced on the fifth rank, if the opponent has weakened the square B3 by advancing his Knight's Pawn, so that the player of the advanced Pawn might find an opportunity to lodge a piece on his B6.

Generally speaking, after the minor pieces have disappeared, a centre-Pawn is safer on the fourth than on the fifth rank unless it is solidly anchored through protection by Pawns in back of it. If that protection is lacking, the Pawn is often within reach of the opposing King, who can join his Rooks in attacking it when no hostile minor pieces are near to endanger him.

Let us now return to the position of Diagram 88. We said that White has nothing better than to exchange his centre-Pawn. He need not do so immediately. He can first castle, for as long as Black's King is still on the King's file, White's Pawn cannot be captured with B×Kt; 9. P×B, P×P, because after 10. B×P, Kt×B or Q×Q; 11. R×Q, White would regain his piece through Q—K2 or R—K1. However, after 8. .... Castles, White again faces the problem of protecting the Pawn. Trying to maintain it at all cost with 9. P—B3 would not be wise, because this move would open a long diagonal for Black's King's Bishop and also reduce the mobility of the white Queen. In view of the solid protection of Black's centre-Pawn, there is really little prospect for White to exert more pressure on it than Black can easily balance. Furthermore, with a Bishop on Q3, the Pawn on K4 reduces rather than enhances White's mobility. Thus, 9. P×P is the logical move from every viewpoint. The continuation might be P×P; 10. B—KKt5, P—B3; 11. Q—B3, B—K2; 12. P—KR3, limiting the mobility of Black's Queen's Bishop, B—K3; 13. KR—K1, R—Kt1; 14. QR—Kt1, P—B4; 15. Kt—K2. White has more territory on the King's wing and Black on the Queen's wing. The white position is therefore perhaps slightly preferable, because a territorial advantage is a germ from which an attack might develop, and an attack on the King is more dangerous than an attack on other targets.

In such a situation, the correct policy for the player who has the preponderance on the King's side is to avoid the exchange of pieces, particularly of the Queen, because after every exchange the chance for a successful attack on the King grows smaller.

ILLUSTRATIVE GAME (SCOTCH OPENING)

This point is instructively illustrated by the following game which I played in 1911, in a match for the championship of Paris against Frédéric Lazard, who had the white pieces.

The opening moves were those which lead to the position of Diagram 88. After 8. **Castles, Castles,** White played 9. **B—KKt5.** This was a positional mistake, because it enabled me to exchange all minor pieces except the white Bishops. The resulting position was bound to be to my advantage for two reasons. The Pawns on White's Queen's wing are on white squares, where they are attackable by Black's Bishop. The black Queen's side Pawns are on black squares, out of reach of White's Bishop. Furthermore, the black Bishop can prevent White's Rooks from invading the seventh rank, Black's QKt2 and Q2 being white squares. The corresponding squares in White's camp are black, so that Black will probably find a chance to occupy one or the other of them. Black can block the King's file by placing his Bishop on K3, from where it cannot be driven away unless White succeeds in opposing his own Bishop. White's Bishop cannot block the Queen's file by posting itself on Q3 because Black can drive it away with his QB Pawn.

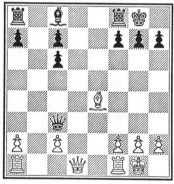

Diagram 89

The continuation was:

| 9. ...... | B × Kt |
| 10. P × B | P × P |

Now White must first exchange on B6 or he loses a piece.

| 11. B × Kt | Q × B |
| 12. B × P | Q × QBP |

Now White should try avoiding the exchange of Queens and working up an attack on the King's side, perhaps with Q—R5, followed by QR—Kt1 and KR—K1, with a view to bringing one of the Rooks up to the third rank and then over to the King's wing. Instead, White played

13. **Q—B3**

He probably expected that after exchanging Queens I would attempt to hold my extra Pawn with B—Kt2 or B—Q2. This would have given him the opportunity to get his Rooks into play first.

| 13. ...... | Q × Q |
| 14. B × Q | R—Kt1! |

A player who is not familiar with chess-strategic principles would almost automatically protect the Pawn. But this thought should be dismissed instantly when considering that the Bishop's mobility would be curtailed on Kt2 as well as on Q2, and that the opportunity of obtaining control of one of the open files would be lost to the opponent. Neither a Bishop nor a Rook should ever be relegated to the role of defending a Pawn except as a last resort, when the alternative of a counter-attack does not exist.

15. B×P

If White opposes his Rook in the Knight's file instead, the reply would be B—K3, and if White then advances the Queen's Rook's Pawn, Black plays B—Q4.

15.	R—Kt7
16. B—K4	B—K3
17. P—QR3	KR—Kt1

Now Black definitely controls the Knight's file. To take advantage of his Rook on the seventh rank he must drive the white Bishop from the diagonal on which it protects the Queen's Bishop's Pawn. For this purpose he will have to advance his Queen's Bishop's Pawn to QB5 and then play P—KB4. White's only counter-chance is to post a Rook on his QB3. But he cannot get there in time to avoid material loss.

18. KR—K1	P—QB4
19. P—KR3	

An awkward necessity in positions of this kind. Before the Rook can venture out, a loophole must be provided for the King to avoid mate.

19.	P—B5
20. R—K3	R—Kt8 ch!

A timely exchange of one of the Rooks. P—B4 without this exchange would give White the counter-play for which he hopes. He could double Rooks in the King's file effectively after Black's Bishop no longer enjoys the protection of the King's Bishop's Pawn.

21. R×R	R×R ch
22. K—R2	P—B4
23. B—B3	K—B2
24. B—K2	

Threatening R—QB3, which would win the Bishop's Pawn.

24.	R—Kt2
25. R—QB3	K—B3

More exact would have been K—K2, to go to Q5 via Q3 and B4. White cannot play B × P because R—B2 would win the Bishop. Neither can he bring the King over to the defence of his Rook, as Black can place his Rook in the Queen's file.

| | 26. P—B4 | R—Q2 |
| | 27. K—Kt3 | R—Q5 |

Preparing to transfer the King to the other wing in back of the Rook.

	28. K—B3	K—K2
	29. R—K3	K—Q3
	30. K—Kt3	R—Q7
	31. P—B3	

At last Black has secured the typical advantage connected with an invasion of the seventh rank by a Rook. He can attack the Pawns of the enemy from the rear. But as long as the opponent has two pieces on the board, even the most obvious move must be carefully checked to avoid trappy combinations of the type illustrated in the preceding chapter. Had I played R—R7, I would have thrown away the fruits of eight hours of hard work. White would have won immediately by 32. R × B ch, followed by B × P ch, etc. (Compare Diagram 75.)

| | 31. ...... | B—B2! |
| | 32. P—QR4 | P—Kt3! |

The Rook's Pawn will not run away. By protecting the King's Bishop's Pawn, Black avoids the possibility that White might win a tempo through R—K5 and swing the Rook over to QR5, at a moment when his Bishop is not attacked by Black's Rook.

| | 33. B—B3 | R—R7 |
| | 34. B—Q1 | B—Q4! |

This wins a Pawn no matter how White defends himself.

| | 35. R—K2 | R—R8 |
| | 36. R—Q2 | |

Or B—B2, R—R6; 37. R—K3, B—B3, etc.

| | 36. ...... | K—B4 |

Not R—R6 on account of B—B3, winning the Bishop.

| | 37. K—B2 | |

If B—B3, B × B; 38. K × B, R—R6; 39. R—Q7, R × P ch; 40. K—B2, P—QR4; 41. R × P, R—Q6; 42. R—KKt7, R—Q3, and the passed Pawn decides quickly.

37.	......	R—R6
38.	R—B2	R×P

and Black won after considerable further struggle by placing the Rook on QKt6 and advancing the Queen's Rook's Pawn.

To recapitulate: In the opening employed in this game, usually referred to as 'Scotch opening', the important thing to keep in mind is that Black, after exchanging his King's Pawn for White's Queen's Pawn, should play P—Q4 and not P—Q3, in order not to let White remain with the advantage of a Pawn in the centre. The move P—Q4 is the key to all defences of Black in King's Pawn openings in which White has forced him to give up his own centre-Pawn. Going back to the first opening of this type we examined, the 'Centre-Game', after White plays 1. P—K4, P—K4; 2. P—Q4, P×P; 3. Q×P, Kt—QB3; 4. Q—K3, Black should continue with Kt—B3; 5. Kt—QB3, B—K2!, so as to be able to play P—Q4 in answer to 6. B—Q2. Even against 6. B—B4, which covers Q5 for the third time, P—Q4 could be tried, because after 7. P×P, Kt—QKt5 would threaten Kt×BP ch as well as Kt×QP, and if 7. Kt×P, Black would obtain a strong attack with Kt×Kt; 8. B×Kt, Kt—Kt5; 9. Q—QKt3, Castles. His advantage in development probably outweighs the Pawn sacrificed (Diagram 90). Black's Rooks may have a chance to become disagreeably active in the centre-files before White's King can castle into safety. For example:

10. B—Q2, Kt×B; 11. Q×Kt, Q× Q; 12. P×Q, B—QB4, threatening R—K1 ch and followed soon by B—KB4. Black will have no difficulty in regaining his Pawn. Or: 11. P×Kt, P—QB3!, and whether White continues with 12. P×P, P× P; or 12. P—QB4, P×P; 13. P×P, B—KB4, Black, with his two Bishops and open files for his Rooks, will probably not only regain his Pawn but maintain his superior position. It would be very dangerous for White to castle on the Queen's side, into Black's open file. And

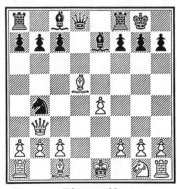

Diagram 90

if he prepares castling on the King's side with 14. Kt—B3 or Kt—K2, Black replies B—K5. White has hardly time to prevent this move with 14. P—B3, as B—Kt4! and occupation of the King's file with the Rook would be altogether too much for him to stand.

Equally unsuccessful would be an attempt on White's part to get his King into safety immediately by playing 10. Kt—B3. The consequence

would be **P—QB3; 11. B—QB4, P—QKt4; 12. B—K2, B—K3,** with
a devastating attack.

BLACK'S COUNTER-STROKE P—Q4

The counter-stroke P—Q4 against White's centre-Pawn is the best
weapon for an inexperienced player in all King's Pawn openings in
which a more seasoned opponent tries to obtain an early advantage
by sacrificing his Queen's Pawn to clear the centre for his pieces.   For
example:

1. **P—K4**		**P—K4**
2. **P—Q4**		**P × P**
3. **B—QB4**		**Kt—KB3**
4. **P—K5**		**P—Q4!**
	or	
1. **P—K4**		**P—K4**
2. **P—Q4**		**P × P**
3. **P—QB3**		**P—Q4!**
	or	
1. **P—K4**		**P—K4**
2. **Kt—KB3**		**Kt—QB3**
3. **P—Q4**		**P × P**
4. **P—B3**		**P—Q4!**

If, in the last two variations, White replies P—K5 to P—Q4, Black
can continue with P × P without danger because his development is no
longer hindered.   To accept the gambit offered by White would bring
White's Queen's Knight into play and make the advance P—Q4
impossible.   While with best play Black may succeed in completing
his development satisfactorily and remaining a Pawn ahead, the
beginner is more likely to miss the right way and to succumb to
White's attack.

THE GIUOCO PIANO

To place obstacles in the way of Black's advance of his Queen's
Pawn, White often plays B—QB4 before removing Black's centre-
Pawn with P—Q4.   In this opening, the '*Giuoco Piano*', Black has
much greater difficulty in equalizing the position than in the variations
discussed up to now.

In the position of the Diagram, Black will play either **B—B4** or
Kt—B3.   In the former case White could not force Black to give up
his centre-Pawn with 4. P—Q4, because Black could capture with the
Bishop.   But White can prepare P—Q4 with 4. **P—B3,** and Black must
then be very careful not to allow White to storm forward with both
of his centre-Pawns, annexing so much territory that the black pieces
cannot find satisfactory developing squares.

For example, after **Kt—B3; 5. P—Q4, P×P; 6. P×P,** he must not retreat with the Bishop to Kt3. The consequence could be 7. P—Q5, Kt—K2; 8. P—K5, Kt—Kt1; 9. P—Q6, Kt—Kt3; 10. Q—Q5, and Black must sacrifice a Knight with Kt—R3; 11. B×Kt, Castles to avoid mate. Or: 7. .... Kt—Kt1; 8. P—K5, Kt—Kt1; 9. P—Q6, with a hopeless position for Black. Instead of B—Kt3, Black must play 6. .... **B—Kt5 ch,** to follow this up again with P—Q4. This ever-desirable advance of the Queen's Pawn would also be the proper reply if White plays 6. P—K5 instead of recapturing the Pawn. 7. B—QKt5 is then met with Kt—K5.

To accept the sacrifice which White could offer after 6. .... B—Kt5 ch with 7. **Kt—B3** is dangerous, though with best play Black can draw. Kt×P; 8. Castles, B×Kt; 9. P—Q5 leads to a wild attack in which an inexperienced player is sure to lose his way.

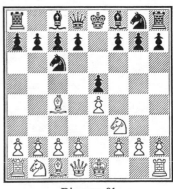

Diagram 91

In Diagram 91, a player should undertake 3. .... **Kt—B3** instead of B—B4 only if he is thoroughly familiar with the vicissitudes of the attack which White can initiate with 4. **Kt—Kt5.** The only way to defend the King's Bishop's Pawn is by P—Q4. After 5. **P×P,** Black is exposed to a terrific onslaught if he recaptures the Pawn, because White can sacrifice his Knight on KB7 and then force the black King out into the open with the check by the Queen on B3 which also attacks the Knight on Q5. With the best defence, Black can probably live through the attack, and then he would win as he is a piece ahead. After 5. .... Kt×P, White can strengthen the attack by playing first 6. **P—Q4,** but **B—Kt5 ch; 7. P—B3, B—K2; 8. Kt×P, K×Kt; 9. Q—B3 ch, K—K3; 10. Castles, Kt—R4** leaves probably nothing better for White than perpetual check with 11. **Q—Kt4, K—B2; 12. Q—B3 ch,** etc.

The move 4. Kt—Kt5 really violates our fundamental strategic law which calls for the rapid development of as many pieces as possible before starting an attack. Black's move 3. .... Kt—B3 was certainly a sound move from the point of view of development, and if there is any justice in chess—which I should not like to doubt—the move 4. Kt—Kt5 should be bad. In tournament play, however, no master has taken the chance of exposing himself to the attack 4. .... P—Q4; 5. P×P, Kt×P; 6. Kt×BP as far back as I can remember. The generally accepted line of procedure has been for Black to sacrifice the Queen's Pawn and to try to gain a telling advantage in development by 4. .... P—Q4; 5. P×P, Kt—QR4; 6. B—Kt5 ch, P—B3; 7. P×P, P×P; 8. B—K2, P—KR3; 9. Kt—KB3, P—K5; 10. Kt—K5, B—Q3. The last word has not been said in this variation. Reuben Fine suggests that White can obtain a superior position by giving back the Pawn with 11. P—KB4, Castles; 12. Castles, B×Kt; 13. P×B, Q—Q5 ch; 14. K—R1, Q×KP; 15. P—Q4. However, Black might continue to put obstacles in the way of White's development with 10. .... Q—B2; 11. P—KB4, B—QB4 rather than taking back his Pawn.

My advice to the beginner is to play B—B4 and not Kt—B3 in the position of Diagram 91, not only to avoid the complications just touched upon, but also because of an equally complicated alternative at White's disposal, which is known as the '*Max Lange Attack*'. White can answer 3. .... Kt—B3 with 4. P—Q4, P×P; 5. Castles, B—B4; 6. P—K5, and whilst the rejoinder P—Q4; 7. P×Kt, P×B had been considered favourable for Black for many years, the line has been shunned since Frank Marshall introduced an innovation at the Hamburg tournament, 1910, when he won against Tarrasch with 8. R—K1 ch, B—K3; 9. Kt—Kt5, Q—Q4; 10. Kt—QB3, Q—B4; 11. QKt—K4, Castles QR; 12. Kt×QB, P×Kt; 13. P—KKt4, Q—K4; 14. P×P, KR—Kt1; 15. B—R6. This is Marshall's move (see Diagram 92).

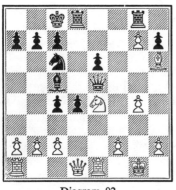

Diagram 92

Whether the position is better for White or Black is anybody's guess. There are so many possibilities for either side that analysis is almost impossible. At any rate, such analysis does not belong to a discussion of strategy but to books which tabulate analysed openings.

THE RUY LOPEZ

We have seen that Black's counter-stroke P—Q4, in all openings in which White makes this move at an early stage, nullifies the advantage White gains through exchanging Black's King's Pawn. Let us now look into an *indirect* attack on Black's centre-Pawn which White can institute by the threat of removing Black's protecting Queen's Knight. The opening based on this idea—the most important of all King's Pawn openings—is the '*Ruy Lopez*', recommended several hundred years ago by the Spanish master of that name. He certainly did not know what headaches he was going to cause future generations of chess fans. The moves characterizing the opening are 1. P—K4, P—K4; 2. Kt—

KB3, Kt—QB3; 3. B—Kt5. This does not threaten to win Black's centre-Pawn *immediately* by exchanging the Bishop for the Knight defending the Pawn. For 4. **B** × **Kt, QP** × **B; 5. Kt** × **P** would be met by **Q—Q5**, which regains the Pawn and leads to an obvious advantage for Black due to the possession of two Bishops ready to enter the fray.

However, the Bishop's move is liable to exert an undesirable pressure on Black's centre-Pawn later; for as soon as the black Queen's Pawn moves to Q3, the Queen's Knight will be pinned. With P—Q4 White will then force the exchange of the Pawns on Q4, and in recapturing with his Knight he will attack Black's Knight for the second time. Black would have to reply B—Q2, a move which does not develop the Queen's Bishop effectively. Furthermore, Black cannot develop his King's Bishop beyond K2, and the result is that his game remains cramped for a long time unless he takes energetic counter-measures from the start. If Black played 3. .... B—B4, he would only invite 4. P—B3 and 5. P—Q4, which would leave White in complete possession of the centre. A white Pawn on White's Q4 is doubly undesirable for Black in this opening because of the threat P—Q5, which would win the Knight if Black moved his Queen's Pawn before 'unpinning' the Knight. For Black to play 3. .... B—Kt5 is naturally out of question, again because of 4. P—B3, which drives the Bishop and at the same time prepares P—Q4.

The most natural plan for Black to consider is a counter-attack on White's centre, beginning with 3. .... **Kt—B3,** again with the intention of playing P—Q4 as soon as possible. Let us see whether such a plan can be executed without Black getting into trouble through the pin of his Queen's Knight.

Rather than protecting the King's Pawn with 4. Kt—B3 White will play 4. **Castles,** for as long as Black's King remains in the King's file, the capture of the King's Pawn will give White's Rook an opportunity to exert pressure in that file. For example: 4. .... **Kt** × **P; 5. R—K1, Kt—Q3; 6. Kt** × **P, Kt** × **Kt** (Kt × B?; 7. Kt × Kt discovered ch, winning the Queen); 7. **R** × **Kt ch, B—K2; 8. Kt—B3, Kt** × **B?; 9. Kt—Q5!, Castles; 10. Kt** × **B ch, K—R1; 11. Q—R5,** threatening mate through Q × RP ch and R—R5. If Black defends with **P—KKt3,** White continues with 12. **Q—R6,** whereupon **P—Q3** would lead to the position of Diagram 58 in which White forces mate in two moves.

Better than 6. .... Kt × Kt, which adds to the mobility of White's Rook, would be B—K2 followed by Castles, when Black may eventually extricate himself from his cramped position.

Instead of occupying the King's file with the Rook after 4. .... **Kt** × **P,** White usually first plays 5. **P—Q4,** in order to lure Black's King's Pawn away and clear the King's file for the Rook. Black's best reply would then be the developing move **B—K2** which closes the

King's file. 5. .... P×P; 6. R—K1, P—B4; 7. Kt×P, Kt×Kt; 8. Q×Kt, P—B3; 9. P—KB3 would obviously be to White's decided advantage.

In Diagram 93, if Black does not take White's King's Pawn immediately but first closes the King's file with **B—K2,** White protects the Pawn and then proceeds to force the exchange of Black's centre-Pawn

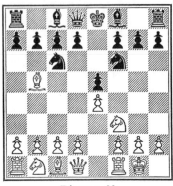

<table>
<tr><td>Diagram 93</td><td>Diagram 94</td></tr>
</table>

with P—Q4, thus obtaining the fundamental advantage in the formation of the Pawn skeleton which we discussed in connection with Diagram 87. Play might proceed as follows:

5. **R—K1**	**P—Q3**
6. **P—Q4**	**B—Q2**
7. **Kt—B3**	

and now P×P is forced. For if Black castles, White wins a Pawn by a long-winded combination first shown by Tarrasch: 8. B×Kt, B×B; 9. P×P, P×P; 10. Q×Q, QR×Q; 11. Kt×P, and if now B×P?; 12. Kt×B, Kt×Kt; 13. Kt—Q3 (R×Kt?, R—Q8 mate), P—KB4; 14. P—KB3, B—B4 ch; 15. Kt×B (K—B?, B—Kt3!), Kt×Kt; 16. B—Kt5, R—Q4; 17. B—K7, R—B2; 18. P—QB4, winning at least the exchange.

7.	**P×P**
8. **Kt×P**	**Castles**
9. **Kt×Kt**	**B×Kt**
10. **B×B**	**P×B**
11. **Kt—K2!**	**Q—Q2**

Not Kt×P on account of 12. Kt—Q4 which wins a piece (P—Q4; 13. Kt×P, Q—Q2; 14. Kt×B ch, Q×Kt; 15. P—KB3, Q—B4 ch; 16. B—K3).

12. **Kt—Kt3**

followed by P—QKt3 and B—Kt2 with much the freer game.

MORPHY DEFENCE

The opening assumes quite a different aspect if Black plays 3. ....
P—QR3 in answer to White's B—Kt5, in order to have the option of
relieving the pin of his Knight through P—QKt4 at a suitable moment.
We have already seen that White cannot win a Pawn with 4. B×Kt
followed by 5. Kt×P, because of Q—Q5. The only advantage White
can establish after the exchange on B6 is the removal of Black's centre-
Pawn through 5. P—Q4, P×P; 6. Q×P, Q×Q; 7. Kt×Q. White's
plan will then be to exchange as many pieces as possible, in order to
arrive at an end-game with four against three Pawns on the King's
wing. He has very good prospects of stopping Black's Pawn majority
on the Queen's wing by avoiding Pawn exchanges on that part of the
board. However, Black has an advantage in his two Bishops which
might tell in the middle-game. Experience has shown that it is
extremely difficult for Black to obtain more than a draw in this
'exchange variation', and in modern tournaments contestants who want
to play for a win often avoid the Ruy Lopez altogether for this reason
when they have the black pieces.

If White retreats with 4. B—R4, Black has a choice between various
strategic plans. He can either try to maintain his centre-Pawn, or he
can give it up and take White's King's Pawn in turn, or he can submit
to the exchange of his Pawn for
White's Queen's Pawn on White's Q4.
The latter alternative, which leaves
White with his King's Pawn on
K4, is the least desirable, for reasons
explained in the discussion of Diagram 78.

Black has several manœuvres at
his disposal with which to hold his
centre-Pawn. He can play 4. ....
P—Q3 (Steinitz Defence deferred),
with the intention of meeting 5. B×
Kt ch, P×B; 6. P—Q4 with P—
B3, or, if White delays exchanging on
B6, he can continue with 5. Castles,

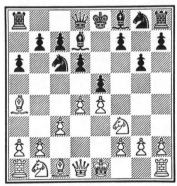

Diagram 95

Kt—B3; 6. B×Kt ch, P×B; 7. P—Q4, Kt—Q2. Another possibility
is 5. P—B3, B—Q2; 6. P—Q4, P—KKt3 (Diagram 95).

It should be noted that after 4. .... P—Q3 White cannot advance
his Queen's Pawn to the fourth before exchanging on B6 unless he is
prepared to sacrifice a Pawn for the sake of rapid development.
5. Castles, Kt—B3; 6. P—Q4 would lead to P—QKt4; 7. B—Kt3,
QKt×P; 8. Kt×Kt, P×Kt, and now White would lose a piece if he

recaptured the Pawn, through P—B4 and P—B5 (Noah's Ark trap).

However, White obtains sufficient compensation for the Pawn with 9. P—QB3, P×P; 10. Kt×P, B—K2; 11. Q—B3, B—Kt2; 12. Q—Kt3, Castles; 13. B—R6, Kt—K1; 14. P—B4, etc.

TCHIGORIN DEFENCE

Perhaps the most thoroughly analysed variation of the Ruy Lopez is Tchigorin's Defence: 4. .... **Kt—B3; 5. Castles, B—K2; 6. R—K1, P—QKt4; 7. B—Kt3, P—Q3; 8. P—B3, Kt—QR4; 9. B—B2, P—B4; 10. P—Q4, Q—B2** (Diagram 96).

Now Black's centre-Pawn is anchored at K4, and the black position,

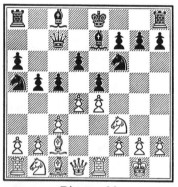

Diagram 96

when properly handled, will stand up against any attempt on White's part to break it open in a King's side attack. That is why this line has been the favourite defence in master tournaments for two generations.

White will try to lodge his Queen's Knight on Q5 or KB5, via Q2, KB1 and K3, and he will attempt an attack on the King's side in view of the fact that there he can bring most of his pieces to bear, whilst the territorial advantage of Black on the Queen's wing invites a disposition of considerable black forces on that wing. White's Queen's Bishop will find employment on KKt5 or it will be useful on K3 to support the Queen's Pawn against which Black might operate with B—KKt5 and Kt—QB3. White will want to hold the Queen's Pawn on Q4 if possible, to tie up black pieces for defence of the King's Pawn and to keep Q5 open for the Knight.

Black in turn will invite the advance of White's Queen's Pawn, in order to have a free hand for manœuvring on the Queen's wing. He might play his King's Knight over to QKt3 and then push his Queen's side Pawns, but he must be careful not to denude his King of defensive forces. If White takes advantage of the exposed position of Black's Queen's Knight's Pawn by playing P—QR4, Black will try to maintain the Pawn on Kt4 as long as possible with QR—Kt1 and B—Q2, rather than advancing it, in order not to lose control of his QB5. Another plan he might follow is to open the Queen's Bishop's file by exchanging once on Q5.

I tried this line in a game against Emanuel Lasker in the New York tournament, 1924, and obtained a very promising position after 11. P—KR3, Castles; 12. QKt—Q2, BP×P; 13. P×P, B—Q2; 14. Kt—B1, KR—QB1; 15. R—K2, Kt—KR4!; 16. P×P, P×P; 17. Kt×P, B×P; 18. Kt×P, B—K3; 19. Kt—Kt5, B—B5; 20. B—Q3, R—Q1; 21. R—B2!, Kt—B5; 22. B×Kt, Q×B; 23. Kt—R3, Q—K4; 24. B×B ch, Kt×B; 25. Q—K2, R—Q5; 26. P—B3, QR—Q1. These moves were practically all forced after 15. .... Kt—KR4. But White's 15th move was not the best. Instead of R—K2 he should have played B—Q3.

In the position of Diagram 96, White's move 11. P—KR3 is dictated by the desire to prevent the exchange of the Knight which Black threatens to pin, because the Knight is important to maintain the Queen's Pawn on Q4. Furthermore, the move comes in handy as a preparation for an attack with P—KKt4 which would be designed to support the occupation of KB5 by the Queen's Knight. White might even try this King's side attack without protecting his Queen's Pawn, and Black's game is by no means easy to defend: 11. QKt—Q2, Castles; 12. Kt—B1, B—Kt5; 13. Kt—K3, B×Kt; 14. Q×B, BP×P; 15. P×P, P×P; 16. Kt—B5!

After 11. P—KR3, Castles; 12. QKt—Q2, there is little inducement for Black to confine himself to purely defensive play with Kt—B3; 13. P—Q5, Kt—Q1 (possibly with the continuation 14. P—QR4, R—Kt1; 15. P—B4, P—Kt5; 16. Kt—B1, Kt—K1; 17. P—Kt4, P—Kt3; 18. Kt—Kt3, Kt—KKt2). It may be extremely difficult for White to pierce the armour protecting Black's King, but the chances are all on his side. That is why modern practice prefers opening the Bishop's file with 12. .... BP×P as indicated above.

Play might go on with 13. P×P, Kt—B3; 14. P—Q5, Kt—QKt5; 15. B—Kt1, P—QR4; 16. P—R3, Kt—R3; 17. P—QKt3, Kt—B4; 18. Kt—B1, B—Q2, or 13. .... B—Q2; 14. Kt—B1, KR—B1; 15. B—Q3 might be inserted before continuing with Kt—B3, etc., as above. Black obtains quite a satisfactory game, with counter-play on the Queen's wing. With the Queen's Bishop's file open, White should not go into the attack with P—KKt4, etc., but he should play Kt—Kt3 and then contest the open file with his Queen's Rook. Otherwise Black invades White's camp on that file and obtains the upper hand.

MARSHALL'S COUNTER-ATTACK

An ingenious innovation enhancing Black's prospects in the Ruy Lopez considerably was introduced by Marshall in 1918. He proposed to profit from the fact that White's move 8. P—B3 in the Tchigorin Defence delays the development of his Queen's wing, and he felt that Black could successfully assume the initiative by castling on his seventh

move and answering P—B3 with 8. .... **P—Q4!** (Diagram 97) instead
of leading into the position of Diagram 96 with P—Q3.   Marshall's
move involves the sacrifice of the King's Pawn.   He anticipates that
the loss of time which White incurs when accepting the sacrifice will
give Black an opportunity to institute a fast King's side attack.   Following the moves

9. **P×P**		**Kt×P**
10. **Kt×P**		**Kt×Kt**
11. **R×Kt**		

Black is ready to start the assault with B—Q3 and Q—R5, after first
defending his Knight with either Kt—B3 or P—QB3.   The former
alternative was refuted by Capablanca in the famous game in which
Marshall, after much secret preparation, tried his innovation for the
first time.   But the improvement 11. .... **P—QB3** poses a difficult

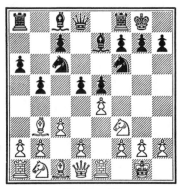

Diagram 97

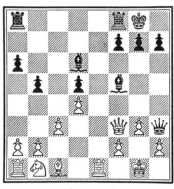

Diagram 98

problem, and its final solution is still wanting.   The attack leads to
such complications that few players dare go into it, whether playing
White or Black, because in tournament games the clock does not allow
them sufficient time for adventures in unexplored regions.

White has the choice between 12. B×Kt and 12. P—Q4.   After
12. **B×Kt, P×B;** 13. **P—Q4, B—Q3;** 14. **R—K1,** Black continues
with **Q—R5;** 15. **P—KKt3, Q—R6;** 16. **Q—B3, B—KB4!** (Diagram
98), when White cannot reply 17. Q×P because of QR—K1, followed
by B—K5.   If he plays 17. Q×P instead, Black can keep up the
pressure with Q—R4!   Again, 18. Q×P would be very dangerous.
The continuation might be QR—Q1; 19. Q—Kt2, B—R6; 20. Q—R1,
B—KKt5!; 21. Kt—Q2, KR—K1, with a devastating attack.   White's
best plan is probably 18. P—B3, though even then B—R6; 19. Q—B2,
P—B4 maintains a strong initiative.

It has been suggested that White might play 14. R—K3 instead of

R—K1, in order to answer Q—R5 with 15. P—KR3. But Black can reply 14. .... P—B4 and 15. .... P—B5, when White's defence becomes extremely difficult.

The alternative line, beginning with 12. **P—Q4**, leads to variations which are still more complicated. After 12. .... **B—Q3; 13. R—K1, Q—R5; 14. P—Kt3, Q—R6,** White's best strategy is rapid development with 15. **Q—Q3, B—KB4;** 16. **Q—B1, Q—R4;** 17. **B—K3, QR—K1;** 18. **Kt—Q2** (Diagram 98A). A game between Christoffel and H. Steiner continued: 18. .... R—K3; 19. P—QR4, B—KR6; 20. B—Q1!, Q—B4; 21. Q—K2. At this point, Black played Kt—B5 and lost. With 21. .... B—B5 he could have regained his Pawn.

In Diagram 97, after 9. P × P, White must beware of a second Pawn

Diagram 98A

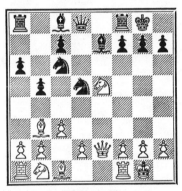

Diagram 98B

sacrifice which Black might offer with P—K5; 10. P × Kt, P × Kt. This Pawn is poisoned, for 11. **Q × P, B—KKt5;** 12. **Q—Kt3, R—K1;** 13. **P—B3, Q—Q6!** gives Black a strong attack. 13. P—KB4?, B—Q3; 14. R—K5, B × R; 15. P × B, Kt—R4! would lose for White. But 11. **P—Q4!** and rapid development of the Queen's wing refutes Black's tactics.

Against best play, the idea of Marshall's counter-attack can not be carried out when White, on his sixth move, continues with **Q—K2** instead of R—K1. Here, after P—QKt4; 7. B—Kt3, Castles, White would not prepare the advance of his Queen's Pawn with P—B3, but play 8. **P—Q4!** immediately. Then P × P; 9. **P—K5, Kt—K1;** 10. **P—B3!** secures a winning positional advantage.

The continuation 8. **P—B3, P—Q4!;** 9. P × P is dangerous for White. After **Kt × P;** 10. **Kt × P** (Diagram 98B), Black might play **Kt × Kt;** 11. **Q × Kt, B—Kt2;** 12. **P—Q4, P—QR4!;** and his Queen's Rook will enter into the battle via QR3. Playable is 9. P—Q3, P × P; 10. P × P, P—R3; 11. R—Q1, B—Q3, with an even game.

THE OPEN VARIATION OF THE MORPHY DEFENCE

The Ruy Lopez assumes an entirely different aspect if Black accepts White's challenge and captures the King's Pawn which White leaves unprotected when castling on the fifth move. 5. .... Kt×P; 6. P—Q4, P—QKt4; 7. B—Kt3, P—Q4; 8. P×P, B—K3 then leads to the position of Diagram 98c.

Black has emerged from the opening with free play for his pieces, but unless he can bring his Queen's Bishop's Pawn up to B4, White is likely to obtain a strong attack by placing his Knight on Q4 and advancing the King's Bishop's Pawn.

The classical continuation is 9. **P—B3**, which prevents the exchange of the King's Bishop through 9. .... Kt—R4. Then Black's King's Knight is dislodged by 10. QKt—Q2 and 11. Q—K2, or 11. B—B2.

In the World Championship Match Tournament of 1948, the Russians introduced the move 9. Q—K2 successfully in conjunction with some new attacking ideas, such as 9. Q—K2, B—K2; 10. R—Q1, Castles; 11. P—B4!, or 9. .... Kt—B4; 10. R—Q1, Kt×B; 11. RP×Kt, Q—B1;

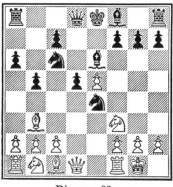

Diagram 98c

12. P—B4!, QP×P; 13. P×P, B×P; 14. Q—K4, with a strong attack.

Most natural for Black seems to answer 9. **Q—K2** with **Kt—R4,** to continue with 10. **R—Q1, B—QB4;** 11. **B—K3, B×B;** 12. **Q×B, P—QB4.**

In Diagram 98c, if White plays P—B3, the following continuations are typical:

Be continually on the alert against the move P—QR4. White can also initiate a dangerous attack by playing Kt—Q4 without bothering to protect his King's Pawn first. These considerations suggest the following two lines of play which are typical of the possibilities which the position of the Diagram offers:

9.	P—B3	B—K2
10.	QKt—Q2	Castles
11.	Q—K2	Kt—B4
12.	Kt—Q4	Kt×B!

13. Kt×QKt would now be refuted through Kt×B.

13.	QKt×Kt	Q—Q2
14.	Kt×Kt	Q×Kt
15.	B—K3	

and while White has succeeded in keeping Black's Queen's Bishop's Pawn from advancing, and the menace of a Pawn storm on the King's side remains in the air, Black has counter-play on the Queen's wing where his Pawn majority will constitute a real threat if he succeeds in exchanging Queens, thereby minimizing the prospects of a white King's side attack. With this idea in mind he might continue at this point with Q—B5.

White's alternative referred to above—involving the sacrifice of the King's Pawn for the sake of immediate pressure by advance of the King's Bishop's Pawn—looks more promising. The tactical execution of this plan might take the following form:

9. P—B3	B—K2
10. P—QR4	P—Kt5
11. Kt—Q4	Kt×P
12. P—KB4	B—Kt5
13. Q—B2	P—QB4

giving back the Pawn to stem White's attack by exchanges.

14. P×Kt	P×Kt
15. P×QP	Castles

White has perhaps slightly better chances, due to his command of more territory on the King's wing. Black cannot take advantage of the open Queen's Bishop's file as White controls his QB2 and QB3 so that Black's Rooks cannot invade White's Queen's wing.

In Diagram 98c, Black can answer White's move 9. **P—B3** with **B—QB4** instead of B—K2. The idea of this more aggressive continuation is to counter 10. **QKt—Q2, Castles; 11. B—B2** with either P—B4 or even Kt×BP. In either case there are wild possibilities which have been insufficiently tested in master play to allow definite conclusions. For example: 11. .... **P—B4; 12. Kt—Kt3, B—Kt3; 13. QKt—Q4, Kt×Kt; 14. Kt×Kt, B×Kt; 15. P×B, P—B5; 16. P—B3, Kt—Kt6!; 17. P×Kt!, P×P; 18. Q—Q3, B—B4; 19. Q×B, R×Q; 20. B×R, Q—R5; 21. B—R3, Q×P ch; 22. K—R1, Q×KP; 23. B—Q2, P—B4; 24. QR—K1, Q×P; 25. B—B4, P—QB4!**, or 11. .... **Kt×KBP!; 12. R×Kt, P—B3; 13. P×P, Q×P; 14. Kt—B1, B×R ch; 15. K×R, Kt—K4 (15. .... P—KKt4?; 16. B×KtP!).**

Less desirable for White appears 14. **Q—B1,** because of B—KKt5; 15. K—R1, B×R; 16. Q×B, QR—K1; 17. Q—Kt3, Kt—K4; 18. B—Q1, P—KR4; 19. P—KR3, P—KR5; 20. Q—B2, Kt—Q6; 21. Q—Kt1, R—K8; 22. Kt×R, Kt—B7 ch; 23. K—R2, Q—K4 ch; 24. P—Kt3, P×P ch; 25. Q×P, Q×Kt, winning.

We have here two examples of long-winded analyses which a master must know in order not to be drawn into a lost position from which he has no chance of extricating himself within the time limit of a tournament game.   How difficult it is even for a player of World Championship calibre to unravel the problems offered by a prepared variation may be seen from the game which Euwe lost to Keres in the match tournament of 1948.   This was a Steinitz Defence deferred (see p. 83), in which Keres answered 5. P—B3 with P—B4, instead of playing the usual B—Q2.   Euwe continued with 6. P×P, B×P; 7. P—Q4, P—K5; 8. Kt—Kt5, P—Q4; 9. P—B3, when Keres offered the interesting sacrifice P—K6, to take advantage of the awkward position of White's King's Knight.   Subsequent analysis showed that White should emerge with the superior game, but Euwe missed the right way.

The move P—KB4 has been tried in the Ruy Lopez by enterprising players as early as on the third turn.   After 1. **P—K4, P—K4;** 2. **Kt—KB3, Kt—QB3;** 3. **B—Kt5, P—B4** (Schliemann Defence), the continuation 4. **Kt—B3, Kt—B3;** 5. **P×P, B—B4** gives Black a good deal of play for the Pawn he has sacrificed.   There might follow: 6. Q—K2, Q—K2; 7. B×Kt, QP×B; 8. Kt×P, B×P; 9. P—Q3, Castles.

THE PETROFF

In the openings which we have considered so far we have taken for granted that after 1. **P—K4, P—K4;** 2. **Kt—KB3** Black will defend his King's Pawn.   It is only natural that attempts have been made by Black to counter-attack White's centre-Pawn instead.   He can do so either by developing his King's Knight or by advancing the Queen's Pawn or the King's Bishop's Pawn.   We can eliminate the advance of the Queen's Pawn from our consideration, as we have seen that even White drifts into a disadvantageous position if he plays 2. P—Q4 rather than first preparing this move with Kt—KB3 in order to recapture on Q4 with his Knight.   From this viewpoint of general strategic principles we will also condemn 2. .... **P—KB4,** because this move does not add to the development of any of the black pieces.   White obtains indeed a better game by simply getting his pieces out as fast as possible. For example: 3. **Kt×P, Q—B3;** 4. **P—Q4, P—Q3;** 5. **Kt—B4, P×P;** 6. **Kt—B3, Q—Kt3;** 7. **B—B4, Kt—KB3;** 8. **Kt—K3,** and as soon as Black tries to anchor his King's Pawn with P—Q4, White will prevent this by playing P—Q5 himself, so that Black's King's Bishop remains condemned to inactivity for quite some time.

The opening in which Black counter-attacks with 2. .... Kt—KB3 is called 'Petroff'.   An important point to know in this opening is that after 3. **Kt×P** Black cannot recapture the Pawn immediately, because Kt×P would be answered by 4. Q—K2 which wins a Pawn. If the Knight moves, White wins the Queen with the discovered check Kt—B6, and if Black protects the Knight with P—Q4, White attacks it with 5. P—Q3, forcing Q—K2; 6. P×Kt, Q×Kt; 7. P×P, etc.

Black must therefore drive White's Knight first with **P—Q3**, and capture the Pawn after White retreats with 4. **Kt—KB3.** White can now win a developing tempo with 5. **Q—K2, Q—K2**; 6. **P—Q3, Kt—KB3**; 7. **B—Kt5.** This threatens to disrupt Black's Pawns with B×Kt, since the Queen is pinned and cannot recapture. After 7. .... **Q×Q ch**; 8. **B×Q** on the other hand, White is two moves ahead in development.

If White is not satisfied with this slight advantage, he might proceed with the obvious developing moves 5. P—Q4 and 6. B—Q3, in an attempt to undermine the advanced position of Black's Knight by pressing against his Queen's Pawn with P—QB4 and QKt—B3. In this case he must be prepared to defend the King's wing against violent attacks which Black is apt to work up, because after 5. **P—Q4, P—Q4**; 6. **B—Q3, B—Q3,** Black is really one move ahead in development. This is due to the fact that White has made three moves with his Knight, landing again on KB3 where it was after its first move. With best play on both sides, the game should be equalized before long.

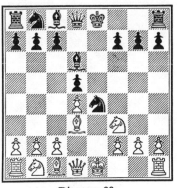

Diagram 99

White has an alternative in dealing with the Petroff Defence. He can refrain from capturing Black's King's Pawn on the third move and, instead, defend his own King's Pawn with 3. **Kt—B3.** However, in that case Black has no difficulty in equalizing the game either. He could reply **B—Kt5,** turning the opening into a Ruy Lopez with colours reversed, or he could play **Kt—B3,** which would lead to a position discussed in the Scotch game if White continues with 4. P—Q4, P×P; 5. Kt×P, B—Kt5; 6. Kt×Kt, KtP×Kt; 7. B—Q3.

FOUR KNIGHTS GAME

After 3. .... **Kt—B3** (Diagram 100) White must not play 4. **B—B4,** because this would enable Black to exchange White's King's Pawn for a less important Pawn of his own. He would reply **Kt×P!,** and after 5. **Kt×Kt** he would regain the piece with **P—Q4.** If then 6. B×P, Q×B, Black remains with the advantage of two Bishops in addition to that of a Pawn in the centre. And if 6. B—Q3, P×Kt; 7. B×P, Black also has the superior game, as White cannot very well enforce the equalizing move P—Q4 without exchanging his Bishop for Black's Queen's Knight.

Instead of capturing Black's Knight immediately after 4. .... **Kt×P,** White might first sacrifice his Bishop on KB7, since he would have to give back a piece anyway. But Black would again emerge with the advantage of two Bishops, and the disadvantage that he cannot castle is not very serious in this case as he can complete his development just as fast as White. The continuation might be 5. **B×P ch, K×B;** 6. **Kt×Kt, P—Q4;** 7. **QKt—Kt5 ch, K—Kt1,** and White cannot prevent Black from freeing himself with P—KR3 and K—R2. There is a trap in this position which Black, however, can easily avoid. In answer to 8. Q—K2 Black must not play P—K5, because 9. Kt×P would follow, and Black cannot take the Knight on account of 10. **Q—B4** check and mate.

Diagram 100

Diagram 101

THE PIN OF THE KING'S KNIGHT

As calm and simple as this '*Four Knights*' opening looks in its initial stage which Diagram 100 depicts, it carries the seed of many wild developments. If White continues with 4. **B—Kt5,** Black can imitate White's moves for a while, but unless he desists at the right moment he is lost. This opening is a most instructive illustration of the advantage conferred upon White by the first move. After 4. .... **B—Kt5;** 5. **Castles,** Black must also castle. If he plays **P—Q3** instead, White obtains an overwhelming attack through 6. **P—Q4, P×P;** 7. **Kt—Q5!,** threatening the Bishop, **B—QB4;** 8. **B—Kt5** (Diagram 101). As Black cannot relieve the pin, White can tear open the chain of Pawns which protects Black's King. The immediate threat is to bring a third piece to bear upon the pinned Knight, perhaps with Kt—R4 and Q—B3. Another threat is Kt×QP, attacking Black's Queen's Knight for the second time. All Black can do is try to drive White's Knight from its dominating post in the centre and advance the Queen's Pawn so as to be able to bring back his King's Bishop for the defence of the King. He might start with 8. .... **P—QR3.** There would be no sense in playing P—KR3, as White would reply Kt×Kt ch and then retreat with the Bishop to KR4, maintaining his pressure on KB6. In answer to P—QR3, White will not hesitate exchanging with 9. **B×Kt ch, P×B; 10. Kt×Kt ch, P×Kt; 11. B—R4,** because if Black now continued with P—Q4, he would only help White's Rook to get into play with 12. R—K1. The only other plans at Black's disposal would be to castle and protect the pinned Pawn with K—Kt2, or to play R—KKt1 and then R—Kt3, or to prepare castling on the Queen's side with Q—K2.

None of these plans would save Black. If he castled, White would first put Black's King's Bishop out of action with 12. P—QKt4!, B—Kt3 (B×P?; 13. Q×P, B—QB4; 14. Q—B3 or Q—Kt2, etc.), and then he might play 13. Kt—Q2, with the idea to attack KB6 further with P—K5! and Kt—K4 or with P—KB4 and then P—K5. Black is helpless.

In reply to 11. .... R—KKt1 White will try to open the King's file for his Rook in order to take advantage of the fact that Black's King is exposed to attack in the middle of the board. At the same time he will try to continue operating against the pinned black Pawn. But he must also take defensive measures against Black's counter-threat in the file which he has just occupied with his Rook. This threat consists in B—R6. As long as White's Rook is on B1, he cannot reply P—KKt3 which he would much rather play than protecting his Knight's Pawn with B—Kt3, unpinning Black's Bishop's Pawn.

The obvious move for White would seem R—K1, to follow this up with P—K5. But then Black could drive the Rook with B—QKt5, and after R—K2 the continuation QB—Kt5 would give Black a good deal of counter-play.

White will therefore first again play 12. P—QKt4! If then B—Kt3, the manœuvre 13. R—K1, B—R6; 14. P—KKt3 will leave Black without defence against P—K5. For example, 14. .... B—K3; 15. P—K5, QP×P; 16. Kt×P, Q—K2; 17. Q—B3, B—Q4; 18. Q—B4, and the pinned Pawn falls.

Should Black attempt 12. .... B×P, the consequence might be 13. Q×P, B—QB4; 14. Q—B3. Black can now disregard the attack on his Bishop's Pawn temporarily and play B—KR6. For if White played 15. B×P Black could reply B×KtP!, threatening mate through B×Kt. But White can protect the threat with 15. Kt—K1, and in the end Black's Bishop's Pawn will fall after all and P—Kt will open the centre for White's Rooks.

This leaves 11. .... Q—K2 to be tried. Again White would play to open the King's file: 12. Kt×P, B—Q2; 13. Kt—B5, B×Kt; 14. P×B, K—Q2; 15. R—K1, Q—Q1; 16. Q—R5 is only one of many possibilities at White's disposal. Black's two ills—the weakness of the Pawns on the King's side and the inability of his Rooks to co-operate —are incurable.

I have given these variations, which might result from the pin of the King's Knight, in considerable detail, not because I want the reader to memorize any of them. They will serve to illustrate the troubles which are liable to ensue after the exchange of the King's Knight is forced in a way which breaks up the chain of Pawns protecting the King, and which leaves the pinning Bishop on the board to exploit the weakness of these Pawns.

If the Bishop is exchanged against the Knight, so that the pin on B6 is relieved, the weakening of the squares B3 and R3 is often compensated for—and sometimes outweighed—by the advantage of the file opened for the Rooks through the exchange. The Four Knights opening which we are discussing furnishes examples for such cases also. From Diagram 100 play might proceed as follows: 4. **B—Kt5, B—Kt5;** 5. **Castles, Castles;** 6. **P—Q3, P—Q3;** 7. **B—Kt5,** and Black might defend himself against the threat of Kt—Q5 with **Kt—K2.** This allows 8. **B×Kt,** but without his Queen's Bishop White cannot force control of the squares KR6 and KB6. In answer to 8. .... P×Kt; 9. Q—Q2, for example, Black might play K—Kt2. Or, if 9. Kt—KR4, the continuation Kt—Kt3; 10. Kt×Kt, RP×Kt would give Black an open Rook's file. After 11. P—B4, B—B4 ch; 12. K—R1, K—Kt2 followed by R—R1, Black should find an opportunity for a King's side attack.

A very dangerous procedure for Black would be to disregard White's threat Kt—Q5 on the 7th move and to imitate White's manœuvre, playing 7. .... **B—Kt5;** 8. **Kt—Q5, Kt—Q5.** Diagram 102 shows the position reached at this stage.

Both players will try to find an opportune moment for exchanging on KB6, i.e. a moment when they can play the Queen over to the King's wing and attack one or both of the points KB6 and KR6 which have been weakened by the disappearance of the King's Knight's Pawn.

White could start with 9. **B—QB4,** placing the Bishop, which is attacked by the Knight, on a square where it is likely to aid in the coming attack on the King. If Black imitates this move again, White will consider both Kt×Kt ch and B×Kt. After 9. .... **B—QB4;** 10. **Kt×Kt ch, P×Kt,** he would have to choose between B—R6 and B—R4. While the latter move maintains the pin, Black can keep White's Queen out of his territory with K—Kt2 as soon as White attacks R6 with Q—Q2. The other alternative, 11. **B—R6,** relinquishes

the pin whilst Black still maintains it, and in view of the fact that the
Knight's file is open for Black's Rooks, this continuation is likely to
be in Black's favour. For example: 11. .... **R—K1**; 12. **P—B3,
Kt×Kt ch**; 13. **P×Kt, B—R4!**, and it is Black who has a slight initiative. 14. P—Q4, B—QKt3; 15. K—R1, K—R1; 16. B—K2, Q—Q2;
17. Q—Q2, Q—R6; 18. R—KKt1, R—KKt1; 19. R—Kt3, Q—R5
or Q—K3 would probably be the best line for White, with chances
for both sides. Black should not consider countering 14. P—Q4 with
P×P; 15. P×P, R×P! The reply 16. P×R!, B×Q; 17. QR×B would

pose a problem which Black would
find hard to solve. The possession
of the open Knight's file, in conjunction with the Bishop of the colour
of Black's weak squares KR3 and
KB3, would easily offset the slight
theoretical superiority of a Queen
over Rook and Bishop. Black could
not very well retreat with his Bishop
because after 17. .... B—Kt3;
18. K—R1, Q—Q2; 19. R—Kt1 ch,
K—R1; 20. B—Kt7 ch, K—Kt1;
21. B×P (B6) ch, K—B1; 22. R—
Q3, he would be helpless against
the threat QR—KKt3 and check on

Diagram 102

Kt8. Neither would 17. .... Q—Q2 be of avail, which threatens
perpetual check on Kt5 and B6. White would again reply 18. K—R1,
and whilst Black can then exchange one of the Rooks with K—R1;
19. R—KKt1, R—KKt1; 20. R×R ch, K×R; 21. R—Kt1 ch, K—
R1, he would lose his Bishop and the fight with the Queen against
Rook and two Bishops would be hopeless.

In the position of Diagram 102, after both players have moved their
Bishops back to QB4, White can hardly expect to derive an advantage
from 10. B×Kt, P×B, because Black can again defend his R3 with
K—Kt2, and, besides, he can relieve his KB3 from pressure by driving
White's Knight with P—B3.

But White can prepare his onslaught with 10. **Q—Q2**, which
threatens to occupy R6 with the Queen after the exchange on B6. This
move Black can no longer imitate, because if Q—Q2, White continues
with 11. B×Kt, B×Kt; 12. Kt—K7 ch and mate in three moves, as
shown in connection with Diagram 59, unless Black gives up his Queen.

10. .... B×Kt is no satisfactory defence either. White plays 11.
B×Kt, and now P×B is followed by 12. Q—R6 with the threat Kt×P
ch and Q×RP mate.

More promising looks 10. .... Kt×Kt ch; 11. P×Kt, B×P (B6).

Then 12. B×Kt, P×B; 13. Q—R6 fails because of K—R1! and R—Kt1 ch. But White has time. He need not exchange on B6 until he is compelled to. Thus, he can make room for his King with 12. P—KR3, in order to play his Rook to KKt1. Black might make similar preparations with K—R1; 13. K—R2, R—KKt1; but with 14. R—KKt1 White threatens at last to force the win through 15. B×Kt, P×B; 16. R×R ch, Q×R; 17. R—KKt1, Q—Q1; 18. Q—R6. Thus, Black must play 14. .... P—B3, and then White wins through the old threat against B6: 15. Kt×Kt, P×Kt; 16. B—R4, Q—K2 (to protect the Bishop's Pawn); 17. R—Kt3! The point of the combination. This Rook cannot be taken, because after R×R; 18. P×R there is no defence against R—KB1 which finally conquers the point B6. On the other hand, after 17. .... B—R4 White forces that point through 18. Q—R6, B—KKt3; 19. R—B3, and Black must lose his Queen against the Bishop.

No matter what Black plays after 10. Q—Q2, White will obtain a winning game because he is a move ahead of Black and so his attack comes first. He will be the first to gain advantage from the open Knight's file if he makes the right moves. These moves are again dictated by considerations of mobility. One of the most interesting illustrations of the many possibilities hidden in this position is this: Black might force a decision on White's part after 10. Q—Q2 by playing P—B3 immediately. After 11. Kt×Kt ch, P×Kt; 12. B—R4, B×Kt; 13. Q—R6 he can then protect his KB3 by interposing his Knight: Kt—K7 ch; 14. K—R1, B×P ch; 15. K×B, Kt—B5 ch; 16. K—R1, Kt—Kt3. Now the position of Diagram 103 is reached, in which Black has succeeded in blocking the Knight's file, and in which a direct assault against his KB3 with P—B4 would be frustrated by Kt×B. On the other hand, White can also attack in the Rook's file, by playing a Rook to KR3. He cannot get the King's Rook there very well, because after 17. R—KKt1, which threatens R×Kt ch, P×R; Q×P ch and mate in two, Black defends himself with 17. .... P—Q4, relieving the pin of his King's Bishop's Pawn. 18. R—Kt3 is then countered with B×P, so that R—R3 is refuted through B×B.

The winning manœuvre is suggested—as in most cases of mating attacks—by an attempt to bring to the scene the *Queen's Rook*, which is not yet developed. This Rook has no square on the third rank via which to reach its objective. But White can free a square for it. He accomplishes this with 17. P—Q4!, B×P; 18. P—QB3, B—B4; 19. QR—Q1, which at the same time holds back Black's Queen's Pawn. Now the threat is 20. R—KKt1, K—R1; 21. R—Q3, Q—K2; 22. R—R3 and mate through B×P ch and Q×P. It does not help Black to anticipate this threat with Q—K2, because 20. R—KKt1, K—R1; 21. R—Q3, R—KKt1; 22. R—R3, Kt×B?; 23. Q×RP ch!, K×Q; 24.

R×Kt mates, and if, instead, 22. .... R—Kt2, then 23. R—B3 again conquers the square B6 for the Bishop, as Kt×B is now not possible on account of Q×R mate.

All these difficult and rather complicated variations seem to bear out the conclusion one would reach on a purely logical basis, that it cannot be good for Black to imitate White's moves in a hand-to-hand fight. Most analyses of this opening were worked out in the years 1910 and 1911 by Leonhardt, Emanuel Lasker's brother Berthold, and myself. I remember it occurred to me at that time, that in Diagram 102, after 9. B—QB4, Black might try to anticipate White's whole combinative syndrome by replying 9. .... Q—Q2, although after the moves 10. Kt×Kt ch, P×Kt; 11. B×P, P—KR3, this permits the fork P—B3. Diagram 104 shows this critical position. 12. P—B3

Diagram 103

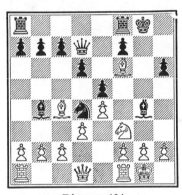

Diagram 104

would now be followed by Kt×Kt ch; 13. P×Kt, B—KR4; 14. K—R1, K—R2; 15. R—KKt1, R—KKt1, just as in one of the variations just discussed, when the colours were reversed. 16. R—Kt3 would be answered with R—Kt3, and after 17. P×B, R×B; 18. Q—K2, R—KKt1; 19. QR—KKt1, R×R; 20. R×R, P—B3, White would have a difficult game, because Black has more mobility. White's Rook is bottled up on the King's wing, while Black's Rook is free to participate in activities on the Queen's wing. White's extra Pawn is doubled and cannot advance, so that it hardly constitutes an advantage which compensates for Black's greater mobility. We concluded that in this opening, which we called the 'inimitable', White obtained no advantage in the position of Diagram 102 by continuing with 9. B—QB4, and that 9. P—B3 was probably the best way for White to demonstrate that imitation would lead Black into trouble. After 9. P—B3, Kt×B; 10. Kt×B, P—B3; 11. Kt—B2, Kt—B2; 12. Kt—K3, Black's Bishop is attacked. If Black persists in imitation and plays Kt—K3,

White breaks the symmetry with 13. B×Kt, B×Kt; 14. Q×B, Q×B; 15. Q×Q, P×Q (Diagram 105) weakening Black's KB3 and KB4. He will be able to lodge his Knight on KB5 whilst Black does not control the corresponding square, since White can play P—KKt3. If Black tries to obtain counter-play in the centre, the game might proceed as follows: 16. P—KKt3, QR—Q1; 17. P—KB4, P—Q4; 18. P×QP BP×P; 19. P×P, P×P; 20. Kt—Kt4, and White wins a Pawn.

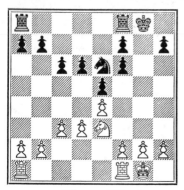

Diagram 105

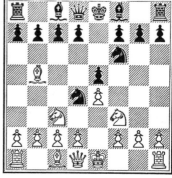

Diagram 106

RUBINSTEIN'S COUNTER-ATTACK

If Black does not want to content himself with a draw from the start he will, of course, try to avoid symmetry of position as soon as the opportunity presents itself. Rubinstein has shown that in the position of Diagram 100 Black can play **Kt—Q5** in reply to 5. **B—Kt5** and obtain at least equality. To say that this move violates a strategic principle, by moving a piece twice before development is completed, would be a misinterpretation of this principle. Dangerous loss of time results only if a second move of a piece lands it on a square from which it can be driven by a *developing* move of the opponent, or if that square could have been reached by the piece in one move instead of two. If, on the other hand, the second move advances the piece to a desirable square which it would try to reach in the middle-game anyway, no harm may be done by anticipating that move. It might be included under the heading of developing moves. A second move with a Knight into the centre of the board belongs in this category, as does the move R—K1 after castling, before the pieces of the Queen's wing are developed.

In the position reached after Rubinstein's move, the only questions for Black to concern himself with are whether White can safely capture the King's Pawn whose protection Black has just relinquished, or whether White can secure an advantage by exchanging Knights and advancing the King's Pawn. In either case Black has a perfectly satisfactory reply. After 5. **Kt × P, Q—K2; 6. Kt—B3, Kt × B; 7. Kt × Kt, Q × P ch; 8. Q—K2, Q × Q ch; 9. K × Q, Kt—Q4**, White accomplishes nothing by attacking Black's Knight with P—B4, because Black has the reply P—QR3. In fact, the position is probably slightly in favour of Black, due to his two Bishops. 5. Kt × Kt, P × Kt; 6. P—K5, P × Kt; 7. P × Kt, Q × P, followed by P—B3 and P—Q4, also gives Black a perfect development. The wild continuation 5. Kt × P, Q—K2; 6. P—B4, Kt × B; 7. Kt × Kt, P—Q3; 8. Kt—KB3, Q × P ch; 9. K—B2 leads to Black's advantage, if after Kt—Kt5 ch; 10. K—Kt3, Q—Kt3; 11. Kt—R4, Q—R4 White tries to win the exchange with 12. Kt × P ch, K—Q1; 13. Kt × R. Black obtains a winning attack with P—KKt4; 14. P × P, Q × P.

The question might be raised why Black could not have recourse to the defence Kt—Q5 in the Ruy Lopez also. The answer is that after 1. P—K4, P—K4; 2. Kt—KB3, Kt—QB3; 3. B—Kt5, Kt—Q5; 4. Kt × Kt, P × Kt, White can calmly proceed with his development whilst in the Four Knights opening he must lose time to do something for his King's Pawn and his Queen's Knight, which are both attacked after the exchange on Q4. Thus, in the Ruy Lopez, White remains

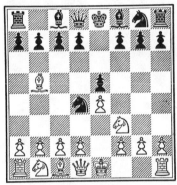

Diagram 107

two moves ahead in development and he retains the advantage of a Pawn on K4. Black does not find time to nullify this advantage by advancing his Queen's Pawn to the fourth. For example: 5. Castles, P—KKt3; 6. P—Q3, B—Kt2; 7. P—QB3, Kt—K2; 8. P × P, B × P; 9. Kt—B3, P—QB3; 10. B—QB4, P—Q4; 11. P × P, P × P; 12. Q—R4 ch, B—Q2; 13. B—QKt5, B—Kt2; 14. B—Kt5, with the customary troubles resulting from such pins. Black cannot free himself through exchanges, because he cannot castle into safety: B × Kt; 15. P × B, B × B; 16. Q × B ch, Q—Q2; 17. Q—B5!, R—QB1; 18. Q—K3, K—B1; 19. KR—K1, Kt—B4; 20. Q—K5, R—KKt1 (K—Kt1; 21. B—B6); 21. P—Kt4, P—KR3; 22. B—B1, etc., or 21. .... Kt—Kt2; 22. P—KR3, and Black is hopelessly tied up.

THE KING'S GAMBIT

Before turning to openings in which Black answers 1. P—K4 with moves other than P—K4, let us review shortly the 'King's Gambit' and related openings in which White attacks the black centre-Pawn with P—KB4 instead of P—Q4. If White plays P—KB4 on the second move, he offers a real gambit, because after P×P Black can hold the Pawn with P—KKt4. White has gained an advantage in mobilization, as a result of two Pawn moves by Black which do not add to his development. Whether this advantage leads to a winning attack is a question which decades of analysis have failed to solve. In modern master practice the King's Gambit is rarely seen, because Black can readily equalize the game by returning the gambit Pawn and counterattack White's centre with P—Q4. For example: 1. **P—K4, P—K4; 2. P—KB4, P×P; 3. Kt—KB3, P—Q4!; 4. P×P, Kt—KB3.** If Black plays 3. .... Kt—KB3 first, White can displace the Knight with 4. P—K5, Kt—R4. Then 5. P—Q4, P—Q4! (Diagram 108) leaves Black with a Knight which is not ideally placed on the edge of the board,

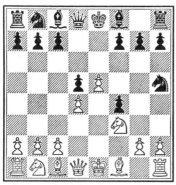

Diagram 108

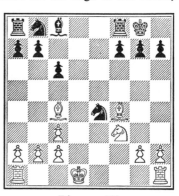

Diagram 109

but White can make no headway with an attack in the King's Bishop's file until he removes the Pawn from KB4, and on that occasion Black's Knight will be exchanged. Meanwhile Black will find an opportunity of attacking White's advanced centre-Pawn with P—KB3, and in that way he will open his own Bishop's file also. Black's defence is harder if White first plays 5. P—KKt4!! and after P×P e.p.; 6. P—Q4, P—Q4 continues with 7. Kt—Kt5, P—KKt3; 8. Q—B3, followed by 9. P×P. This possibility has not yet been tested sufficiently in masterplay.

In reply to 1. **P—K4, P—K4; 2. P—KB4, P×P; 3. B—B4,** Black again frees his game with **P—Q4!** Then 4. **B×P, Kt—KB3; 5. Kt—QB3, B—QKt5; 6. Kt—B3, B×Kt; 7. QP×B, P—B3; 8. B—B4, Q×Q ch; 9. K×Q, Castles; 10. B×P, Kt×P** leads to a position with equal chances for both players (Diagram 109).

MUZIO GAMBIT

If Black tries to hold on to the gambit Pawn, he exposes himself to a violent attack, which is the natural consequence of relinquishing the centre-Pawn and delaying his development. The most striking attack at White's disposal is the 'Muzio Gambit' in which he sacrifices a whole piece: 1. **P—K4, P—K4**; 2. **P—KB4, P×P**; 3. **Kt—KB3, P—KKt4**;

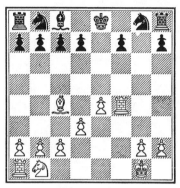

Diagram 110

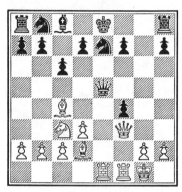

Diagram 111

4. **B—B4, P—Kt5**; 5. **Castles, P×Kt**; 6. **Q×P, B—R3**; 7. **P—Q3, Q—B3**; 8. **QB×P, B×B**; 9. **Q×B, Q×Q**; 10. **R×Q**. White wins the Bishop's Pawn, and Black will have no easy time getting a draw even though he is a piece ahead. Instead of exchanging Queens, White can complicate matters still further through 8. **P—K5, Q×P**; 9. **Kt—B3, Kt—K2**; 10. **B—Q2, P—QB3**; 11. **QR—K1**. An ideally developed position if there ever was one. It should lead to a win for White. For example: **Q—B4 ch**; 12. **K—R1, P—Q4**; 13. **Q—R5, Q—Q3**; 14. **B×QP, P×B**; 15. **Kt×P** or **Kt—Kt5**, and Black is in hot water.

Another way in which White can conduct the attack is with 4. **P—KR4**. In reply to **P—Kt5** (Diagram 112) White can then continue either with 5. **Kt—Kt5, P—KR3**; 6. **Kt×**

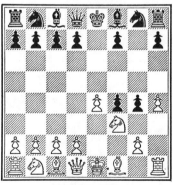

Diagram 112

P, K×Kt; 7. **B—B4 ch** or **P—Q4,** or he can play 5. **Kt—K5, B—Kt2**; 6. **Kt×KtP** or **P—Q4**. These attacks are full of fascinating possibilities, but the inexperienced player is bound to lose his way in the complicated combinations through which he must see to avoid pitfalls on almost every step.

For this reason, he does better to decline the gambit altogether. This is all the more commendable, as our general principles point the way to the proper method of development very clearly.

White's move 2. P—KB4 does not threaten to remove Black's centre-Pawn immediately, because Q—R5 ch would follow, forcing the King to move, as P—Kt3 would lose a Rook through Q×KP ch. Therefore Black has time to develop his King's Bishop before protecting his King's Pawn with P—Q3. After **B—B4; 3. Kt—KB3, P—Q3** Black will be able to get his minor pieces out one move ahead of White, as the latter must still advance his Queen's Pawn for the purpose. Diagram 113 shows the position reached after both players have made the plausible developing moves 4. **B—B4, Kt—KB3; 5. P—Q3, Kt—B3; 6. Kt—B3.** Black's King's Bishop prevents White from castling

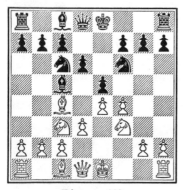

Diagram 113

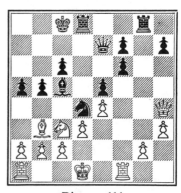

Diagram 114

on the King's side, and in order to preserve the Bishop against the exchange which White might force through Kt—QR4 Black could now play P—QR3. Somewhat more aggressive would be B—KKt5. If then 7. P—KR3, Black has the choice between B—K3 and B×Kt. After B—K3 White would have no advantage from the double Pawn he could create by exchanging on K6 and K5. Black would control the squares Q5 and KB5, while White would not have the corresponding squares at his disposal. Furthermore, White has a glaring weakness on his KKt3, of which Black threatens to take advantage at the first opportune moment with Kt—KR4.

7. .... B×Kt; 8. Q×B, Kt—Q5; 9. Q—Kt3!, Q—K2! is also

playable for Black. White's threat Q×P is now harmless, as the King's Bishop's Pawn is defended. Black's threat Kt×P ch, on the other hand, forces White to move 10. K—Q1, and then Castles QR gives Black the superior development. White will experience difficulties in getting his Queen's Rook into play. In one of the games of my match with Marshall for the U.S. Championship, in which I adopted this defence, the continuation was 11. P×P, P×P; 12. R—KB1, KR—Kt1; 13. B—KKt5, P—B3; 14. Q—R4, P—QKt4; 15. B—Kt3, P—QR4; 16. B×Kt, P×B (Diagram 114), whereupon Marshall felt obliged to give up his Bishop for two Pawns with 17. P—KKt4, P—R5; 18. Q×BP, Q×Q; 19. R×Q, P×B; 20. RP×P. If he had attempted 17. Q×BP, Q×Q; 18. R×Q, P—R5; 19. B×BP, he would have lost the game very quickly through R×P, and if he had saved the piece with 16. P—R3, the consequence would have been Kt×B; 17. P×Kt, followed by R×P ch, etc. He should have played 13. P—QR4! to prevent P—QKt4.

If White, after 2. .... B—B4; 3. Kt—KB3, P—Q3, spends time on the preparatory move 4. P—B3, Black secures sufficient counter-play by attacking the King's Pawn with Kt—KB3, or even P—KB4.

FALKBEER COUNTER-GAMBIT

Another method of declining the King's Gambit is the 'Falkbeer Counter-Gambit' 2. .... **P—Q4**; 3. P×QP, **P—K5** or **P×P**. Whilst this looks like a logical manner in which to take advantage of White's second move, Black, as a rule, must be much more careful than White when offering a Pawn for the sake of development. White, being a move ahead from the start, may not suffer enough of a set-back in development to balance the extra Pawn. Feasible continuations in the two variations suggested above would be 3. .... P—K5; 4. P—Q3, Kt—KB3; 5. P×P, Kt×KP; 6. Kt—KB3, B—QB4; 7. Q—K2, B—B4; 8. Kt—B3, Q—K2; 9. B—K3, or 5. Kt—Q2, P×P; 6. B×P, Q×P (Diagram 115) or Kt×P, and 3. .... P×P; 4. Q—B3, Kt—KB3; 5. B—Kt5 ch, B—Q2; 6. Kt—B3,

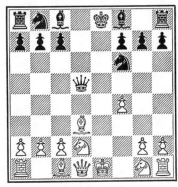

Diagram 115

B—QKt5; 7. KKt—K2, Castles; 8. B×B, QKt×B; 9. Castles, Kt—Kt3; 10. Kt×P (Diagram 116), and Black will finally regain his Pawn with B—Q3 or Q—Q2 and QR—Q1.

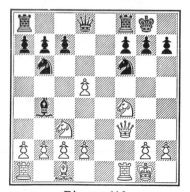

Diagram 116

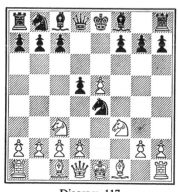

Diagram 117

White can delay the move P—KB4 and play first QKt—B3, or B—B4, or both. Again Black will reply with a counter-attack against White's King's Pawn. For example: 1. **P—K4, P—K4;** 2. **QKt—B3, KKt—B3;** 3. **P—B4, P—Q4;** 4. **P×KP, Kt×P;** 5. **Kt—B3** (Diagram 117). White will try to drive the black Knight from the centre with P—Q3 or Q—K2, and to anchor his King's Pawn with P—Q4. After placing his Bishop on Q3 and castling, he would then have an excellent chance for a King's side attack. Black can counteract this plan in

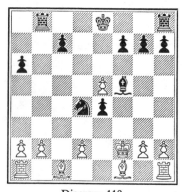

Diagram 118

different ways. With Kt—QB3; 6. P—Q3, Kt×Kt; 7. P×Kt, P—Q5 he can try to keep White's King's Bishop shut in and to prevent him from rounding out his Pawn-skeleton with P—Q4; or he can permit P—Q4 and open his own Bishop's file with 7. .... B—K2; 8. P—Q4, P—B3. 6. Q—K2 would be futile, as Black can maintain his hold on K5 with B—KB4. Then 7. Q—Kt5 would be risky on account of P—QR3; 8 Q×KtP, Kt—Kt5! This regains the Pawn with much the superior position. After 9. Kt×

Kt, P×Kt; 10. Kt—Q4, R—QKt1; 11. Q—R7, B—B4!; 12. Q×B, Q×Kt; 13. Q×Q, Kt×P ch; 14. K—B2, Kt×Q, Black is three or four moves ahead in development, because of the time White has lost by making six Queen's moves against one of Black's. It is interesting to note that due to his advantage in development Black has all sorts of combinations at his disposal with which to win material. White cannot take the Rook's Pawn with his Bishop, because 15. B×P,

Kt—B7; 16. R—QKt1, Kt—Kt5 wins a piece through the threat P—K6 ch. 15. P—QKt3 is practically the only move with which White can hope to complete his development. But Kt—B7; 16. R—QKt1, Kt—Kt5; 17. R—R1, R—Q1 again ties up the Bishop, and if 18. P—QR3, Kt—Q6 ch; 19. B×Kt, R×B; 20. P—QKt4, K—Q2 followed by K—K3 and KR—Q1 will soon win a Pawn. I might mention in passing, that with the Rooks on the board, the fact that the Bishops are of opposite colour will not give White the drawing chance which he would have without the Rooks. In fact, an attack with Rooks and a Bishop often succeeds more readily when the opponent has a Bishop of different colour, because that Bishop can then rarely be made effective for defence.

EVANS GAMBIT

We have seen that in the King's Gambit and related openings Black fares quite well when declining the gambit rather than accepting it. It can be stated quite generally that it is preferable to decline a gambit, when one has the choice, because accepting it means spending time upon the capture of a Pawn instead of continuing the development. The 'Evans Gambit' is an example. The moves defining this gambit are 1. **P—K4, P—K4; 2. Kt—KB3, Kt—QB3; 3. B—B4, B—B4; 4. P—QKt4.** The idea of the Pawn-sacrifice is to lure either the black Bishop or Knight to Kt5, so that 5. P—B3 can be played in preparation of P—Q4 without permitting Black a developing move in reply.

After 4. .... **B×P; 5. P—B3, B— R4; 6. P—Q4, P×P; 7. Castles** (Diagram 119), Black has difficulties in getting his King into safety. If, for example, P—Q3; 8. P×P (threatening Q—R4 and P—Q5), B—Kt3; 9. Kt—B3, Kt—R4 (KKt—K2?; 10. Kt—KKt5, Castles; 11. Q—R5); 10. B—KKt5, P—KB3; 11. B—K3, Kt×B; 12. Q—R4 ch and Q×Kt, White's superior mobility is worth more than the Pawn sacrificed.

If Black continues 'eating Pawns' in the position of the Diagram, he only increases his troubles. After

Diagram 119

7. .... P×P; 8. Q—Kt3, Q—B3; 9. P—K5 followed by Kt×P and B—R3, White has by far the better winning chances.

On the other hand, if Black simply retreats with his Bishop to Kt3 in reply to 4. P—QKt4, White remains with a somewhat disrupted Pawn position without having gained anything for it. Sooner or later he must do something for his Knight's Pawn.   Protecting it with P—QR3 would be a waste of time which would give Black the initiative that by right is White's; and advancing the Pawn to Kt5 is likely to make the Pawn a target for Black's pieces.

After 4. .... **B—Kt3; 5. P—Kt5, Kt—R4** (Diagram 120), White cannot very well proceed with 6. Kt×P, although Black must lose time to protect his King's Bishop's Pawn before he can try to take advantage of the hanging position of White's pieces.   6. .... Kt—R3 would win a piece, because of the double threat P—Q3, driving the Knight which is the only protection of the Bishop, and B—Q5, attacking Rook and Knight simultaneously.   White can get four Pawns for the piece through 7. P—Q4, P—Q3; 8. B×Kt, P×Kt; 9. B×KtP, R—KKt1; 10. B×P ch, K×B; 11. B×P.   But at this early stage of the game, Pawns are not a sufficient compensation. With a piece ahead, Black will either find an opportunity of regaining a Pawn or two before the end-game is reached, or he will succeed in working up an attack against which the Pawn majority of White will form no effective barrier.

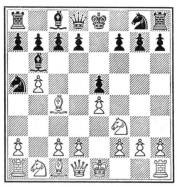

Diagram 120

Further examples showing how in openings beginning with 1. P—K4, P—K4 the strategic principles dealing with mobility and centre-control point the way to proper handling will be found in the chapter containing illustrative games.   They give additional evidence to support the conclusion that Black can gradually nullify the advantage which the first move gives White, although he is often unable to avoid the exchange of his King's Pawn for White's Queen's Pawn, which leaves White with superior mobility. The subsequent course of the game then hinges upon the success or failure of Black's attempts to free himself with P—Q4, which contests the control exerted by White's King's Pawn upon the centre.

CENTRE-COUNTER GAME

It is not surprising that effective ways and means have been sought to answer 1. **P—K4** with moves other than P—K4, so as to avoid placing a target in the centre which White readily attacks with natural developing moves, and to prevent White from opening the Queen's file for his Rooks with P—Q4.

An ideal plan for this purpose seems to play **P—Q4** as early as possible.   This move wrests the control of White's Q5 and KB5 from

White and in turn aims at control of Black's K5 and QB5. Advancing the Pawn to Q4 on the first move is not likely to be good, because after 2. P×P, Q×P White wins a developing tempo with 3. Kt—QB3—just as we saw it with colours reversed in the 'Centre-Game' (1. P—K4, P—K4; 2. P—Q4, P×P; 3. Q×P, Kt—QB3). Black might delay recapturing the Pawn and play 1. **P—K4, P—Q4; 2. P×P, Kt—KB3.** White's simplest method of development would then be 3. **P—Q4, Kt×P; 4. P—QB4** or Kt—KB3 and later on P—QB4. As a result, he would have a centre-Pawn—in this case the Pawn on Q4—and Black would have no chance to get his own centre-Pawn to the fourth rank. The position would therefore be definitely in White's favour.

After 2. .... **Kt—KB3,** most inexperienced players would try to hold on to the Pawn with 3. **P—QB4, P—B3; 4. P×P.** According to our strategic principles, this would be a most dubious procedure. With 4. .... **Kt×P** (Diagram 121) Black secures an ideal development. White's Queen's Pawn cannot advance to the fourth, and there is the danger that his game will be cramped in a manner similar to that which, with colours reversed, we observed in connection with Diagram 86. 5. **Kt—QB3, P—K4; 6. P—Q3, B—QB4** already threatens P—K5 as well as Q—Kt3, and White must play with great circumspection to stem Black's onslaught.

Diagram 121

In reply to Black's 3. .... **P—B3,** White can retain the initiative which is his prerogative, if instead of winning a Pawn he simply develops his pieces: 4. **P—Q4, P×P; 5. Kt—QB3,** etc.

FRENCH DEFENCE

This 'Centre-Counter' opening is rarely seen in modern tournaments. If Black wants to assail White's King's Pawn from the start he usually prepares P—Q4 with either 1. .... **P—K3** or 1. .... **P—QB3.** The former move characterizes the 'French Defence', the latter the 'Caro-Kann' opening. After 2. **P—Q4, P—Q4** we attain the positions set out in Diagrams 122 and 123, the study of which will offer useful and interesting examples of the struggle for possession of the centre. As early as on the third move White must make an important decision. Should he play P—K5 and prevent the opening of the King's file or the Queen's file for a long time to come, or should he proceed to develop his pieces and leave Black the option of playing P×P, thus avoiding the blocking of the centre?

Let us first investigate the consequences of P—K5, starting with the French Defence, after which the Caro-Kann will be easily understood.

Diagram 122

Diagram 123

The position which ensues in the centre after 1. **P—K4, P—K3**; 2. **P—Q4, P—Q4**; 3. **P—K5** divides the board diagonally, and it is easy to recognize roughly the main lines of play which will govern the game. On the King's side, White has more territory at his disposal than Black. Therefore his pieces will have greater mobility there, and

Diagram 124

he will be able to work up an attack against the black King. Black, on the other hand, has more scope on the Queen's wing, and he will seek his chances there. Both sides will have to advance Pawns on a wing in order to obtain mobility for the Rooks, as the centre-files are blocked.

The obvious moves to this end are: for White the advance of the King's Bishop's Pawn, for Black that of the Queen's Bishop's Pawn. Thus, we get the Pawn-skeleton illustrated in Diagram 124.

Here White's prospects are superior, because his Pawn-advance involves a direct assault on the King. That is why Black will try to ward off White's advance either by playing P—KB4 or by attacking White's centre with P—KB3. In the former case, White can make a breach in the black barrier only by playing P—KKt4 as well. The resulting Pawn-formations are shown in Diagrams 125 and 126.   The all-important point for Black is to play P—QB4.   Otherwise his game will be hopelessly cramped, not only because the Queen's Rook cannot find a field of activity, but also because the base of White's Pawn-centre, the Queen's Pawn, must be attacked in order to make advanced King's Pawn insecure and thereby rob White's attack of some of its sting.

If White can maintain his centre-formation Q4—K5, he usually gets the upper hand, mainly because Black's Queen's Bishop is condemned to inactivity for a long time, whilst both of White's Bishops find easy employment.   White's King's Bishop occupies a commanding diagonal on Q3 from where it always threatens Black's King's Rook's Pawn, and his Queen's Bishop often helps the attack indirectly by exchange

Diagram 125

Diagram 126

against Black's King's Bishop.   The absence of the latter makes itself felt disagreeably because Black's King's Knight cannot aid in the defence of the King from its usual post on KB3 as long as White has a Pawn on his K5.

Typical constellations of the pieces around the above Pawn-skeletons may be observed in the following examples:

1. P—K4, P—K3; 2. P—Q4, P—Q4; 3. P—K5, P—QB4; 4. P—QB3, Kt—QB3; 5. Kt—B3.   Here P—KB4 would not be advisable, because it would block the diagonal of the Queen's Bishop and enable Black to place his King's Knight favourably on KB4 via KR3.   After 5. P—KB4, Kt—R3; 6. Kt—B3, P×P; 7. P×P, Kt—B4, White must do something to avoid losing the Queen's Pawn through Q—Kt3.   He could either play P—QKt3 and B—Kt2, or he could play Kt—B3 and answer Q—Kt3 with Kt—QR4.   In either case Black has time to play P—KR4 so that White cannot dislodge the Knight from B4 for quite some time.

In reply to 5. Kt—B3, Black will aim at the same type of arrangement of his pieces: Q—Kt3; 6. B—K2, P×P; 7. P×P, KKt—K2; 8. P—QKt3, Kt—B4; 9. B—Kt2, B—Kt5 ch; 10. K—B1, P—KR4; 11. P—Kt3, B—Q2; 12. K—Kt2, R—QB1, and Black has equalized the position more or less, though the inability of his Queen's Bishop to get into play is liable to tell against him if White finally gets an attack on the King's side going, possibly starting with P—KR3 and P—KKt4. Without first dislodging Black's Knight, White has difficulties in getting his Queen's wing developed (Diagram 127).

More interesting fights are produced when White brings out his Queen's Knight before advancing his King's Pawn to the fifth rank.

Diagram 127

Diagram 128

In this case Black has time for Kt—KB3. From here the Knight goes to Q2 when attacked with P—K5, and adds to the pressure on White's King's Pawn, besides keeping an eye on the possibility of reaching QB5 via QKt3. The sequence of the moves might be: 1. **P—K4, P—K3;** 2. **P—Q4, P—Q4;** 3. **Kt—QB3, Kt—KB3;** 4. **P—K5, KKt—Q2;** 5. **QKt—K2** (to be able to hold the Pawn on Q4 with P—QB3), **P—QB4;** 6. **P—QB3, Kt—QB3;** 7. **P—KB4, B—K2;** 8. **KKt—B3, P—B3;** 9. **Kt—Kt3, Castles;** 10. **B—Q3** (Diagram 128).

In this line-up the lack of mobility of Black's Queen's Bishop is more glaring than in Diagram 127. White threatens a direct attack against the King: 11. Kt—Kt5, P×Kt; 12. Q—R5. Black can defend himself with 10. .... P—B4 or Q—K1, but White's game is stronger. As a result of P—KB4, his centre is greatly relieved and he can devote his attention undisturbed to preparations for storming the King's wing. In answer to Q—K1 he might exchange on B6, castle, and pile up his Rooks in the King's file.

If White defers the advance of the King's Pawn for another move and plays 4. **B—KKt5,** Black does best to avoid the cramping move

P—K5 altogether by exchanging Pawns.   After **P×P; 6. Kt×P, B—
K2; 7. B×Kt, P×B,** Black has at least the two Bishops as compensation for the loss of his centre-Pawn.   4. .... **B—K2; 5. P—K5, Kt—
Q2** offers White several advantageous lines of play.   He can either
exchange Bishops with 6. B×B, Q×B and continue with 7. Q—Q2,
Castles; 8. P—B4, P—QB4; 9. Kt—B3, Kt—QB3; 10. Castles QR,
P—B3; 11. P×P, Kt×BP (Diagram 129), or he can even sacrifice
a Pawn with 6. **P—KR4!** Acceptance of the sacrifice gives White too
great an advantage in development.   6. .... **B×B; 7. P×B, Q×P;
8. Kt—R3, Q—K2; 9. Kt—B4, P—QR3** (to prevent Kt—Kt5 in reply
to P—QB4); **10. Q—Kt4, P—KKt3; 11. Castles QR.** It is most unlikely
that Black can stem White's attack (Diagram 130).

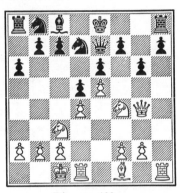

Diagram 129   Diagram 130

Even if Black declines the sacrifice offered by White on the 6th move
and plays **P—KB3,** it is questionable whether he can defend himself
satisfactorily.   White would continue with 7. **B—Q3!** and force Black's
King to B1 with the Queen-check on R5 on the next move.   He can
bring the King's Rook into play on KB3 via R3, and so it is wisest for
Black to keep the Bishop's file closed as long as he can.   After 7. ....
P—QB4; 8. Q—R5 ch, K—B1; 9. KP×P, Kt×P; 10. B×Kt, B×B;
11. P×P, Kt—Q2; 12. Castles QR, Kt×P; 13. Kt—B3, Black still
has great difficulties in getting his King's Rook out and finding a safe
spot for his King (Diagram 131).

All in all, the defences against 3. **Kt—QB3** which we have considered
do not give Black an inviting game.   In every one of them he suffers
from the cramping effect of P—K5 and from the inactivity of his Queen's
Bishop.   Now, let us see whether Black has some other continuation
besides 3. .... Kt—KB3, which might equalize the game.   He might
try 3. .... **B—Kt5,** with the idea to attack White's Q4 with P—QB4,
Kt—QB3, Q—Kt3 and KKt—K2—B4, as in the line which led to

Diagram 127. But this plan does not work, for White can force the exchange of the Bishop for the Knight. Then Black's King's wing is badly weakened, partly because one of the defending minor pieces is missing, and partly because Black's centre-Pawns are locked on white squares. In the absence of the King's Bishop, the black squares are inadequately defended.

White would reply 4. **P—K5, P—QB4**; 5. **P—QR3, P×P** (for B×Kt see Chapter 5, game Smyslov—Botvinnik); 6. **P×B, P×Kt**; 7. **Kt—B3!**, offering a Pawn sacrifice for the sake of rapid development. After the plausible sequence Q—B2; 8. Q—Q4, Kt—K2; 9. B—Q3, Kt—Q2; 10. Castles, Kt—QB3; 11. Q×BP, Black suffers again from the troubles characteristic of the French Defence. His Queen's Bishop is shut in

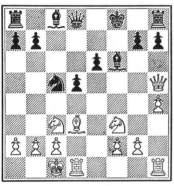

Diagram 131

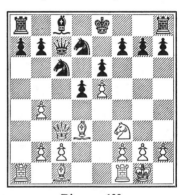

Diagram 132

and his centre is badly cramped. In Diagram 132, which shows the position reached at this stage, Black cannot play Kt (Q2)×P, as P—Kt5 would win a piece. The same move refutes 11. .... Q—Kt3, for 12. .... P—Q5 would be met with 13. Kt×P, Kt×Kt; 14. B—K3, and 12. .... Kt—K2; 13. B—K3, Q—Q1 would give White an overwhelming game. Naturally, White would not continue with 14. B×QRP, because P—QKt3 would cut off the Bishop and lead to its exchange after B—Kt2 and Kt—QB1. Instead, White would simply bring the Queen over to the King's side, and possibly also the Queen's Rook, via QR4.

A simple way to prevent White from playing P—K5 and from shutting in Black's Queen's Bishop seems to exchange Pawns on the third move, in reply to 3. **Kt—QB3**. But after **P×P**; 4. **Kt×P**, White has the typical advantage resulting from possession of a centre-Pawn where the opponent has none. All he has to do is to develop his pieces one by one and he is bound to obtain a far superior position. The usual counter-play, which we saw Black initiate in the other lines, i.e.

P—QB4, would be of doubtful value in this '*Exchange Variation*', because White would obtain a majority of Pawns on the Queen's wing by QP×P. The ending would be clearly in his favour.

CARO-KANN DEFENCE

Let us now return to Diagram 123 and see whether we can apply to the Caro-Kann opening the knowledge gained from our discussion of the French Defence.

The fundamental difference between the two openings is that in the Caro-Kann Black can bring out his Queen's Bishop, while in the French Defence he cannot. On KB4 Black's Bishop is well posted for the defence of the King's wing which is generally subject to attack when the King's Knight cannot take up the natural defensive post on B3. For this reason the move P—K5 is not likely to be effective in the Caro-Kann. After 3. **P—K5, B—B4** White can rid himself of this Bishop only through 4. **B—Q3.** However, in this way he loses one of the most important aids in any attack which he might try to institute on the black King's wing. Besides, the exchange leaves White weak on white squares, since his Pawn-skeleton rests on black ones. A plausible continuation would be: 4. .... **B×B** (not B—Kt3 on account of 5. P—K6!, hemming in Black's King's wing and breaking up his protective Pawn-chain); 5. **Q×B, P—K3** (Diagram 133); 6. Kt—QB3 or Kt—K2 or KR3 (in order to leave the King's Bishop's Pawn free to advance). Black can then either play P—QB4 immediately, to follow this up with Kt—QB3 and later KKt—K2—B4 and R—QB1, or he can first play Q—Kt3 and offer the exchange of Queens with Q—R3 or even Q—Kt4. Accepting this offer would leave White with an inferior game, as he would not have

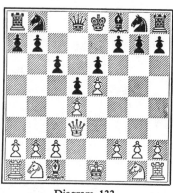

Diagram 133

enough material left to organize a promising King's side attack, whilst Black would be sure to obtain considerable pressure on the Queen's wing.

There are two logical strategic plans which White might choose from, rather than advancing his King's Pawn on the third move. He can either force Black to give up his centre-Pawn by 3. Kt—QB3, or he can play 3. P×P, P×P; 4. P—QB4, in order to provoke P—K3 which would again shut-in Black's Queen's Bishop, as in the French Defence.

In answer to 3. **Kt—QB3** Black has hardly an alternative to P×P, because if he played P—K3 or Kt—B3, White would continue with P—K5 and lead into the French Defence with a move to the good, as Black will have to make a second move with his Queen's Bishop's Pawn to get it to B4.

After 3. .... **P×P**; 4. **Kt×P**, White will try to take advantage of his greater freedom in the centre by developing as rapidly as possible. If Black plays 4. .... **Kt—B3**, the most promising continuation, and one which fits the strategic idea best, is probably 5. **B—Q3, Q×P**; 6. **Kt—KB3, Q—Q1**; 7. **Q—K2, Kt×Kt**; 8. **B×Kt**. White's superior development should outweigh the Pawn sacrificed (Diagram 134). White can, of course, play more conservatively 5. Kt—Kt3 or Q—Q3 or Kt×Kt. But then he is not likely to obtain an advantage in development. The only feature in his favour is that sooner or later Black

Diagram 134 Diagram 135

will have to play P—QB4 to challenge White's centre-Pawn, and after the exchange of the Pawn White remains with three against two Pawns on the Queen's wing. With 5. Kt×Kt, KtP×Kt, Black's Pawn position is weakened for the end-game, but the open file which Black obtains for the Rook offsets this disadvantage because it offers opportunities for attack in the middle-game.

More promising for White is the other alternative which we mentioned: 3. **P×P, P×P**; 4. **P—QB4**. This opening has certain similarities with the Queen's Gambit which is discussed later. Black's Queen's Bishop cannot very well get out because its Queen's side needs protection against the pressure White can exert with Q—Kt3. For example: 4. .... **Kt—KB3**; 5. **QKt—B3, B—B4**; 6. **Q—Kt3**, and Black is already in trouble. If Black plays 5. .... **Kt—B3**, White can force P—K3 with 6. **B—Kt5**. Black could not answer this move with P×P, because 7. P—Q5 would completely disorganize his line-up.

White gets the better game also after **P—K3,** either by 7. **P—B5** (Diagram 135), which gives him a dangerous Pawn majority on the Queen's wing, or by simply continuing his development with Kt—B3, etc. Due to the fact that Black's Queen's Bishop is shut in and that the King's file is available to White's Rooks for a transfer to the King's wing, White has every expectation of a successful King's side attack.

SICILIAN DEFENCE

Our next subject is the '*Sicilian Defence*', characterized by the moves 1. **P—K4, P—QB4.** This is one of the most interesting King's Pawn openings, giving rise—in some of its variations—to Pawn formations altogether different from the ones we have seen before. At first glance, the move of the Bishop's Pawn seems inferior because it opens a line only for the Queen, a piece which ought not to be brought out at an early stage of the game. But there are other arguments in favour of the move. As soon as White plays P—Q4, a line will be opened for Black's Queen's Rook by exchanging the Bishop's Pawn for the Queen's Pawn. In the open file White's Pawn will be subject to pressure as long as it remains on B2, and so will the Queen's Knight on B3, as we shall soon observe. Besides, the exchange of a wing-Pawn for a centre-Pawn is favourable in itself. Black remains with two Pawns in the centre against one of White, and if Black succeeds in exchanging his Queen's Pawn for White's King's Pawn by playing P—Q4 at the first opportune moment, he is likely to obtain the better game. An opportune moment, however, is only one which permits Black to recapture on his Q4 with a piece. If he must do so with the King's Pawn, he remains with an isolated Pawn in the Queen's file. This represents a lasting weakness. Also, the advance of the Queen's Pawn should preferably be timed so that White cannot answer it with P—K5 and institute a crushing advance of all King's side Pawns. Such an advance —P—KB4, P—KKt4, P—KB5, etc.—is very frequently the best plan for White in the Sicilian, even where the King's Pawn cannot advance to the fifth rank. With the centre more or less blocked, White must attack on the King's wing, where he has the territorial advantage, whilst Black is bound to get the upper hand on the Queen's wing, due to the open Bishop's file.

If White could block this file, he would have much the better prospects, because he could then pursue the attack against the King without worrying about Black's manœuvres on the Queen's wing. For this reason Black must not permit White under any circumstances to set up a Pawn-chain on QR2—QKt3—QB4, which incidentally would also make P—Q4 impossible for Black.

In view of the fact that White is likely to obtain a strong attack on the King's side, it is advisable for Black to play P—KKt3 and B—Kt2 ('King's fianchetto') in order to have as many minor pieces as possible on that side for defence. From KKt2 the Bishop also acts aggressively, keeping an eye on White's Q4 and aiding in the pressure which Black will try to develop in the Queen's Bishop's file against White's QB3.

These considerations lead to the following line-up of the forces which represents a typical example of many variations based on the same theme:

         2. Kt—KB3   **Kt—QB3**

With this move Black keeps the option of either playing P—Q3 and P—KKt3, B—Kt2, or P—K3 and B—K2.

         3. P—Q4   **P×P**
         4. Kt×P   **Kt—B3!**

In order to bring out White's Queen's Knight and thus prevent P—QB4. If White tried to hold the King's Pawn with P—KB3, to follow this up with P—QB4, Black would foil his plan by 5. ..... P—Q4!

         5. Kt—QB3   **P—Q3**

Black cannot carry out his intention to play P—KKt3 without this preparatory move, because White would otherwise be able to disorganize Black's line-up with 6. Kt×Kt and 7. P—K5.

         6. B—K2   **P—KKt3**
         7. B—K3   **B—Kt2**
         8. Castles   **Castles**

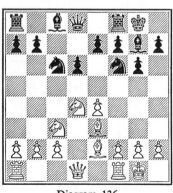

Diagram 136

P—Q4 would have been premature. White would have won a Pawn through 9. P×P, Kt×P; 10. Kt×Kt, Q×Kt; 11. B—B3, Q—B5; 12. Kt×Kt, P×Kt; 13. P—QKt3, Q—B6; 14. Q—Q3, Q×Q; 15. P×Q, B×R; 16. B×P ch and B×R.

The Diagram shows the Pawn-formation characteristic of all variations of the Sicilian Defence in which Black fianchettos his Bishop. Black is ready to push the Queen's Pawn. White will try to prevent this before starting to push his King's side Pawns. For example: 9. **Kt—Kt3**, **B—K3**; 10. **P—B4, Kt—QR4** (here P—Q4 would be premature because P—K5 would be the reply, forcing the Knight to K1); 11. **P—B5, B—B5,** and now White obtains a slight advantage with

12. **B—Q3!**, a line shown by Spielmann which runs: Kt×Kt; 13. RP×Kt, B×B; 14. P×B, P—Q4; 15. B—Q4, P×P; 16. P×P, Q—B2; 17. P—K5, QR—Q1; 18. P×Kt, B×P; 19. R—R4, P—QKt4; 20. Kt×P, Q—Q2; 21. Q—K2, P—QR3; 22. B×B, P×Kt; 23. B×P, P×R; 24. B×KR.

For this reason it is safer for Black to play his Bishop only as far as Q2 on the 9th move, so that it will not be attacked by the advancing King's Bishop's Pawn of White. The continuation might then be 10. P—B4, R—B1; 11. B—B3, P—QR3; 12. P—Kt4, Kt—QR4 or P—QKt4, with chances for both sides.

The defence takes on a different face if Black plays P—K3 instead of P—Q3, with the idea of enforcing P—Q4 at the earliest possible moment. After 2. **Kt—KB3, P—K3**; 3. **P—Q4,** Black could advance the Queen's Pawn, but 4. KP×P, KP×P would enable White to isolate the Pawn and make it a target difficult to defend. The following procedure would be indicated: 5. B—K2, Kt—KB3; 6. Castles, Kt—B3; 7. R—K1, B—K3; 8. B—KKt5, B—K2; 9. P×P, Castles; 10. QKt—Q2, B×P; 11. Kt—Kt3, B—K2; 12. KKt—Q4.

Diagram 137

In this position Black has little hope for counter-play. White can block the Queen's Bishop's file with P—QB3 at any time he sees fit to do so, and he can leisurely pile-up his Rooks in the Queen's file and place the King's Bishop on B3. His pressure on K6 is also strong. If Black does not defend this point without delay he will lose a Pawn. For example: 12. .... R—B1?; 13. P—QB3, P—KR3?; 14. B×Kt, B×B; 15. Kt×B, P×Kt; 16. B—Kt4, etc. This method of playing against an isolated Pawn by blocking its advance and then concentrating forces against it should be carefully followed. The reader will find many opportunities of applying this stratagem.

Now, let us see whether Black can force P—Q4 a little later without disadvantage. After 3. .... **P×P;** 4. **Kt×P,** the advance would still be premature, for P—Q4; 5. B—Kt5 ch, B—Q2; 6. P×P would again isolate the Pawn. Incidentally, B×B; 7. Kt×B, P×P, would lose a Pawn because of a combination which occurs rather frequently: 8. Q×P!, Q×Q; 9. Kt—B7 ch, etc. The logical continuation for Black would be 4. .... **Kt—KB3.** White cannot reply P—K5 because Q—R4 ch would win the Pawn. If he defends with 5. **Kt—QB3,** Black must again delay P—Q4 because of B—Kt5 ch. It would not be advisable for him to play B—Kt5, because 6. P—K5, Kt—Q4 (Kt—K5?, 7. Q—Kt4!, to White's advantage); 7. B—Q2, Kt×Kt; 8. P×Kt, B—K2; 9. Q—Kt4, P—KKt3; 10. B—KR6 would cramp his game badly. Instead, he would first prevent P—K5 with 5. .... **Kt—B3.** Now 6. B—K2, B—Kt5; 7. B—B3 would no longer stop P—Q4. That is why 6. **Kt×Kt, KtP×Kt; 7. P—K5, Kt—Q4;** 8. **Kt—K4** is preferable for White. This leads to the position of Diagram 138, which looks

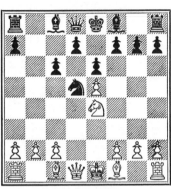

favourable for White because Black's game is still constricted whilst White threatens to complete his development rapidly and then to attack on the King's wing. If Black tries to free himself by removing White's King's Pawn with Q—B2; 9. P—KB4, P—KB4; 10. P×P e.p., Kt×P (3); 11. Kt×Kt ch, P×Kt; 12. Q—R5 ch, K—Q1, White can maintain his pressure with 13. Q—R4, B—K2; 14. B—Q2, P—Q4 (at last!); 15. B—B3, P—K4; 16. Castles QR, when Black's King remains exposed to attack for quite some time. Posi-

Diagram 138

tions of this type usually give rise to sacrificing combinations. Such a combination would end the game very quickly if Black hastily advanced his Queen's Pawn to Q5. White would reply 17. P×P, P×P; 18. R×P ch!, B—Q2; 19. R×B ch!, K×R (Q×R?; 20. B—R5 ch); 20. Q—Kt4 ch, K—K1; 21. Q—Kt7, R—KB1; 22. B×P, followed by B—K2.

MODERN CHESS OPENINGS

The Sicilian Defence is an opening which has several features characteristic of 'modern chess', as distinguished from the classical chess represented by all the other openings we have so far examined. One of these features is Black's delay in declaring what form he intends to give his Pawn-skeleton in the centre—whether he wants to direct his efforts against White's K4 or Q4, and whether he aims at occupying his own K4 or Q4 with a Pawn. Another feature is the fianchetto-development of the Bishop. This was formerly regarded as dubious because it involves an additional Pawn-move in the opening and because the advance of the Knight's Pawn weakens the squares R3 and B3. The modern masters, who came into their own after the First World War, showed that the principle of rapid development had to be taken *cum grano salis*; that in openings in which centre-files were not available to the Rooks through an early exchange of centre-Pawns, the time-loss entailed in the fianchetto-development of the Bishop was well compensated by the pressure the Bishop exerted sooner or later on the opponent's centre; and that the fianchetto-position made an attack on the King very difficult, because it reduced the effectiveness of the opposing King's Bishop and kept an additional minor piece ready for defence in front of the King. As long as the Bishop remains on Kt2, the squares R3 and B3 are defended. As explained during the discussion of the Four Knights opening, in case the Bishop is exchanged for the adversary's Queen's Bishop, the weakness of those two squares is not serious because they can usually be defended by the King itself.

The feature which makes the fianchetto-position more readily a target for attack than the original Pawn-position, on the second rank, is the exposure of the Knight's Pawn to exchange by the advancing Rook's Pawn of the opponent, which would open a file. However, this advance presupposes, as a rule, that the King of the attacking player castles on the other side of the board, and there the fianchettoed Bishop usually exerts some pressure.

A delay in advancing one or both centre-Pawns always gives the opponent more freedom of movement in the centre. This may enable him to work up a fast attack, preceded by the advance of his own centre-Pawns for the purpose of cramping defensive movements. On the other hand, as we have had occasion to observe in various openings, a Pawn advancing to the fifth rank is more exposed to attack than when it remains in its home territory, on the fourth rank. There is always the possibility that an opposing Pawn in a neighbouring file will exchange itself for the advanced Pawn and thereby open that file for a Rook.

The uncertainty whether an advanced Pawn will bring about a decisive advantage in the middle-game or prove a fatal weakness in the end-game often remains with a player even when he has reached a high level of playing strength. It takes a master's positional feeling to make the correct decision.

ALEKHINE'S DEFENCE

An opening in which the idea of provoking a premature advance of White's centre-Pawns is more clearly expressed than in any other is 'Alekhine's Defence', 1. P—K4, Kt—KB3. Here White has occasion to chase Black's Knight, bringing forward his King's Pawn, Queen's Pawn and Queen's Bishop's Pawn, whilst Black has no time for further development. Diagram 139 shows the position reached after 2. P—K5, Kt—Q4; 3. P—QB4, Kt—Kt3; 4. P—Q4. If White's Pawn were on K4 instead of K5, his position would be so vastly superior that it is doubtful whether Black could survive. But on K5 the Pawn is

subject to attack by P—Q3 as well as P—KB3. If, after 4. .... **P—Q3,**
White permits Black to exchange (5. P—B4) instead of exchanging
himself, White's Queen's Pawn offers a target for Black, in addition
to the King's Pawn. Naturally, Black will bring out his Queen's
Bishop before advancing the King's Pawn: 5. P—B4, P×P; 6. BP×P,
Kt—B3; 7. B—K3 (not Kt—KB3, on account of B—Kt5), B—B4;
8. Kt—QB3, P—K3; 9. Kt—B3, B—K2; 10. B—K2, Castles; 11.
Castles, P—B3, and Black finally rids himself of White's King's Pawn.

Diagram 139

It is therefore probably a better
plan for White to play 5. **P×P** in
answer to P—Q3. After KP×P
White has slightly more freedom in
the centre, and Black's Knight is
not doing any useful work on Kt3,
but after normal development of all
pieces—Black might play his Queen's
Knight over to KB3—Black will be
able to equalize the game completely
through P—QB3 and P—Q4. If
White prevents this through P—Q5,
Black obtains the use of his K4 and
QB4 for his pieces.

I should perhaps point out that,
of course, White need not accept Black's invitation to advance his
Pawn to K5. He could simply protect his King's Pawn with 2. **Kt—
QB3,** which would most likely produce one or the other classical
defences. For example: 2. .... P—K4; 3. Kt—KB3 or B—B4. Or
2. .... P—Q4; 3. P—K5, KKt—Q2; 4. P—Q4, P—K3, which leads
into the French Defence.

When playing the latter variation, Black must be prepared to fight
an uphill battle with retarded development in return for a Pawn. White
could sacrifice a Pawn with 4. P—K6, in order to delay the development of Black's King's Bishop. The doubled King's Pawn has little
chance to advance, for after 5. P—Q4 and 6. Kt—B3 White's K5
remains in White's possession.

A Pawn-sacrifice of this type must be guarded against whenever the
opponent has advanced a centre-Pawn to the fifth rank and one's own
Pawn in the file in question has not yet moved.

We encountered a similar example in the Caro-Kann Defence after
1. P—K4, P—QB3; 2. P—Q4, P—Q4; 3. P—K5, B—B4; 4. B—Q3,
B—Kt3?; 5. P—K6!. To give just one more typical example: In the
position of Diagram 91, after 3. .... B—B4; 4. P—B3, Kt—B3; 5.
P—Q4, P×P; 6. P×P, B—Kt3?; 7. P—Q5, Kt—QKt1; 8. P—K5,
Kt—Kt1; 9. P—Q6!, Black would be hopelessly boxed up.

There are no replies to 1. P—K4, outside of those we have investigated, which require especial mention. They can all be properly dealt with by the application of our general strategic principles in the manner which we have observed in the examples cited.

We turn now to '*Queen's Pawn-openings*'. Again we will first assume that Black answers 1. P—Q4 with the same move, in an attempt to maintain a Pawn in the centre, and we will examine whether White has ways and means of luring that Pawn away, as we saw he had in most King's Pawn-openings.

In this fight for control of the centre, there is a fundamental difference between the two types of opening. After 1. **P—Q4, P—Q4,** the players cannot advance the other centre-Pawn to the fourth rank until they have protected the square K4, while after 1. P—K4, P—K4, the Queens back the Pawn advance to Q4 from the start.

As a result, the centre-files are likely to remain closed in Queen's Pawn-openings for some time, and it is necessary to prepare the opening of a file for the Rooks other than the King's or Queen's file. This consideration calls for P—QB4 on the part of White as well as Black, similar to Black's strategy in the French Defence. P—QB4 not only enables opening the Bishop's file at a suitable moment, but it attacks the opposing centre-Pawn and is thus in line with the fundamental strategy of any opening. It does not follow that the advance of the King's Pawn to the centre should be dismissed from consideration. On the contrary, this advance remains a major aim of both players in all Queen's Pawn-openings. White tries to enforce the advance after covering K4 with Kt—QB3 and B—Q3 or B—KKt2, sometimes also with Q—QB2 and even P—KB3. Black tries to prevent the execution of the plan by Kt—KB3, B—KB4 or B—QKt2, and sometimes P—KB4, depending upon the manner in which White deploys his men.

After 2. **P—QB4** the first impulse of an inexperienced player would be to capture White's Pawn, because it is not protected. However, White easily regains the Pawn with a superior game. This opening, though called '*Queen's Gambit*', is therefore not a gambit in the original sense of the word. 2. .... P×P; 3. **Kt—KB3, Kt—KB3;** 4. **P—K3, P—QKt4?** would lead to 5. **P—QR4, P—B3;** 6. **P—QKt3, P×KtP;** 7. **P×P, P×P;** 8. **B×P ch, B—Q2;** 9. **Q×P** (Diagram 140).

The beginner might ask why, after 2. .... P×P, White could not play 3. P—K4 instead of Kt—KB3, since Black's Queen's Pawn has given up control of White's K4. The answer is that then Black also could play P—K4, for if White captures the Pawn, Black exchanges Queens, and follows this up with Kt—QB3, development of the Queen's Bishop, and Castles QR, whereupon the luckless white King would soon succumb to Black's attack. For the same reason White would not play 3. P—K3. After 3. Kt—KB3, however, he really threatens P—K4, and that is why Black prevents this advance first with Kt—KB3 before making other developing moves.

Diagram 140

In the position of the Diagram, White has a Pawn in the centre of the Board and Black has not. Black's Queen's Rook's Pawn is a target for White in the open Rook's file, so that Black's Rook will have to be kept in that file for defensive purposes and cannot oppose White who will place his King's Rook in the Queen's Bishop's file after castling. Thus, Black should not consider this line of play at all.

In any case—even though dismissing from the start the thought of holding on to the Gambit-Pawn—Black will hesitate accepting the Gambit, because by relinquishing his centre-Pawn he would be conceding superior mobility to White. This general tenet holds naturally in Queen's Pawn-openings as well as in King's Pawn-openings. Therefore, unless attempts at maintaining his Pawn at Q4 should entail difficulties in the development of his pieces, Black will play either 2. .... P—K3 or 2. .... P—QB3.

The distinction which strikes us in comparing these moves is the same as the one we noted between the French Defence and the Caro-Kann: P—K3 shuts-in the Queen's Bishop, P—QB3 does not. However, as we shall see, White can often force Black to shut-in his Bishop with P—K3 even after he has played P—QB3, and this advantage of the first player is the reason why Queen's Pawn-openings dominate the scene in all modern master tournaments. Black has much greater difficulties than in King's Pawn-openings in securing a satisfactory development, and White's winning chances are therefore greater.

The Pawn-skeleton which White normally forms against the defence 2. .... P—K3—and which Black would like to form, but can attain only if White plays indifferently—is shown in Diagram 141. In a famous game played in Lodz, 1907, between Rotlewi and Rubinstein, the latter continued in this position with 4. .... Kt—QB3. A modern master would have chosen Kt—KB3, in order to answer 5. BP×P with

Kt×P. After 4. .... Kt—QB3; 5. BP×P, KP×P, Black is bound
to remain with a weak Queen's Pawn. We saw a similar situation in
the Sicilian Defence after 1. P—K4, P—QB4; 2. Kt—KB3, P—K3;
3. P—Q4, P—Q4.

White actually replied 5. **Kt—B3,** and the game continued **Kt—B3;
6. QP×P, B×P;** 7. **P—QR3, P—QR3.** (No doubt played to avoid
8. P—QKt4, 9. P—QB5, 10. P—QKt5, but P—QR4 seems stronger.)
After 8. **P—QKt4, B—Q3;** 9. **B—Kt2, Castles,** White still should have
played P×P, when the black Queen's Pawn would have been per-
manently weak. (He could not have captured the Pawn with his Queen

Diagram 141

Diagram 142

after exchanging on Q5, because Black would have won the Queen
with B×P ch.) Another promising continuation would have been
10. Q—B2, to follow this up with R—Q1. Instead, he played 10.
Q—Q2, a move which decreases rather than increases the mobility of
the Queen, and which was refuted by Rubinstein in what is no doubt
one of the most beautiful games ever played: 10. .... Q—K2!; 11.
B—Q3, P×P; 12. B×P, P—QKt4; 13. B—Q3, R—Q1; 14. Q—K2,
B—Kt2; 15. Castles KR, Kt—K4; 16. Kt×Kt, B×Kt; 17. P—B4,
B—B2; 18. P—K4, QR—B1; 19. P—K5, B—Kt3 ch; 20. K—R1,
Kt—Kt5!!; 21. B—K4, Q—R5; 22. P—Kt3, R×Kt!!; 23. P×Q, R—
Q7!!; 24. Q×R, B×B ch; 25. Q—Kt2, R—R6; and mate at R7.

TARRASCH DEFENCE

Curiously enough, it was Rubinstein who a few years later himself
refuted the '*Tarrasch Defence*' which is characterized by the advance
of the Queen's Bishop's Pawn on the third move, before the King's
Knight has been developed. Rubinstein originated the development
of White's King's Bishop on Kt2, from where it aids the attack of

Black's Queen's Pawn: 1. **P—Q4, P—Q4;** 2. **P—QB4, P—K3;** 3. **Kt—QB3, P—QB4;** 4. **BP × P, KP × P;** 5. **Kt—B3, Kt—QB3;** 6. **P—KKt3, Kt—B3;** 7. **B—Kt2, B—K2;** 8. **Castles** (Diagram 142), and now White threatens P × P followed by Kt—QR4, B—K3 and Kt—Q4. If Black plays 8. .... P—B5, White replies 9. Kt—K5 and P—K4. Black has no counter-play whatever. He can consider himself lucky if he barely succeeds in saving himself.

ORTHODOX DEFENCE

Realizing that P—QB4 is premature on the 3rd move, Black will await a more opportune moment and first make as many natural developing moves as offer themselves without interfering with the advance of the Bishop's Pawn. White, on the other hand, will try to keep Black's Bishop's Pawn from the fourth rank as long as he can. In answer to 3. .... **Kt—KB3** White will play 4. **B—Kt5.** Now P—B4 is not possible because 5. P × QP, KP × P; 6. B × Kt would force Black to recapture with the Pawn, breaking up the Pawn formation on his King's wing in addition to leaving the Queen's Pawn as weak

as ever. Therefore 4. .... B—K2 or QKt—Q2 is indicated. The former is probably better because it restores the mobility of the King's Knight and defers the decision whether to develop the Queen's Knight to Q2 or to B3 until it is quite certain that the Bishop's Pawn cannot advance to the fourth rank. 4. .... **B—K2;** 5. **P—K3** still does not permit P—B4, as P × BP followed by P × QP and B × Kt would win a Pawn. This threat persists after 5. .... **Castles;** 6. **Kt—B3,** when the position of Diagram 143 is reached.

Diagram 143

Now Black has two lines of play which will eventually make possible the advance of the Bishop's Pawn to B4. One is the continuation of the development with **P—QKt3,** and the other the more aggressive **Kt—K5.** Against the former, White's best plan is to play 7. **P × P,** so that the long diagonal remains closed in case Black maintains his centre-Pawn by recapturing with the King's Pawn. Otherwise Black would have the option of opening the diagonal with P × P and placing his Bishop effectively on Kt2. After **P × P;** 8. **B—Q3** White has good expectations for a strong King's side attack which he can initiate by placing his Knight on K5 and fortifying it with P—B4, unless Black takes early measures against this strategy. For example: 8. .... **P—B4;** 9. **Kt—K5, B—K3;** 10. **P—B4** (Diagram 144), **KKt—Q2;** 11. **Q—R5,** and Black is in a bad way. Better is 8. .... **B—Kt2,** in order to follow this up with Kt—K5. If Black played 8. .... **B—K3,** White would have to reply Kt—K5 without delay or Black would extricate himself with QKt—Q2. After 9. Castles, for example, 9. .... QKt—Q2; 10. Kt—K5, Kt×Kt; 11. P×Kt, Kt—Q2; 12. B×B, Q×B; 13. P—B4, P—KB4 stops White's attack and gives Black good chances on the Queen's wing.

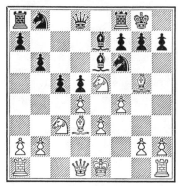

Diagram 144

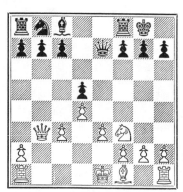

Diagram 145

LASKER DEFENCE

Black has less difficulties in equalizing the game in the position of Diagram 143 when continuing with 6. .... **Kt—K5,** a move introduced by Emanuel Lasker. After 7. **B×B, Q×B;** 8. **P×P, Kt×Kt;** 9. **P×Kt, P×P;** 10. **Q—Kt3** (Diagram 145), Black must not play passively P—QB3, because then White obtains strong pressure on the Queen's side with P—B4—B5. Instead, Black must continue to threaten P—QB4, for example with **Q—Q3** or **R—Q1.** In the latter case, if 11. **P—B4,** Black can force the exchange of Queens through **Kt—B3** (or first P×P and then Kt—B3) which threatens both Q—Kt5 ch and Kt—R4. In reply to 11. .... Kt—B3, 12. P—B5 would permit the Pawn-sacrifice B—Kt5; 13. Q×KtP, B×Kt; 14. Q×Kt, B—K5 which gives Black a strong attack (15. P—B3?, B×P!). But after the more or less forced series of moves 12. **P×P, Q—Kt5 ch;** 13. **Kt—Q2, Q×Q;** 14. **P×Q!, Kt—Kt5;** 15. **R—B1, Kt×P;** 16. **P—K4, R—K1;** 17. **B—K2, Kt—B3;** 18. **P—K5, Kt—Q4;** 19. **B—B3,** Black is in trouble. P—QB3 would be followed by 20. B×Kt and R—B7, and it is very unlikely that Black can draw the ending, 17. .... Kt—B5; 18. R×P, Kt×P ch; 19. K—Q1, Kt—B5; 20. P—Q5, does not look very bright either. For this reason the alternative 11. .... **P×P**; 12. **B×P, Kt—B3** is preferable for Black. If then 13. **Q—B3,** Black obtains counter-play with **B—Kt5**; 14. **Castles, B×Kt**; 15. **P×B, R—Q3**, etc. (Diagram 146.)

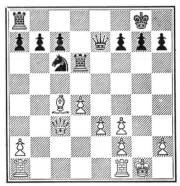

If the move 6. ...., P—KR3; 7. B—R4 is interposed and play continued to the position of Diagram 145 (with Black's Pawn on KR3), the ingenious line 11. ...., R—Q1; 12. P—B4, B—K3; 13. Q×P, P×P!!; 14. Q×R, Q—R6!! fails against 15. R—QKt1, B—Q4; 16. Q×B!, R×Q; 17. R×Kt ch, K—R2; 18. R—QKt1, Q×P ch; 19. Kt—Q2.

Diagram 146

These examples should suffice to illustrate the tactical possibilities with which Lasker's Defence abounds. If White deploys the whole weight of his forces on the Queen's wing, he is liable to be subjected to a King's side attack, because Black has obtained freedom of movement in the centre so that he can swing his men over to the King's wing with comparatively few moves.

Let us now return to Diagram 143 and see whether Black can enforce an early advance of P—QB4 by playing 6. .... **QKt—Q2.** The only move which foils Black's plan for the time being is 7. **R—B1.** If White played 7. Q—B2 instead, P—B4 can neither be refuted by 8. BP×P nor by 8. R—Q1. In answer to the former Black can avoid an isolated Queen's Pawn with Kt×P; 9. Kt×Kt, B×B or 9. B×B, Kt×B; and against 8. R—Q1 he has the defence P—KR3; 9. B—R4, Q—R4. Now 10. B—Q3 is met by Kt—Kt3; 11. BP×P, QKt×P, to follow this up with Kt—QKt5.

The reply P—QB4 is insufficient against 7. R—B1, because of 8. P×BP, P×P; 9. P—B6!, Kt—Kt3; 10. Q×Q and 11. Kt—K5, or 9. .... P×P; 10. B×P, when Black has no compensation for the weakness of his isolated Pawn in the Bishop's file.

Thus, Black must wait for his opportunity still further. In view of the fact that his Queen's Bishop can find employment only in the long diagonal—unless White frees it by exchanging with BP×P—the plan to open the diagonal with QP×P and then to place the Bishop on Kt2 seems the most plausible at this moment. Black might play **P—QR3** first, because if possible he will want to win a tempo by delaying the capture on B5 until White's King's Bishop has moved, so that the latter reaches B4 in two moves instead of one. White, however, can also make a waiting move. With 8. **P—QR3** he can threaten P—QKt4, which would make it once and for all impossible for Black to get his Bishop's Pawn to the fourth rank. But then Black can finally realize his aim by **P×P; 9. B×P, P—QKt4; 10. B—K2, B—Kt2; 11. Castles, P—B4** (Diagram 147). Now, if White does not play 12. **P×P**, Black advances his Bishop's Pawn. He then has better prospects for the ending due to the Pawn-majority on the Queen's wing. 12. .... **Kt×P** followed by 13. .... **R—B1** completely equalizes the game.

Diagram 147

Diagram 148

To prevent the advance of Black's Bishop's Pawn, White has no other means than 8. **P×P**. After the exchange on Q5 White can always isolate Black's Queen's Pawn by capturing the Bishop's Pawn if the latter advances to B4. This line of play is indeed probably White's strongest, although Black's Queen's Bishop is then no longer shut-in. The trouble is that Black has no particularly good square for this Bishop. After 8. .... **P×P; 9. B—Q3, P—B3; 10. Q—B2, R—K1; 11. Kt—K5, Kt—B1** (Diagram 148), only K3 is available to the Bishop, and there it is in the way of Black's Rook which has only the King's file to work in. Besides, on K3 the Bishop is almost reduced to the role of a Pawn. White, by way of contrast, has excellent scope for all of his pieces. Since his open file on the Queen's side is blocked by Black's Bishop's Pawn, it will be a good plan for him to make this Pawn the target of his operations. He will advance his Queen's Knight's Pawn to Kt5, after preparing this with P—QR4. If Black captures twice on his QKt4, both his Queen's Pawn and Queen's Knight's Pawn will be isolated and therefore weak, and White will have accomplished his aim of opening the Bishop's file for his Rooks. On the other hand, if Black permits White to make the Pawn exchange, he will remain with a backward Pawn on B3 which is destined to fall, a victim of the white Rooks.

Black would have to seek his counter-chances in the King's file. In the position of the Diagram he will therefore try Kt—K5 against almost any continuation White might choose. If, for example, 12. **Kt—R4**, in order to occupy the strong point B5, White cannot win a Pawn in reply to **Kt—K5** by exchanging Bishops and capturing twice on K4, because he would lose a piece through P—B3. White will not hesitate exchanging Bishops, as Black's Pawn-skeleton is based on white squares. A black Bishop is here more valuable to Black than to White, whose Pawn-skeleton is based on black squares. After 13. **B × B, Q × B** White might also exchange the other Bishop for the Knight and then play Kt—B5, or he might play Kt—B5 immediately. Exchanging pieces is in White's favour, as long as he leaves Black with his bad Bishop and keeps a Knight for operations on black squares. Black cannot do much to prevent the advance of White's Queen's side Pawns alluded to above, but he might be able to get his pieces together for an attack on the King's side. Thus, the more exchanges, the better White's prospects.

In the Queen's Gambit, Black must always be on guard against the type of Queen's side attack just discussed when he has played P—QB3. He can rarely recapture with this Pawn in reply to BP × QP without yielding control of the Bishop's file to White, so that the latter can invade the seventh rank with his Queen or Rook. With this possibility in view, the tendency for White in recent years has been to exchange Pawns on Q5 as early as possible. This strategy has been rewarded with success so frequently that the defence 2. . . . . P—K3 is nowadays seen only rarely.

SLAV DEFENCE

Where Black plays 2. . . . . **P—QB3** ('*Slav Defence*') instead, White can also exchange Pawns immediately, but then a symmetrical Pawn-skeleton results and though we shall see that Black is forced to shut-in his Queen's Bishop with P—K3 in order not to weaken his Queen's wing, he does not yield control of the Queen's Bishop's file to White, and the game is equalized at an early stage.

If White does not exchange Pawns, Black must do so himself in order to get his Bishop out. Otherwise he gets the worst of it as follows: (1. P—Q4, P—Q4; 2. P—QB4, P—QB3); 3. **Kt—KB3, Kt—B3; 4. Kt—B3, B—B4; 5. P × P, P × P; 6. Q—Kt3** (Diagram 149). If now P—QKt3, White can exploit in short order the weakness of Black's QB3 created by this Pawn move by training his King's Knight and King's Bishop on this square with 7. Kt—K5 and 8. P—K4!, followed by B—QKt5.

There is no other plausible way of protecting the Knight's Pawn. 6. . . . . **Q—Kt3** loses the Queen's Pawn, and although Black gains two developing moves in turn (7. Kt × P, Kt × Kt; 8. Q × Kt, P—K3;

9. Q—Kt3), the exchange of the Queens does not permit him to work-up an attack which compensates for the loss.

On the other hand, if Black plays 4. .... **P×P**, he can develop his Bishop without getting into difficulties on the Queen's side—for one thing because White's Queen cannot occupy the favourable spot Kt3 at this moment. Moreover, if White does not take immediate steps to recapture the Pawn, Black might find an opportunity of holding on to it without submitting to an attack of the type which led to the

Diagram 149

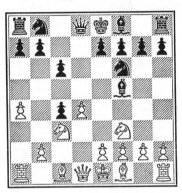

Diagram 150

position of Diagram 140. White could continue with 5. **P—K3, B—B4; 6. B×P** or 5. .... **P—QKt4; 6. P—QR4, P—Kt5; 7. Kt—R2,** followed by **B×P.** Most masters prefer holding back Black's Queen's side Pawns with 5. **P—QR4.** After Black replies B—B4, the position of Diagram 150 is reached in which White will try to reduce Black's Bishop to inactivity by advancing his King's Pawn to K4 while Black will do what he can to prevent this. Having given up his own centre-Pawn, Black should direct his efforts at White's centre-Pawn, in this case with P—QB4 or P—K4, depending upon the opportunities White's continuation might give him.

These considerations explain the following lines of play: 6. **Kt—K5, P—K3; 7. P—B3, B—QKt5!** Now 8. P—K4 is not possible because Black would reply B×P; 9. P×B, Kt×P and obtain more than enough compensation for the piece sacrificed. Instead, White would play 8. **Kt×P (B4).** The simplest plan of development for White is: 6. **P—K3, P—K3; 7. B×P, B—QKt5; 8. Castles, Castles; 9. Q—K2,** to be followed soon by P—K4, or 9. Kt—K5, with the idea of attacking with P—B4 and P—Kt4. The important thing for Black is to place his King's Bishop on QKt5, so as to exert pressure on K5 and delay the advance of White's King's Pawn until the black pieces are sufficiently developed to make the counter-thrust P—K4 or P—QB4 feasible. In many of the variations which are likely to ensue, Black is forced to give up his King's Bishop for White's Queen's Knight, leaving White in the possession of two Bishops, with the better chances to work up an attack. For example: 9. Q—K2, P—B4; 10. Kt—R2, Kt—B3; 11. R—Q1, Q—K2; 12. Kt×B, Kt×Kt; 13. P×P, Q×P; 14. P—QKt3 followed by B—Kt2.

A fundamental trouble with Black's opening from the point of view of a stronger player is that, in the position of Diagram 150, White can practically force a draw by repetition of moves if he continues with 6. Kt—R4. Black has nothing better than to return with the Bishop to B1, when White can play the Knight back to B3, so that Black is forced to shut-in his Bishop with P—K3 if he wants to avoid the draw.

QUEEN'S GAMBIT ACCEPTED

However, if Black is satisfied to give up the centre-Pawn with P×P without getting his Queen's Bishop developed on KB4, he may as well save himself the move P—B3 altogether, aiming at a line-up of his men similar to that shown in Diagram 147. In other words, he may as well accept the Queen's Gambit immediately and play 1. **P—Q4, P—Q4**; 2. **P—QB4, P×P**; 3. Kt—KB3, Kt—KB3; 4. **P—K3, P—K3**; 5. **B×P, P—B4**; 6. **Castles, P—QR3,** to follow this up with P—QKt4, B—Kt2, QKt—Q2 and possibly P—B5, or he might exchange Pawns in order to isolate White's Queen's Pawn.

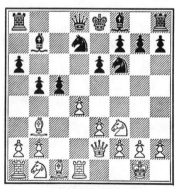

Diagram 151

In the former case, the continuation might be 7. **Q—K, P—QKt4**; 8. **B—Kt3, B—Kt2**; 9. **R—Q1, QKt—Q2,** leading to Diagram 151. In this position Black has the advantage—as compared with Diagram 147—that White's Queen's Bishop is shut-in. If White is not discriminate in the manner in which he continues his development he is liable to find himself with a badly cramped game. For example: 10. Kt—B3, Q—B2; 11. B—Q2, B—Q3; 12. QR—B1, as played by Horowitz against Edward Lasker in the New York State Championship, 1942, leaves Black with much the better prospects. Instead, White should play 10. P—QR4, P—Kt5; 11. QKt—Q2 and Kt—B4, which eliminates Black's threat to get the better ending through a Pawn majority on the Queen's wing and gains a good square for the Queen's Knight.

If Black isolates White's Queen's Pawn with 6. .... **P×P**; 7. **P×P**, White will enjoy the freer play for his pieces which goes with the possession of a Pawn in the centre, but if Black succeeds in exchanging enough pieces to avoid a dangerous attack against his King he will emerge with the better end-game. Should Black play P—QR3 and P—QKt4, and develop the Bishop to Kt2, it is again advisable for White to place his Queen's Knight on QB4 after forcing Black's Queen's Knight's Pawn to Kt5 with P—QR4, thus: 7. .... **P—QR3**; 8. **Q—K2, P—QKt4**; 9. **B—Q3, B—Kt2**; 10. **P—QR4, P—Kt5**; 11. **QKt—Q2, B—K2**; 12. **Kt—B4** (Diagram 152). Black will now play P—QR4 to avoid having

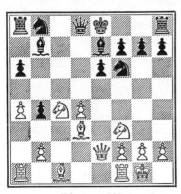

Diagram 152

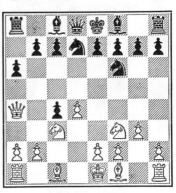

Diagram 153

his Knight's Pawn isolated through P—R5, and he will then move his Queen's Knight to Q4 via Q2 and Kt3. Meanwhile White will line up his forces advantageously with B—B4, KR—Q1, QR—B1, etc., and the fact that he may be able to utilize the third rank for swinging a Rook over to the King's wing will force Black to exercise the greatest care in protecting his King.

For this reason, the method of development illustrated in Diagram 151 is probably preferable for Black. This method looks also most plausible against another system of attack which some masters have favoured in the accepted Queen's Gambit in recent years: 1. **P—Q4, P—Q4**; 2. **P—QB4, P×P**; 3. **Kt—KB3, Kt—KB3**; 4. **Kt—B3, P—QR3**; 5. **Q—R4 ch, QKt—Q2**; 6. **P—KKt3** (Diagram 153).

Of course, Black cannot now continue with P—QKt4? because of 7. Kt×P, Kt—Kt3?; 8. Kt—Q6 mate. After 6. .... **P—K3**; 7. **B—Kt2**, he must again prepare the advance of the Knight's Pawn: **R—QKt1**; 8. **Q×BP, P—QKt4**; 9. **Q—Q3, B—Kt2**; 10. **Castles, P—B4**. Now, to avoid P—B5 followed by the advance of the other black Queen's side Pawns, White has nothing better than to exchange with 11. **P×P, Kt×P**; 12. **Q×Q ch, R×Q**, when Black equalizes the game without difficulty by completing his development with B—K2 and Castles.

Before the exchange of Pawns on White's Q5 and the Queen's side attack discussed in connection with Diagram 148 had proved a strong weapon in White's hands, a variety of defences held the stage which were based on the Pawn-skeleton shown in Diagram 154.

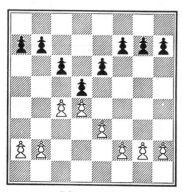

Diagram 154

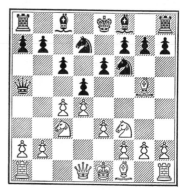

Diagram 155

CAMBRIDGE SPRINGS DEFENCE

The constellation of the pieces around this skeleton depends mainly upon whether White brings out his Queen's Bishop or not. After 1. **P—Q4, P—Q4; 2. P—QB4, P—K3; 3. Kt—QB3, Kt—KB3; 4. B—Kt5, QKt—Q2; 5. Kt—B3, P—B3; 6. P—K3,** Black can start an early counter-attack with **Q—R4,** bringing further pressure on White's Queen's Knight to bear with his King's Bishop and King's Knight (Diagram 155). White cannot blithely continue his development with 7. B—Q3, because Kt—K5 would threaten to win a piece through Kt×B and P×P, so that he would have to give up his Bishop for the Knight with 8. B×Kt, P×B; 9. Kt—K5, etc. White's best continuation in the Diagram is probably 7. **P×P, Kt×P; 8. Q—Kt3, B—Kt5; 9. R—B1.** Black must then take steps to get his Queen's Bishop out, and the most effective way is **P—K4!,** offering a Pawn which White will hardly want to accept, as Black would annoy his Queen either with Kt—B4 or B—K3 and gain a considerable advantage in development. 10. B—QB4, Castles; 11. Castles would be a plausible continuation.

MERAN DEFENCE

If White shuts-in his own Queen's Bishop in this opening with 1. **P—Q4, P—Q4; 2. Kt—KB3, Kt—KB3; 3. P—QB4, P—K3; 4. Kt—B3,**

P—B3; 5. **P—K3, QKt—Q2** (Diagram 156), he will still have an opportunity of utilizing the Bishop effectively by developing it on QKt2 from where it can support the King's Knight on K5 for a King's side attack.

Black's line-up of Pawns on the Queen's side, however, precludes a similar development of the Queen's Bishop. Therefore he must try to free his game with either P—QB4 or K4, as usual.

Diagram 156

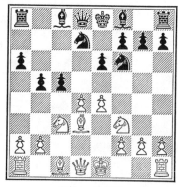

Diagram 157

The former manœuvre is more readily executed. For example: 6. **B—Q3, P×P; 7. B×P, P—QKt4; 8. B—Q3, P—QR3; 9. P—K4, P—B4** (Diagram 157). Now 10. **P—K5** gives rise to many wild combinations which in practical play have generally turned out in favour of White. After **P×P; 11. Kt×KtP!**, Black can play either P×Kt or Kt×P.

The continuation Kt×P invites White's King's Knight to a favourable spot, and has been practically abandoned since Reshevsky introduced the line 11. .... Kt×P; 12. Kt×Kt, P×Kt; 13. Q—B3, B—Kt5 ch; 14. K—K2, R—QKt1; 15. Q—Kt3!, which leaves Black with weak Pawns without compensation.

11. .... P×Kt, with the continuation 12. P×Kt, Q—Kt3, introduced by Keres, was considered Black's best defence until Botwinnik demolished this line in one of his World Championship games with Euwe. He played 13. P×P, BP×P; 14. Castles, Kt—B4; 15. B—KB4, B—Kt2; 16. R—K1, and Black was never able to castle. He could not do so on the 14th or 15th move, because of the sacrifice B×P ch, which gives White a killing attack. 16. .... Kt×B; 17. Q×Kt would not permit Black to castle either, as 18. Kt—Kt5 would win. After 16. .... R—Q1; 17. R—QB1, R—Q4, Botvinnik again made castling appear too dangerous to Euwe with 18. B—K5 (Castles; 19. B×B, K×B; 20. Kt—K5, and three of Black's pieces are cut off from the King's wing where they are needed for defence), B×B;

19. R × B, R × R; 20. Kt × R, Kt × B; 21. Q × Kt (if Black castles now, he loses through 22. Q—Kt3 ch, K—R1; 23. R—B7!); 21. .... P—B3; 22. Q—KKt3!!, and there is nothing to be done against Q—Kt7 followed by R—B7.

This game may have sounded the death-knell to the Meran Variation based on the move 6. .... P × P with subsequent P—QB4, and in Diagram 156 Black may have to be satisfied with imitating White's 6. B—Q3. Naturally, after 6. .... B—Q3, White will be the first to be able to push the King's Pawn: 7. Castles, Castles; 8. P—K4. However, with P × KP; 9. Kt × P, Kt × Kt; 10. B × Kt, P—QB4, or with 8. .... P × BP; 9. B × P, P—K4, Black secures equality.

COLLE'S SYSTEM

A very similar line of play, with colours reversed, so that White enjoys the advantage of an extra move, could occur in 'Colle's System' of the Queen's Pawn-opening, in which White deliberately permits Black to play P—QB4 and assumes the role of the defender of a Queen's Gambit. He does this in the expectation that the additional move will tell in his favour. However, experience has shown that Black has no particular difficulty in equalizing the game. After 1. **P—Q4, P—Q4; 2. Kt—KB3, Kt—KB3; 3. P—K3, P—B4; 4. P—B3, P—K3; 5. QKt—Q2, Kt—B3; 6. B—Q3, B—Q3; 7. Castles, Castles; 8. P × P, B × P; 9. P—K4,** for example (Diagram 158), Black can prevent P—K5 with either Kt—KKt5 or Kt—Q2 and then play KKt—K4 and B—Q2. With the white Knight on Q2 Black may try to hold his Pawn on Q4, although it can be isolated there through P × P. Then his centre-Pawn controls White's K4, the square White needs for his Knight in preparation for an attack on the King's wing. Positionally safer would be the continuation 9. .... P—K4; 10. P × P, Kt × P; 11. Kt—K4, B—K2, followed by P—B4.

Diagram 158

There are many other ways in which White can lead into variations of the Queen's Gambit with colours reversed and with a move to the good, but Black is always able to equalize by advancing his Queen's Bishop's Pawn to B4 on the second or third move. The safest way for Black is to play Kt—KB3 before P—QB4, as otherwise White can sometimes institute a strong attack by sacrificing his King's Pawn on

K4 in order to cramp Black's game with **P—Q5.** For example: 1. **P—Q4, P—Q4;** 2. **B—B4, P—QB4;** 3. **P—K4!** (Diagram 159). As early as on his third move Black has a wealth of possibilities from which to choose. He will want to consider BP×P, QP×P, Kt—QB3, Kt—KB3 and P—K3. As usual, general principles will be the best guide. **BP×P** is not likely to be good, as it develops White's Queen. After 4. **Q×P, Kt—QB3;** 5. **B—QKt5** the Queen will not be easily dislodged. (5. Q×QP would not be good on account of Q×Q; 6. P×Q, Kt—Kt5.) It is interesting to note that the continuation 5. .... Q—R4 ch; 6. Kt—QB3, Q×B; 7. Kt×Q, Kt×Q; 8. Kt×Kt leaves Black with practically a lost game, just because White has two pieces developed and Black has none. Black cannot defend the threats P×P and Kt—Kt5 at the same time.

Diagram 159

3. .... **P—K3** cannot be good in the position of the Diagram, because White can isolate Black's Queen's Pawn with P×QP, followed later by P×BP.

3. .... **QP×P** deserves strong consideration because it removes a hostile centre-Pawn. True, after 4. **P—Q5** Black cannot play the seemingly logical move P—K3, as the check 5. B—Kt5 would win in short order: B—Q2; 6. P×P!, B×B?; 7. P×P ch, K—K2; 8. P×Kt (Kt) ch!, K—K1 (R×Kt?, B—Kt5 ch, etc.); 9. Q—R5 ch, K—Q2; 10. Kt—QB3 followed by R—Q1, etc.

But Black could develop his game satisfactorily with 4. .... **Kt—KB3;** 5. **Kt—QB3, P—QR3;** 6. **KKt—K2, P—KKt3** and **B—Kt2.** He will lose the Pawn on K5, no doubt, but he will probably win the advanced white Queen's Pawn. On the other hand, if White takes the time to defend the Queen's Pawn with 5. P—QB4, Black can proceed to play P—K3, as the check on White's QKt5 is no longer threatened.

From the point of view of rapid development, the moves 3. .... **Kt—QB3** or **Kt—KB3** are undoubtedly best. In reply to Kt—KB3 White could not very well play 4. P—K5, blocking his Bishop, unless he intends the dubious Pawn sacrifice 5. P—K6. The only continuation in the spirit of his preceding move would be 4. Kt—QB3, whereupon Black can either accept the gambit Pawn, this time exchanging Knights in the process, or he can play the more conservative P—K3. In case White continues with KP×P, Black would recapture with the Knight, to avoid the isolation of his Queen's Pawn.

ALBIN'S COUNTER-GAMBIT

The surprising combination cited above in the line 3. .... P×KP; 4. P—Q5, P—K3? can occur—with roles reversed—in the opening 1. **P—Q4, P—Q4; 2. P—QB4, P—K4,** which is called '*Albin's Counter-gambit*'. Here White would be lost if after 3. P×KP, P—Q5 he continued with P—K3. Instead, 4. Kt—KB3, followed later by P—KKt3 and B—Kt2, gives White a superior game.

THE INDIAN DEFENCES

We turn now to the openings in which Black does not counter 1. P—Q4 with the immediate advance of his own Queen's Pawn. They are to-day the most favoured in master tournaments. Black refrains from playing P—Q4 until he feels that he is prepared to hold the point Q4 against White's pressure—an idea similar to that which prompted replies other than 1. P—K4 in King's Pawn-openings. By way of preparation, Black fianchettoes his King's Bishop or his Queen's Bishop. He either tries to make White's centre-Pawn a target for his initial operations, or he is satisfied to prevent the advance of White's second centre-Pawn to the fourth rank. He may even permit both White's Queen's Pawn and King's Pawn to come forward, hoping to undermine their position later and thus to prove that the advance was premature.

An early attack against White's Pawn on Q4 is feasible with either P—QB4 or P—K4, but, just as in the Queen's Gambit, usually only P—QB4 leads to a satisfactory position.

The prevention of White's P—K4 can be attempted by either Kt—KB3 or P—KB4. The former is obviously superior because it develops a piece, and to-day it is the move chosen against 1. P—Q4 in nine out of ten cases.

A combination of both, the prevention of P—K4 and the attack on White's Q4, forms the basis of most successful defences against 1. P—Q4 which have been evolved.

KING'S INDIAN DEFENCE

The idea of this combination is perhaps most clearly expressed in the following sequence of moves which forms a variation of the '*King's Indian*' Opening called '*Gruenfeld Defence*'.

1. **P—Q4, Kt—KB3; 2. P—QB4.** For White to try to prepare P—K4 with 2. Kt—QB3 would be a serious error, because Black could reply P—Q4, turning the opening into a Queen's Gambit which he himself will offer with P—QB4, whilst White has missed the opportunity of opening the Queen's Bishop's file for his Rooks. With P—QB4 White assumes control of the important centre-square Q5. He

will have an opportunity of exchanging this Pawn for Black's Queen's Pawn, if the latter advances to Q4 to prevent White's P—K4.   2. . . . .
P—KKt3. The fianchetto development of the King's Bishop is in the spirit of the contemplated attack on White's Q4.   3. **Kt—QB3, P—Q4.**
This is Gruenfeld's line, which many masters consider superior to the classic line B—Kt2; 4. P—K4, P—Q3; 5. Kt—B3, Castles; 6. B—K2, P—K4 (compare Game No. 11).

On his fourth move White must choose between forcing the occupation of K4 by his King's Pawn immediately or first trying to prevent Black from freeing himself with P—QB4.

If he plays the obvious 4. **P×P, Kt×P;** 5. **P—K4,** Black secures promising counter-play with **Kt×Kt;** 6. **P×Kt, P—B4;** 7. **Kt—B3, B—Kt2.** He will add further pressure through Kt—B3 and Q—R4, and after exchanging on White's Q4 he will have the better ending with two Pawns against one on the Queen's side.   White will try for an attack on the King's side, but it is doubtful whether he can succeed, in view of the good mobility of Black's pieces.

In Diagram 160, preferable methods of development for White are 4. Kt—B3, B—Kt2; 5. Q—Kt3, or 4. B—B4, B—Kt2; 5. P—K3, Castles; 6. Q—Kt3.

Now Black faces the disagreeable dilemma whether to play P×P, which facilitates the advance of the white King's Pawn, or whether to defend his Queen's Pawn with P—K3, which shuts-in the Queen's Bishop, or with P—B3, which relinquishes the intended attack on White's Queen's Pawn by P—B4 for the time being.

Diagram 160

In reply to P—B3, White can reduce the effectiveness of Black's fianchettoed Bishop by exchanging on Q5, for as soon as Black can no longer play P—QB4, White's Queen's Pawn keeps the black Bishop blocked for a long time to come.

In the last variation suggested above, Black's move 5. . . . . Castles involves the sacrifice of a Pawn, since White could continue with 6. P×P, Kt×P; 7. Kt×Kt, Q×Kt; 8. B×P.   However, delaying the development for the sake of winning a Pawn other than a centre-Pawn is always risky, and in the present case Black would indeed obtain a strong attack.   For example: 8. . . . . Kt—B3; 9. Kt—K2, B—Kt5; 10. P—B3, B×BP; 11. P×B, Q×BP.   The sacrifice of the Bishop keeps White's King in the middle of the board, exposed to the combined onslaught of the black pieces. If White does not succumb to the attack, he will at least have to lose enough Pawns to compensate Black for his Bishop.

The strategic considerations which, in Diagram 160, govern continuations other than those just reviewed, are the same as those which we discussed in connection with the Queen's Gambit, so that a more detailed explanation is here unnecessary.

NIEMZOVICH DEFENCE

A favourite line of play for Black, again suggested by the idea of holding back White's King's Pawn from the fourth rank, is the pinning of White's Queen's Knight with B—QKt5 rather than developing the Bishop to Kt2. In the position reached after 1. **P—Q4, Kt—KB3;**

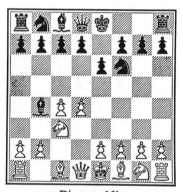

Diagram 161

2. **P—QB4, P—K3; 3. Kt—QB3, B—Kt5** (Niemzovich's variation, Diagram 161), White can either avoid a doubled Pawn on his QB3 by playing 4. Q—B2 or Q—Kt3, or he can continue his development with Kt—B3, P—K3, B—Q3, etc., in the expectation that after B×Kt, P×B the possession of two Bishops will more than offset the disadvantage of a weakened Pawn structure on the Queen's wing. Some masters consider the two Bishops so superior to Bishop and Knight that they provoke the doubled Pawn even at the cost of a tempo, playing 4. **P—QR3.** It is quite true that after **B×Kt ch; 5. P×B,** White's Pawn on B4 might prove difficult to defend, as Black might attack the Pawn with his Queen's Bishop from R3 and his Knight from QR4. But the Pawn on B3 lends strong support to White's centre and enables him to proceed with P—KB3 and P—K4, in preparation of a powerful King's side attack. With two black pieces busy on the Queen's wing hunting for a Pawn, White's King's side attack often succeeds. That is why Black does better to attack White's centre immediately with 5. . . . . . **P—B4,** and to answer 6. P—B3 with P—Q4.

When choosing between 4. **Q—B2** and **Q—Kt3** in the position of Diagram 161, it would be reasonable to select Q—B2 because there the Queen has greater mobility. Black's most logical continuation is then **P—Q4,** to follow this up with P—QB4, which would practically turn the opening into a Queen's Gambit.

QUEEN'S INDIAN DEFENCE

The simple developing move 4. P—K3 ('Rubinstein Variation') poses perhaps the most difficult problem for Black. He can pursue his efforts to keep control of White's K4 either with P—Q4 or with P—QKt3 and B—Kt2. In the latter line—usually leading to the 'Queen's Indian Defence', so called in contrast to the 'King's Indian Defence', which is characterized by the fianchetto development of the King's Bishop—the continuation might be 4. .... **P—QKt3; 5. B—Q3, B—Kt2;** 6. **Kt—B3, Castles; 7. Castles, B × Kt;** 8. **P × B, B—K5; 9. B × B, Kt × B;** 10. **Q—B2, P—KB4,** as played by Alekhine against Reshevsky in the Avro Tournament, 1938.

When playing 4. .... P—Q4 in answer to P—K3, the point Black must keep in mind is to avoid getting an isolated Pawn on Q4, just as in similar lines in the Queen's Gambit. For example, after 5. B—Q3, P—B4; 6. Kt—B3, Castles; 7. Castles, he should play QP × P before continuing his development with Kt—B3.

Against the Queen's Indian Defence, a good alternative for White is to fianchetto his King's Bishop rather than developing it to Q3. After 1. **P—Q4, Kt—KB3; 2. P—QB4, P—K3; 3. Kt—KB3, P—QKt3; 4. P—KKt3, B—Kt2; 5. B—Kt2, B—K2; 6. Castles, Castles; 7. Kt—B3** (Diagram 162), White threatens 8. Q—B2 and 9. P—K4. Again Black can try to prevent this manœuvre with either P—Q4 or occupation of his K5. In reply to P—Q4 White obtains the better chances through 8. Kt—K5, because this opens the diagonal for his King's Bishop whilst that of Black Queen's

Diagram 162

Bishop is blocked. Better for Black is 7. .... Kt—K5; 8. Q—B2, Kt × Kt; 9. Q × Kt, P—KB4, which effectively stems White's contemplated advance in the centre.

Placing the King's Knight on K5, protected by the King's Bishop's Pawn, as in the line-up just described, often gives Black good chances for activity on the King's wing. White will try to take advantage of the greater mobility which he enjoys on the Queen's wing, due to the fact that he has Pawns on Q4 and QB4 while Black's Queen's Bishop's Pawn has not advanced to the fourth rank.

DUTCH DEFENCE

Based on this idea is the 'Dutch Defence', which is characterized by the move 1. **P—Q4, P—KB4.** If White gives Black time for P—Q4 also, the advance of White's King's Pawn to the fourth rank is difficult to enforce. Diagram 163 shows the customary array of the men in this opening, in which Black's strong centre somewhat offsets the disadvantage of the inactive Queen's Bishop.

Diagram 163

Since Black's first move is not a developing move in the real sense of the word, an attempt on White's part to gain a considerable advantage in development by the Pawn sacrifice 2. **P—K4** is worthy of consideration. After **P×P; 3. Kt—QB3, Kt—KB3; 4. B—KKt5, P—K3; 5. Kt×P, B—K2; 6. B×Kt, B×B; 7. Kt—KB3, P—QKt3; 8. B—Q3, B—Kt2,** an interesting position is reached which occurred in a game I played against Sir George Thomas in London, 1912. I continued with

9. **Kt—K5, Castles; 10. Q—R5,** threatening Kt×B and Q×P. With four white pieces amassed against Black's King it looks as if White's attack will be difficult to parry. But Black could have defended himself with KB×Kt; 11. Q or P×B, R—B4. The sacrifice 11. Kt—B6 ch is not sufficient either (R×Kt; 12. Q×P ch, K—B1; 13. Q—R8 ch, K—K2; 14, Q×P ch, R—B2; 15. Q×B, P—Q3). Thomas actually played 10. .... **Q—K2,** enabling the pretty Queen's sacrifice 11. **Q×P ch, K×Q; 12. Kt×B double ch, K—R3** (K—R1; 13. Kt—Kt6 mate); 13. **Kt (K5)—Kt4 ch, K—Kt4; 14. P—R4 ch, K—B5; 15. P—Kt3 ch, K—B6; 16. B—K2 ch, K—Kt7; 17. R—R2 ch, K—Kt8; 18. K—Q2 mate.** Faster would have been 14. P—B4 ch, K×P; 15. P—Kt3 ch, K—B6; 16. Castles mate, or 15. .... K—Kt4; 16. P—R4 mate, or 14. .... K—R5; 15. P—Kt3 ch, K—R6; 16. B—B1 ch, B—Kt7; 17. Kt—B2 mate.

A line which is still more aggressive is the attempt to refute the Dutch Defence with the Pawn sacrifice 1. **P—Q4, P—KB4; 2. P—K4, P×P; 3. P—KB3.** After Kt—KB3; 4. Kt—QB3, P×P; 5. Kt×P. P—K3; 6. B—Q3, B—K2; 7. Castles, Castles; 8. B—KKt5, for example Black would be hard pressed for a satisfactory defence. P—QKt3; 9. Kt—K5, B—Kt2 would this time be fatal on account of 10. B×Kt, B×B; 11. Q—R5, or 10. .... P×B; 11. B×P ch, K×B; 12. Q—R5 ch, K—Kt2; 13. Q—Kt6 ch, K—R1; 14. QR—K1, threatening R—K3, etc.

The wisest thing for Black to do, if he wants to avoid a violent attack, is not to capture White's Bishop's Pawn on the fourth move but to give back the Gambit-Pawn with P—K6.

BUDAPEST DEFENCE

In reply to other irregular defences to the Queen's Pawn-opening, normal rapid development will always point to the proper continuation. Two examples will suffice. 1. **P—Q4, Kt—KB3**; 2. **P—QB4, P—K4** ('Budapest Defence'); 3. **P×P, Kt—Kt5** is best answered with 4. **P—K4, Kt×KP**; 5. **Kt—QB3**, followed by P—B4, Kt—B3, etc., when White controls much more territory. For an inexperienced player this manner of handling the opening would be decidedly preferable to the attempt to hold the Pawn with 4. **B—B4, Kt—QB3**; 5. **Kt—KB3, B—Kt5 ch**; 6. **Kt—B3, B×Kt ch**; 7. **P×B, Q—K2**; 8. **Q—Q5**, when P—B3; 9. P×P, Kt×P (B3) leaves White with rather weak Pawns.

BENONI COUNTER-GAMBIT

Again, if Black offers the Queen's Bishop's Pawn instead of the King's Pawn in answer to 1. **P—Q4** by playing **P—QB4** immediately ('Benoni Counter-Gambit'), White will not take the Pawn which Black could easily regain with P—K3, but he would either turn the opening into a Sicilian Defence with 2. **P—K4**, or into some form of Queen's Gambit with 2. **P—K3**. He could also try to cramp Black's game with 2. **P—Q5**, though this gives Black good counter-chances unless White handles the opening very exactly. Black will attack the Pawn immediately with **P—K3**. After 3. **P—QB4, P×P**; 4. **P×P**, Black will fianchetto his King's Bishop, to take advantage of the fact that the advance of White's Queen's Pawn has given up control of the black centre-squares: **P—KKt3**; 5. **Kt—QB3, P—Q3**; 6. **P—K4, B—Kt2** (Diagram 164). Indifferent play on White's part would now enable Black to exert pressure against White's King's Pawn in the open

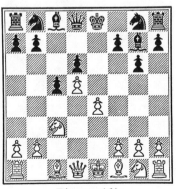

Diagram 164

King's file, besides leaving him with good prospects for the ending due to the Pawn-majority on the Queen's wing. White can hope to get the upper hand only if he succeeds in a King's side attack, probably involving the advance P—B4 and P—K5 at the first opportunity, or if he can convert his Queen's Pawn into a dangerous passed Pawn through B—KB4, Kt—B3 and P—K5. It will take some testing in master-play to arrive at a final verdict.

Similar considerations explain one of the important lines in the 'Reti Opening', 1. **Kt—KB3, P—Q4;** 2. **P—B4, P—Q5.** Here we have the Benoni with colours reversed. As usual, the extra move which White enjoys makes a great difference. After 3. **P—K3, P—QB4;** 4. **P×P, P×P;** 5. **P—KKt3, Kt—QB3;** 6. **B—Kt2, P—K4;** 7. **Castles,** White already threatens Kt×KP, followed by R—K1. This slows down Black's contemplated advance in the centre, but P—B3 gives Black a solid position so that he can complete his development undisturbed, for example with KKt—K2, P—KKt3 and B—Kt2, when the advance of the centre-Pawns remains a menace. If Black tries to turn Reti's Opening into a variation of an ordinary Queen's Gambit by replying 2. .... P—K3 or P—B3, no new strategic problems present themselves in case White plays P—Q4. Reti's idea, however, was to hold back this move and instead play P—Q3, fianchetto both Bishops, and then force P—K4. Emanuel Lasker showed the proper development for Black against this system in one of his games with Reti in the New York Tournament, 1924: 2. .... P—QB3; 3. P—QKt3, B—B4!; 4. P—Kt3, Kt—B3; 5. B—KKt2, QKt—Q2; 6. B—Kt2, P—K3; 7. Castles, B—Q3; 8. P—Q3, Castles; 9. QKt—Q2, P—K4!; 10. P×P, P×P; 11. R—B1, Q—K2; 12. R—B2, P—QR4; 13. P—QR4, P—R3; 14.

Diagram 165

Q—R1, KR—K1; 15. KR—B1, B—R2 (Diagram 165); 16. Kt—B1, Kt—B4. Black has carefully prepared the thrust P—K5. The retreat of the Bishop was intended to avoid the loss of a move which would have been entailed in White's reply Kt—Q4, if P—K5 had been played as long as the Bishop was on KB4. Now the advance of the Pawn threatens to win the exchange, or at least a Pawn, and to tie the white pieces into a Gordian knot. For example: 17. Kt(B3)—Q2, P—K5; 18. P—Q4, Kt—R3; 19. P—K3, Kt—QKt5; 20.

R—B3, Kt—Q6; 21. R—Kt1, B—Kt5; 22. R—B2, Kt—Kt5, etc. The lack of mobility of White's pieces is pitiful. White did the best under the circumstances by sacrificing a Rook for Knight and Pawn with 17. R×Kt, but he did not obtain adequate positional compensation.

Some very interesting lines, leading away from the beaten path, are apt to develop if Black tries to turn Reti's opening into an accepted Queen's Gambit with 2. .... **P×P**, and White, instead of continuing with either 3. P—K3 or 3. Q—R4 ch plays 3. **Kt—R3,** as recommended by Capablanca during the New York Tournament in 1924. The draw-back to this line-up of the white forces, which aims at occupation of K5 with one of the Knights, is that Black can easily keep control of his K4 through P—KB3 and P—K4. Together with P—QB4 and Kt—QB3, this gives Black far greater mobility because he controls more centre-squares. The immediate advance 3. .... **P—K4,** originated by Spielmann, leads to rather wild play the result of which is not quite clear. 4. **Kt×KP** is forced, as Kt×BP would permit P—K5. Against **B×Kt;** 5. **Q—R4 ch** (Diagram 166), Spielmann played P—QKt4. Then

Diagram 166   Diagram 167

6. Q×P ch would lose a piece, because after P—QB3; 7. Kt×QBP, Kt×Kt; 8. Q×Kt ch, B—Q2; 9. Q—K4 ch, Black can interpose his Bishop. Instead, White must play 6. Q×B, when Q—Q4; 7. Q—KB3, Kt—KB3; 8. Q×Q, Kt×Q; 9. P—KKt3, P—B3; 10. B—Kt2, B—Kt2; 11. Kt—Kt4, QKt—Q2 creates a difficult position with chances for both sides.

Very dangerous for White is a little-known continuation involving the sacrifice of the Queen's Bishop's Pawn for the sake of rapid development: **Kt—Q2!;** 6. **Kt×Kt, B×Kt;** 7. **Q×KB, Kt—K2!;** 8. **Q—QB3, Castles;** 9. **Q×BP** (Diagram 167). Now a strange position is reached, in which seven white Pawns are still on their original squares after nine moves have been made. White has considerable difficulties in devising a workable plan to get his pieces out. For example: B—K3; 9. Q—KR4, Q—Q3, followed by Kt—B4 and Kt—Q5. White's best plan is 8. P—K4!, B—K3; 9. P—Q3!, P×P; 10. B—K3!, Castles; 11. Castles.

ENGLISH OPENING

If White omits Kt—KB3 on the first move and plays **P—QB4** immediately, Black need not lead into a Queen's Pawn game at all, but can counter with 1. .... **P—K4,** turning the opening into a Sicilian with colours reversed, in which White is naturally a move ahead as compared with the normal Sicilian Defence. Black's best plan is to play P—Q4 as soon as feasible, for example: 2. **Kt—QB3, Kt—KB3;** 3. **Kt—B3, Kt—B3** (Diagram 168); 4. P—Q3, P—Q4; 5. P×P, Kt×P; 6. P—KKt3, B—K3; 7. B—Kt2, B—K2, etc., or 4. P—K3, P—Q4; 5. P×P, Kt×P; 6. B—Kt5, Kt×Kt; 7. KtP×Kt, B—Q3.

Should White prevent Black's P—Q4 with 4. P—Q4, P×P; 5. Kt×P —now P—Q4 would be met by 6. P×P, Kt×P; 7. Kt×Kt, P×Kt; 8. P—K4—Black can develop himself satisfactorily with B—Kt5; 6. B—Kt5, P—KR3; 7. B—R4, B×Kt ch; 8. P×B, Kt—K4; 9. P—K3, P—Q3, followed by Kt—Kt3 and Kt—K5.

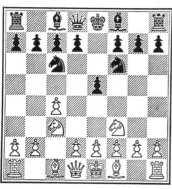

Diagram 168

Diagram 169

FROM'S GAMBIT

Among other irregular first moves which White might choose in order to lead into an opening normally played by Black, but in which he is one move ahead, only 1. **P—KB4** (Bird's Opening) needs special mention. Based on the same reasoning which suggested 2. P—K4 in the Dutch Defence (p. 140), Black can here try 1. .... **P—K4; 2. P×P, P—Q3; 3. P×P, B×P** (From's Gambit), which threatens mate through Q—R5 (P—KKt3, Q×KtP). After 4. **Kt—KB3** Black continues the attack with **P—KKt4** (Diagram 169). If then 5. P—KKt3, Kt—QB3; 6. B—Kt2, P—KR4; 7. P—Q3, White's mobility can be further restrained with P—KB3!, intending 8. P—K4, P—R5!; 9. P×P, P—Kt5; 10. KKt—Q2, P—KB4, which is likely to prove too much for White.

White's best plan is to play 5. P—Q4 in the Diagram, in order to meet P—Kt5 with 6. Kt—Kt5, and it is doubtful whether Q—K2; 7. Q—Q3, Kt—KB3; 8. Kt—QB3, Kt—B3; 9. P—QR3 leaves sufficient attacking possibilities for Black to compensate him for the Pawn.

More conservative is Black's treatment of this opening with 1. .... P—Q4, to prepare P—K4 if possible. After 2. P—K3, Kt—KB3; 3. Kt—KB3 Black will prevent White's Kt—K5 with B—Kt5. Then, 4. B—K2, B×Kt; 5. B×B, QKt—Q2; 6. P—B4 does not stop P—K4, though P—K3; 7. P×P, P×P; 8. Kt—B3, P—B3 is perhaps safer and also sufficient to reach an even game.

There are, of course, quite a number of ways in which either White or Black might deviate from the more or less thoroughly analysed standard openings discussed in this chapter. However, a player who has grasped the meaning of the mobility-principle will be in a position to devise a satisfactory plan of development in any opening, even though he has never seen it before. A player who relies to a large degree upon his memory to guide him through the opening is apt to be at a loss when confronted by a move which deviates from those recommended by 'the book'. Usually he does not realize that the latter is nothing but a collection of variations illustrating the application of the general strategic laws which all good moves must obey. It does not occur to him that on the basis of these laws he can judge himself whether a move not recorded in the books is good, or bad, or indifferent.

We have seen that the two strategic principles which dominate the opening stage are the principle of rapid development and the principle of centre-square control. To recapitulate, the specific rules which we have derived from these principles are:

1. Make only such Pawn-moves as are required
    (a) to open lines for your pieces,
    (b) to restrict your opponent's mobility,
    (c) to control centre-squares.
2. In developing a piece choose a spot from which
    (a) it aids the control of centre-squares,
    (b) It has as many other squares to move to as possible,
    (c) it cannot be driven away by a developing move.
3. Do not move a piece in the opening more than once, unless the additional move
    (a) places it on a square it will want to reach in the early middle-game in any case,
    (b) is required to meet a specific attack,
    (c) leads to a clear advantage in material or position, due to a weak move of the adversary.

From rule No. 1 it follows that P—K4 and P—Q4, when feasible, are always likely to be better than other Pawn-moves; that P—QB4 or P—KB4 may be required in addition, to open a file for the Rooks; that P—QB3 or P—KB3 should not be considered unless necessary to support a centre-Pawn or to drive away an opposing piece menacingly posted in the centre; that P—KKt3 or P—QKt3 are desirable only when Kt2 is a more effective developing square for the Bishop in question than squares accessible through the advance of the King's or Queen's Pawn; and that P—KR3 and P—QR3 are rarely called for unless an opposing Bishop must be kept away from Kt4 to preserve a Knight on B3 who is needed for the support of a centre-square.

From rule No. 2 we deduce that KB3 and QB3 are the most desirable developing squares for the Knights; that the Bishops may be effectively placed on almost any square accessible to them, depending upon the Pawn-skeleton which characterizes the opening; that the Rooks will most frequently find a field of activity in the centre-files or a Bishop's file, and that, like the Queen, they should be confined to the first and second ranks until exchanges of minor pieces make it safe for them to emerge into the open.

It is hardly necessary to elaborate on rule No. 3. It justifies an occasional early occupation of K5 by the King's Knight, or a move of the Bishop from K2 to B3, when some of the other pieces are still undeveloped. The early phase of the middle-game is so often inextricably connected with the opening, that the rule to complete the development of *all* pieces before moving a piece for the second time must not be too strictly applied.

Let us now turn our attention to the middle-game. This part of the struggle is likely to offer the student considerable difficulties, because it lends itself less readily than the opening to the formulation of general strategic principles which might serve as a guide through the maze of continuations open at every step. We shall see, however, that in the last analysis the mobility principle again furnishes the clue to very useful generalizations which help to solve the specific tactical problems we have to face.

5. MIDDLE-GAME AND END-GAME

THE strategy of the middle-game depends a good deal upon whether the defending player can force the exchange of the Queens and a few minor pieces, or whether such a simplification can be avoided.

When the Queens have been exchanged, a decision is usually not reached until the position is reduced to an end-game. In such cases, the strength or weakness of the Pawn-formation is the paramount consideration. With the Queens on the board, the game is often decided by a more or less violent combination before the end-game has been reached. Such a combination need not necessarily imply a mating attack; it may result in a gain of material which makes further resistance useless.

As we have already learned in Chapters 3 and 4, wild attacking combinations are not likely to be successful unless they are staged against a healthy background of superior mobility. We must realize that when the adversary has developed his men logically, in accordance with the dictates of opening-strategy, it would be unjust if the position held a combination detrimental to him; it would probably be a waste of time to look for such a combination. On the other hand, if a player emerges from the opening with a markedly superior development, he should be confident that an opportunity for a successful onslaught will soon offer itself, and he should be on the look-out for surprising sacrificial turns.

These general considerations must again be qualified on account of the special role played by the King. His unique position among the pieces introduces an element inimical to generalization, and sometimes constellations of pieces occur which offer an opportunity for a mating attack not readily inferred from the general characteristics of the position. Diagrams 59 and 60 showed examples to the point, and we shall find more of them as we go along. The number of these constellations—usually referred to as 'traps'—is not large. They have to be memorized, just like the few traps which we encountered during the discussion of the opening, when a seemingly sound developing move led to a forced loss of the game.

We saw that correct treatment of the opening, i.e. rapid development of the pieces and maintenance of control over as many centre-squares as are in the hands of the opponent, ordinarily gives White an advantage, however slight. As a result, White will be quite naturally in a position to assume the initiative in the middle-game. This means merely that as a rule White will be the first to work up an attack. It may be a mating attack, if he can concentrate considerably superior forces on the side on which the adversary has castled; or it may be an attack on the other wing, if he has managed to obtain a Pawn-majority there, or an open file for his Rooks, or an advanced Pawn-chain behind which his pieces have more freedom of movement than those of the other player.

WHERE TO START OPERATIONS

Speaking quite generally, the side of the board on which a player has a Pawn-majority is usually the one on which he should plan operations. For one thing, an advance of the Pawns on this side is likely to result in a passed Pawn. For another, as just mentioned, it increases the territory behind the Pawns and thus also the mobility of the pieces supporting the advance, while at the same time it reduces the territory of the defending player.

On the side on which the King has castled, a Pawn-advance requires stronger support by pieces than on the other side, because the advancing Pawns no longer provide the protective screen around the King of the attacking player which normally relieves most of his pieces of the necessity to do defensive work. In turn, a Pawn-advance on the King's side is more dangerous for the adversary, because his King is in the zone in which the mobility of the attacking pieces is increasing. Usually, if he can mobilize adequate defensive forces and ward off the attack, his King can also block the passed Pawn which, in the end, results from the advance of the Pawn-majority. That is why manœuvres designed to yield a passed Pawn occur most frequently on the Queen's wing.

CASTLING PROBLEMS

In the great majority of all games, both players castle on the King's side. The reason is not only the greater speed with which the King reaches a safe spot and a Rook gets into play, but also the fact that on the Queen's wing a broader front has to be defended—three Pawns instead of only two. Game No. 5 furnishes a typical example of the difficulty of such a defence.

To delay castling beyond the developing stage of the game is dangerous if the opponent can open the King's file and place his Queen or a Rook in it, pinning whatever man of the uncastled King may find himself in that file. Frequently a Pawn-sacrifice serves to produce such a situation, as exemplified in Game No. 20.

With the centre solidly closed, castling may be delayed in favour of middle-game manœuvres designed to secure territorial gain; but if it is put off too long, the attendant lack of co-operation of the Rooks is apt to prove fatal. Without castling, such co-operation can usually be accomplished only by placing the King in the second rank. This is often feasible if Queens have been exchanged early so that the middle-game tends to resolve itself into an end-game. But even without Queens on the board, a King has sometimes difficulties in defending himself on the second rank if the opponent can work up an attack with his Rooks. Game No. 7 is a good example.

As pointed out before, a successful attack against the castled King presupposes either a larger fighting force or, with attacking and defending forces numerically balanced, greater mobility of the attacking forces. A restriction of the mobility of the defending forces is almost always caused by one or more advanced Pawns of the attacker which increase his territory and correspondingly decrease the territory of his opponent. The most common forms of such an advanced Pawn-chain are a pair placed on K5 and KB4 or on K5 and Q4 (see Games Nos. 3 and 4). Sometimes Pawns on K4 and KB5 exert the fatal cramping effect, as in Game No. 10.

Even a single Pawn lodged on the fifth rank in the centre may suffice to secure for the attacker the territorial superiority which he needs to restrict the mobility of the defending player. Game No. 17 offers a most instructive example which clearly illustrates a case of this type.

Ordinarily, of course, a Pawn-pair on Q5 and K4 presages attacking manoeuvres on the Queen's wing, just as a pair on K5 and Q4 is normally a basis for aggression on the King's wing. In fighting the territorial expansion of the aggressor, the defending player will try to break up a Pawn-pair on the opponent's K5 and Q4 with P—KB3 or P—QB4, as pointed out in the discussion of the French Defence. Similarly, a Pawn-pair on the opponent's Q5 and K4 can frequently be weakened or destroyed by P—KB4 or P—QB3 (compare Games Nos. 8 and 9).

Against the Pawn-alignment K4—KB5 the defender must attempt breaking through in the Queen's file (Game No. 11). The corresponding defence against Pawns on Q4 and QB5 would consist in counter-attack in the King's file.

Whether the formation of one of the four advanced Pawn-pairs just discussed is desirable depends upon whether or not that formation can be maintained long enough to serve its original purpose. If it can, it usually entails the advance of the wing-Pawns also (see Games 3, 4, 8, 10, 11, 17), the object being the opening of a file in which a Rook might invade the opponent's territory.

As we saw during the discussion of the openings, an advance of the Rook's or Knight's Pawn on the King's wing, after castling there, should never be undertaken without careful consideration of the weaknesses created by leaving the squares unprotected which the Pawns had been guarding. This guard should be taken over by pieces placed behind the advancing Pawn-chain.

On the Queen's wing, an advanced Rook's or Knight's Pawn—unless it is a passed Pawn—will prove to to be a weakness more often than not, either because the Pawn itself is more readily attacked, or because the enemy can lodge pieces on squares adjoining the file in which the Pawn is located, without being driven away by the Pawn.

PROVOKING WEAKENING MOVES

The novice who has grasped the importance of mobility for his pieces will readily understand that, after completing their initial development, any move which further increases their mobility will improve his chances of getting the better game. But finally he will arrive at a position in which his men seem almost ideally placed, and he will then be at a loss how to proceed.

In Chapter 3 I pointed out that a natural target for attacking combinations is offered either by a man who for one reason or another cannot leave his post, or by two or more men who can be attacked simultaneously. There is little sense in directing one's efforts against pieces which can move to another desirable spot.

If, due to careful handling of the opening, the adversary offers no natural target, a reasonable plan of campaign will always be based on manœuvres which *provoke the creation of a weakness*. Such a weakness might result either from a move which produces a target according to the definition just given, or by a move which gives up the control of a square coveted by the enemy's pieces. In either case it is usually a *Pawn-move* which weakens a position that was otherwise quite sound.

As mentioned above, this is true particularly of the Rook's Pawn or the Knight's Pawn in front of the castled King. The provocation of the advance of one of these Pawns is almost always the necessary prelude for an attack on the King. Less obvious is the indirect weakness which is often produced by the advance of a centre-Pawn to the fifth rank, due to the opportunity it offers the opponent to open the adjoining Bishop's file for his Rook.

The Rook's Pawn is sometimes advanced to the fourth rank for the purpose of maintaining a Knight on B4 (Game No. 8). On the King's wing such an advance has the disadvantage that it surrenders the square Kt4 to the opponent who might lodge a piece there in order to provoke the move P—KB3. This would weaken the square KKt3 very much as the Rook's Pawn no longer guards it. Positional manœuvres of this type frequently provide the key for a winning attack, as the observant reader will realize when playing over the following games.

ILLUSTRATIVE GAMES

To illustrate strategy and tactics in middle- and end-game, I have chosen mostly positions from games I have played myself. It is very difficult to do full justice to games of other masters in an analysis which includes middle-game manœuvres. It takes the sweat and blood a player puts into a tournament-game to appreciate fully the reasons behind his moves. Even the greatest chess-master-authors, while excelling in lucid criticism of the opening strategy employed in the games of others, have often failed to discern the full significance of tactical manœuvres which these players executed in middle-games.

In *Chess for Fun and Chess for Blood* I cited as an instance a game which I played against Emanuel Lasker in the New York Tournament, 1924. Alekhine, for whose chess-genius I have the greatest admiration, devoted some two thousand words to the analysis of the different phases of that game in the tournament book; but he arrived at totally wrong conclusions because he did not evaluate correctly the middle-game manœuvre in which the strategy of the opening culminated. Another example is Alekhine's diagnosis of the critical combination in the following middle-game which I am selecting as the first illustration of the application of general strategic principles to that phase of the contest.

GAME No. 1

The opening had been a 'Philidor Defence': 1. P—K4, P—K4; 2. Kt—KB3, P—Q3; 3. P—Q4, Kt—KB3; 4. Kt—B3, QKt—Q2; 5. B—QB4, B—K2; 6. Castles, Castles. Black's game is cramped, because the Queen's Knight blocks his Queen's Bishop, and time-taking manœuvres are required to get the Bishop into play. For reasons fully discussed in the preceding chapter, Black will try to maintain his King's Pawn in the centre, whilst White will want to provoke the exchange on Q4. Before Black can move his Queen's Knight, he will therefore have to play P—B3 and Q—B2 (compare Diagram 84). The game continued as follows:

7. B—KKt5

As this move does not pin the Knight, it is likely to lead to an

Black: Efim Bogolyubov

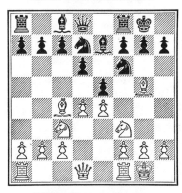

White: Edward Lasker

From a game played in the New York International Masters' Tournament, 1924

Diagram 170

exchange of the Bishop. This would be undesirable for White, because it would somewhat relieve the cramped position of Black's pieces. My best move was probably Q—K2, to follow this up with R—Q1. My plan was to play the Bishop to KKt3, to exert further pressure on Black's centre-Pawn. However, Black succeeds in exchanging the Bishop.

7. ...... **P—B3**

This threatens to win my King's Pawn through P—Kt4—Kt5.

PASSIVE METHODS LOSE INITIATIVE

The proper defence against this threat would have been P—QR4, which, at the same time, would have maintained the Queen's Bishop on B4 where it has excellent mobility. Instead, I retreated with the Bishop to a square of lesser mobility and permitted the expansion of Black's territory on the Queen's wing—certainly a bad decision.

8. B—Kt3   P—KR3

Preparing the exchange of the Bishop through Kt—R4. The advance of the Rook's Pawn does not constitute a weakness here, because I do not have superior fighting forces on the King's wing and cannot hope to evolve a King's side attack unless I succeed in forcing the exchange of Black's King's Pawn on my Q4.

9. B—KR4   R—K1
10. Q—Q3

Alekhine suggested here B—Kt3, in order to counter Kt—R4 with 11. Kt×P, Kt×B; 12. Kt×KBP. In reply to 10. .... P×P he proposed 11. Kt×P, Kt—B4; 12. B—QB4. Perhaps Kt×P was a misprint for Q×P, as the King's Pawn must be protected. But even 11. Q×P, Kt—B4; 12. B—QB4 would enable Black to do away with my King's Pawn through Kt×P; 13. Kt×Kt, Kt×Kt; 14. Q×Kt, P—Q4, and his two Bishops would be ample compensation for the isolated Queen's Pawn

with which he emerges from the exchange. My plan was to make room for one of the Rooks.

10. ......   Kt—R4
11. Q—B4   R—B1
12. B×B   Q×B

While I have forced Black's Rook to return to the square from which it had just moved, my Queen will also have to move again very soon, so that I have not really gained a tempo. Moreover, the exchange of the Bishop, which I could not avoid, freed Black's game. Black has now more mobility on the King's wing. He threatens Kt—B5 which would in the long run provoke the weakening Pawn move P—KKt3. Thus the initiative has passed to Black.

13. Kt—K2   P—R4

My Knight's move was practically forced, to hold back Black's King's Knight. Black probably expected that I would answer his Pawn move with 14. P—B3. But then he would have obtained tremendous pressure in the King's file through P×P; 15. Q×QP, Kt—B4; 16. B—B2, P—B4, and due to the unguarded position of my Queen's Knight, he would have won a Pawn. For example: 17. P—K5, P×P; 18. Q×P, Q×Q; 19. Kt×Q, R—K1; 20. P—KB4, Kt×P, etc., or 17. Kt—Q2, R—K1; 18. P—B3, P—Q4, etc.

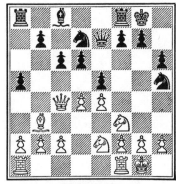

Diagram 171

For this reason I gave up the idea of defending my King's Pawn and tried to induce Black to capture it with the Queen, so that I might obtain tactical threats with my Rook in the King's file. I played

14. **Q—B3**

inviting P×P; 15. QKt×P, Q×P; 16. QR—K1. Then, if Q—Kt3, 17. Kt—K6! would have won at least the exchange. If 16. .... Q—Kt5; 17. P—KR3, Q—Kt3, again 18. Kt—K6 would have won. Neither would 16. .... Q—R2 have been feasible, because of 17. R—K7, again threatening Kt—K6. Kt—B4 would not have helped, because 18. B×P ch!, R×B; 19. R—K8 ch, R—B1; 20. Q—B4 ch would have forced the Bishop or the Knight to interpose (20. .... P—Q4?; 21. R×R ch, K×R; 22. Q×Kt ch, followed by 23. Kt×P!). Then 21. R×R ch, K×R or R×R would in the end lose a Pawn after White captures twice on K6. Finally, in reply to 16. .... Q—B5, the invasion 17. R—K7 again would have afforded compensation for the Pawn sacrificed.

This situation is another good example of the far-reaching influence of delayed development. The opponent obtains tactical opportunities which would otherwise not exist.

Naturally, Bogolyubov saw the dangers involved in the capture of the King's Pawn, and, instead, he simply followed up the chance I had given him to expand his mobility on the Queen's side.

14.	**P—R5**
15. **B—B4**	**P—QKt4**
16. **B—Q3**	**B—Kt2**

The result of my omitting the move P—QR4 is seen in the immobile position of my Bishop. Black threatens P—QB4. P×KP would then not be possible on account of P—B5, and P×BP would be met with Kt×P, followed by Kt×KP and much greater mobility for the black forces. To keep the advanced chain of

black Pawns immobile I continued with

17. **P×P**   **P×P**

and now I should have tried to find a way to open a file for my Rooks. The Queen's file is blocked through my badly placed Bishop, and even if the file is finally cleared, Black can readily contest its control by opposing his own Rooks. That is why my next move cannot be considered in the spirit of the position. A file which I might have opened for my Rooks without Black being able to oppose his own is the King's Bishop's

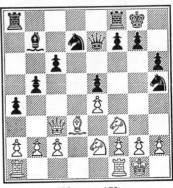

Diagram 172

file. After 18. Kt—Kt3, Kt×Kt; 19. BP×Kt the threat would have been 20. Q—Q2 and then 21. Kt—R4—B5. While Black could have defended this threat with 19. .... P—Kt3 and 20. .... K—Kt2, I would have regained the initiative at least on one wing.

18. **QR—Q1**	**KR—K1**
19. **Kt—Kt3**	**Kt×Kt**
20. **RP×Kt**	

Probably I did not like the isolation of the King's Pawn through BP×P, but the open file may have been worth it.

20.	**Kt—B3**
21. **Kt—R4**	

As suggested above, first Q—Q2 was more subtle. Black would then have had to reply K—R2 in order to be able to play P—Kt3, and on the white square the King was less safely placed in view of the possible advance of my King's Bishop's Pawn and the opening of a diagonal for my Bishop in case Black exchanged Pawns.

21.	P—Kt3
22. Q—Q2	K—Kt2
23. Q—K3?	

Probably intending to invade Black's Queen's wing on Kt6, and overlooking that Black's reply makes this move impossible. I remember I was short of time, with only a few minutes left within which to complete my thirtieth move. For this reason I rejected the plan P—KB4, no doubt, though the open file, after P×P; 24. Q×P might have been a sufficient compensation for the weak Pawns. Another feasible plan was P—KB3, K—B2 and R—KR1, in order to utilize the open Rook's file.

| 23. ...... | Kt—Kt5 |

If the Queen goes to Kt6 she is lost through R—R3.

| 24. Q—Q2 | Q—B4 |

Increasing the mobility of the Queen and preventing P—KB4.

25. B—K2	Kt—B3
26. B—Q3	QR—Q1
27. Q—K2	B—B1

Threatening B—Kt5. Black's pieces have far superior mobility. Mine are condemned to almost complete inactivity.

28. K—R1	B—Kt5
29. P—KB3	B—K3
30. P—R3	R—K2

A simple move which prepares the doubling of the Rooks. Due to time-pressure, Black had to make his thirtieth move without much consideration. Otherwise he might have considered P—Kt5. After 31. P×P, Q×P, I should hardly have been able

to avoid the loss of a Pawn in the long run, with Black in possession of open lines on the Queen's wing, besides threatening the advance of the Queen's Bishop's Pawn. Black's Rook's move gives me a breathing spell which I can utilize for an attempt to exchange the Queens or seize the long diagonal KKt1—QR7 for a counter-attack. I cannot play Q—B2 immediately, because after the exchange of Queens Black would play P—B4—B5, squeezing the life out of my Bishop. But after my Rook moves out of the Queen's file, which is in Black's possession anyway, he cannot advance the Queen's Bishop's Pawn without leaving his Queen's Knight's Pawn 'en prise'.

| 31. QR—K1 | Q—Q5 |

While this wins my Knight's Pawn, I get my counter-attack for it. I think P—Kt5 was still the best.

| 32. Q—B2 | Q×KtP |

Diagram 173

33. Q—B5	R—B2
34. R—QKt1	Q—Q5
35. R×P!	

The point of the combination. Bogolyubov tries a counter-combination, but it involves the exchange of his Bishop for my rather useless Knight and separates his pieces into two unconnected groups, so that it is not likely to turn out well. He should probably have played simply: P×R; 36. Q×R, P—Kt5; 37. P×P, P—R6; 38. Q—R5, P—R7; 39. P—Kt5, R—QKt1!, stopping the advance of my Pawn and threatening R—Kt2 —R2. If necessary, his Knight could have entered the fray via Q2, while my Knight was hopelessly shut out from the scene of battle.

35.	......	P—Kt4
36.	Kt—B5 ch	B×Kt
37.	P×B	Kt—R4

Diagram 174

I cannot defend the Knight's Pawn, as 38. K—R2, Kt×P!; 39. K×Kt, Q—R5 would be mate. Neither can I exchange Queens, because my Rook on Kt5 would then have to move, and Kt×P ch would win the exchange. Therefore I strive for increased mobility of my inactive Rook, and this proves at least good enough to save the game.

38.	R—K1	Kt×P ch
39.	K—R2	Q—R5 ch
40.	K—Kt1	P—B3

Black is completely unaware of my intention to sacrifice my Rook in order to break through his protective Pawn-chain for a mating attack. He should have been suspicious of such a possibility, because his Rooks are not protected and therefore subject to double attacks. Very likely it did not occur to him that the position

really demanded defensive rather than aggressive action on his part, since my pieces were now well co-operating whilst his own were separated. In the heat of battle, the importance of such a cool appraisal of the position is indeed often forgotten.

Diagram 175

Alekhine called Bogolyubov's move an error when he was near his goal, and he suggested that he could easily have won with R—Q4; 41. Q—Kt6, P×R; 42. Q×R, Q—Q5 ch and Kt×P. He overlooked that in reply to P×R I could have checkmated Black through 42. P—B6 followed by Q—Kt8 ch!

41. R×P!!
Had I played R—Kt4 first, Black could have forced a draw with P—K5!; 42. B×P, Kt—K7 ch!; 43. K—B1, Kt—Kt6 ch, etc. 43. R×Kt, of course, would have permitted R—Q8 ch and mate next move. 42. P×P, Q—R8 ch; 43. K—B2, Q—R5 also would have led to a forced repetition of moves.

41. ......   **P×R**
After this Black should have lost the game. His only hope lay in Q—Q5 ch; 42. Q×Q, R×Q; 43. KR—B5, Kt—R4, in order to bring the Knight back into the game via B5.

42. Q × P ch   K—Kt1
43. R—Kt4!

This is what Black had not considered. Q × R would lose on account of Q—Q5 ch and P × R.

43. ......   Q—R8 ch
44. K—B2   R—KB2

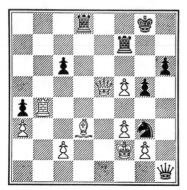

Diagram 176

45. R—Kt8??

I had only a few seconds left within which to make my 45th move before the third hour on my clock had elapsed. I completely overlooked that here I could capture the Knight, as the mate previously threatened through Q—R5 was now protected by my Rook. The exposed position of Black's King would no doubt have very soon sealed his doom. To realize the threat B—B4, I had only to play the King back to B2.

45. ......   R × R
46. Q × R ch   K—Kt2

I had hoped for R—B1; 47. B—B4 ch, K—Kt2; 48. P—B6 ch, followed by 49. Q × R, winning.

47. Q—K5 ch

and the game was drawn by perpetual check on Kt8 and K5. An exciting battle!

The course of this game, typical of many encounters, illustrates two strategic errors. In the opening, I assumed too passive an attitude. By allowing my opponent to expand his territory gradually, I drifted into a position in which I could no longer maintain equality, and I lost a Pawn. However, too sure of his victory, Bogolyubov omitted checking his plans from the viewpoint of general principles, and he pressed the attack on the wrong wing. As a result, his advantage was lost, and he even came near losing the game.

GAME No. 2

The position shown in Diagram 177 was reached after the opening moves:

1. P—Q4	Kt—KB3
2. P—QB4	P—K3
3. Kt—KB3	P—Q4
4. Kt—B3	P—B3
5. P—K3	QKt—Q2
6. B—Q3	P × P
7. B × BP	P—QKt4
8. B—Q3	P—QR3
9. Castles	P—B4

Black: SAVIELLY TARTAKOWER

White: EDWARD LASKER

From a game played in the New York International Masters' Tournament, 1924

Diagram 177

We discussed this opening ('Meran Defence') in connection with Diagram 157. At the time this game was played, the possibilities entailed in the move 9. P—K4, instead of castling, had not as yet been investigated in master-play. In fact, the defence characterized by the above opening-moves had been tried for the first time only a few months previous to the New York Tournament, by the great Akiba Rubinstein, in a game played at Meran, Austria. I had not seen that game, but Tartakower was familiar with it.

The advance of the King's Pawn on the 9th move is sharper and more logical than castling, because after the exchange of Black's Queen's Pawn for White's Queen's Bishop's Pawn there is always the threat that Black may secure a Pawn-majority on the Queen's wing with P—B4—B5, and to counter this threat, White must attack on the King's wing. For this purpose the advance of the King's Pawn to the fifth rank is indicated which drives one of Black's pieces from its post defending the King's side Pawns.

I continued with 10. P—QR4, in order to gain control of the square QB4, and thus to remove Black's threat P—B5 which would become acute as soon as the black minor pieces are developed. However, the provocation of P—Kt5 is much more effective when White hasn't a Knight on QB3 which is chased by the advancing Pawn. When the Knight is still at QKt1, it can readily reach the square QB4 via Q2.

I may have feared that after 10. P—K4, P×P; 11. Kt×QP, Kt—B4; 12. B—B2, Black would win a Pawn through P—Kt5; 13. P—K5, KKt—Q2. However, 14. Kt—K4, Kt×P; 15. Kt×Kt, B×Kt; 16. B—R4 ch, B—Q2 (or Kt—Q2); 17. Kt×P!, followed by 18. Q—R5 ch, would have regained the Pawn with a vastly superior position.

Neither does 10. P—K4, P×P; 11.

Kt×P, Kt—B4; 12. B—B2, P—Kt5; 13. P—K5, P×Kt; 14. P×Kt, Q×P; 15. P—QKt4!, Kt—Q2; 16. B—K4, R—Kt1; 17. Kt—B6 look rosy for Black.

After the natural 10. P—K4, B—Kt2, the continuation 11. P—K5, P×P; 12. Kt×KtP, P×Kt; 13. P×Kt, Q—Kt3 (Diagram 178) would lead to the variation which Botvinnik refuted in his game against Euwe, quoted on p. 133.

Diagram 178

The game actually proceeded as follows (Diagram 177):

| 10. P—QR4 | P—Kt5 |
| 11. Kt—K4 | B—Kt2 |

WHEN NOT TO EXCHANGE PIECES

12. Kt × Kt ch   Kt × Kt

There can be no advantage, during the development stage, in exchanging a Knight that has moved twice, for one that has moved only once. 12. Q—B2 would have been answered by QR—B1, and 12. Kt—Kt3 by B—Q3, preventing the advance of the King's Pawn which, after B×Kt, would lack sufficient protection. But 12. QKt—Q2! would have either enabled P—K4, or, if 12. .... P×P; 13. P×P, it would have led to Kt—B4, possibly followed by Kt—K5.

13. Q—K2

A natural developing move which clears the square Q1 for the Rook.

13. ......   P × P

Q—Q4 would have been stronger. I should have had to take recourse to such complicated manœuvres as P × P, R—Q1 and Kt—K1.

14. Kt × P   Q—Q4
15. P—B3   B—Q3

Black's Bishops are now ideally placed. An attack on my KR2 will provoke another Pawn move in front of my King, and the result is bound to be a dangerous weakness. The only consoling feature for me is that Black's King's Bishop is protected only by the Queen whose position I am about to make uncomfortable by posting my Rook in the Queen's file. However, Tartakower has calculated the resulting possibilities exactly, concluding that he can meet my threats.

16. R—Q1   Castles

In the tournament book Alekhine suggested, correctly, that I could now have won a Pawn with 17. Kt—Kt3, which threatened B × P ch. Q × Kt would lose the Queen through B—B4. I had seen the move but rejected it because I was not certain whether after Q—KR4; 18. B × P ch, K × B; 19. R × B, Kt—Q4 my Rook would extricate itself satisfactorily. Later I saw that with 20. Q—Q3 ch and Q—

Q4 I could have held Black's Queen away from my Rook. Then I could have forced a line of retreat for it with P—K4.

17. B—B4

There seems little sense in chasing the Queen from a square on which she is exposed to all sorts of combinations due to the control of the Queen's file by my Rook. The best continuation was probably 17. P—QKt3, followed by B—Kt2 and P—K4. This development of the Queen's Bishop was particularly strong in view of the possibility that Black might advance his King's Pawn after first preventing Kt—B5 with P—Kt3. The white Queen's Bishop would then exert great pressure in the long diagonal.

17. ......   Q—QB4

In order to provoke a weakening Pawn-move with Q—B2. Simpler seems Q—KR4; 18. P—KKt4, Q—K4. Perhaps Black felt that his Queen was too exposed in the centre of the board.

18. B—Q2   Q—B2
19. P—KKt3   Q—R4

Black makes too many Queen-moves. The obvious developing move was KR—Q1.

20. P—K4   KR—Q1
21. Kt—Kt3   Q—R4

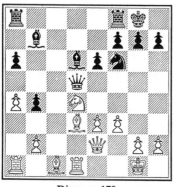

Diagram 179

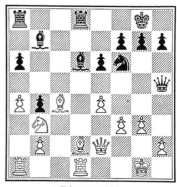

Diagram 180

This position furnishes a good example of the manner in which the principle of mobility can guide a player in making the best selection among the many moves which seem feasible in the middle-game. The maximum increase of mobility for my men I would have obtained through B—K3. This would not only have given my Bishop and Rook full sway, but it would also have prevented Black from improving the position of his Knight with Kt—Q2 which would have left the Bishop on Q3 unprotected. Specifically, B—K3 would have threatened B—Kt6 and doubling of the Rooks in the Queen's file. In meeting this threat with B—B2, Black would have permitted my Bishop to reach B5, attacking the Knight's Pawn. After P—R4, the Bishop would have gone to K7, driving Black's Rook from the Queen's file and enabling the invasion of the seventh rank after removing Black's Knight.

22. QR—B1, the continuation which I actually chose, was not as strong. It was also a developing move but did not restrict Black's mobility and should have enabled Black to exchange enough pieces to secure a draw.

| 22. QR—B1 | Kt—Q2 |

Threatening Kt—K4, so that I must provide for a second defence of my King's Bishop's Pawn.

| 23. Q—B2 | B—B3? |

Kt—K4 would have been answered by B—K2. But Kt—B4 would have easily drawn, as I would have had to submit to the exchange 24. Kt×Kt, B×Kt; 25. B—K3, B×B; 26. Q×B, whereupon Black could have defended both invasion points with Q—R4. 24. P—Kt4, Q—K4; 25. B×KtP would not have worked, on account of Kt×KP! The move chosen by Black, which contemplates the capture of my Rook's Pawn, shows that he underestimates the danger to his unprotected King's Bishop. By sacrificing the Rook's Pawn I can force the exchange of the white Bishops and gain access to QB6 with my Knight, winning at least the exchange.

| 24. Kt—Q4 | B×RP |

The retreat Kt2 was the only move to try saving the game.

| 25. P—Kt3 | B—Kt4 |
| 26. P—Kt4! | Q—Kt3 |

Not Q—R6, because of Kt×B followed by B—B1; nor Q—K4, because of B×B and Kt—B6.

| 27. B×B | P×B |
| 28. Kt—B6 | KR—QB1 |

This loses a whole piece, but there was no saving move. Had I not driven Black's Queen from R4 on the 26th move, he might have saved himself with 28. .... Kt—B4; 29. P—Kt4, Q—R6; 30. R×Kt, B×R; 31. Q×B, Q×P or 30. Kt×R, Kt—Q6, etc.

29. B—K3	P—K4
30. Q—Q2	Q—B3
31. K—Kt2	B—B4
32. Q×Kt	B×B
33. Kt—K7 ch	Q×Kt
34. R×R ch	R×R
35. Q×R ch	Q—B1
36. R—Q8	Resigns.

The winning combination in this game was of a rather frequently recurring type. A piece—in this case Black's King's Bishop—is exposed to attack by a Rook, but it can be defended by uncovering a protecting Rook in the same file. If this protecting Rook could be driven away, both the exposed piece and the piece which was to uncover the Rook would be undefended. To be able to drive the Rook, a fourth piece which guards the key-square must be lured away. This is accomplished with a Pawn sacrifice as bait.

In our case the above combination really provided an untimely end for a middle-game which was still in its formative stage. Due to the loosening of the Pawns in front of the white King, Black had the better attacking chances. If he wanted to avoid the drawish variation given in the note to the 23rd move, he might have planned an attack against my King's Bishop's Pawn, which formed the base of the Pawn-chain blocking his Queen's Bishop, with 23. .... Kt—K4; 24. B—K2, P—Kt4!, threatening Q—Kt3 and P—Kt5. The attack on my K4 with 24. .... P—B4 was also worthy of consideration. 25. P—B4 could have been answered with Kt—Kt5, practically forcing the exchange of my Bishop for the black Knight, whereupon Black's white Bishop controlled the long diagonal, with hardly any counterplay left to me. A splendid illustration, showing how much better the protection is which the horizontal Pawn-chain in front of the King provides, as compared with a diagonal chain!

It should be interesting for the student to note that, just like in our first example, here again a game is lost because a player operates on a part of the board on which he has inferior fighting forces, instead of manœuvring on the wing on which he is stronger. Both of Black's Bishops and the Queen were converging on my King's wing. That was the region toward which Black should have directed his play, beginning with Kt—K4. Instead, he went after my Queen's Rook's Pawn and his game was disorganized within a very few moves.

Another point which the game illustrates is the importance of the time-element in the early middle-game, when the forces are being regrouped in accordance with the exigencies of the attacking or defensive manœuvres planned by the players. Accomplishing this regrouping in as few moves as possible is as necessary here as the speedy development of the pieces during the opening stage.

In the position of Diagram 177, I should not have embarked on an operation involving the exchange of my Queen's Knight for Black's King's Knight, because it meant spending two moves without either increasing the mobility of my forces or increasing the territory controlled by them. The time consumed by the journey of my Knight enabled Tartakower to complete the line-up of his own men ahead of me. Thus, my normal advantage as the player of the white pieces was completely lost, and the initiative went to Black.

The subtle influence of the time-element often manifests itself in a good many other ways far into the middle-game. The *order* in which a series of moves is made when lining up the men for an attack may sometimes be of considerable importance. If chosen properly, it may retard the necessary defensive regrouping of the opponent's men, whilst otherwise it may place no particular difficulties in his way. In the game just discussed, my 22nd move was an example of improper timing.

GAME No. 3

Another instructive illustration will be found in the following game, in which the position of Diagram 181 was reached after: 1. P—K4, P—K3; 2. P—Q4, P—Q4; 3. Kt—QB3, B—Kt5; 4. P—K5, P—QB4; 5. P—QR3, B×Kt ch (regarding 5. .... P×P, see p. 112); 6. P×B, Kt—K2.

As pointed out on various occasions in the preceding chapter, the Pawn-skeleton clearly indicates that White will have to attack on the King's wing, Black on the Queen's wing. If Black castles on the King's

Black: MIKHAIL BOTVINNIK

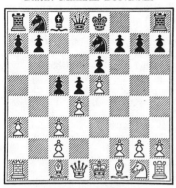

White: SMYSLOV

From a game played in the Russian Championship Tournament at Moscow, 1944

Diagram 181

side, the black King will not have the protection of the Knight whose normal developing square is controlled by White's King's Pawn. Thus, the Pawn-chain in front of the King will form his only protection, unless he can place his Knight on Kt3 or open the King's Bishop's file with P—KB3. Then the Rook could do defensive duty on B2 or B3, apart from possible counter-threats in the Bishop's file.

White's aim will be to provoke a weakening move in Black's protective Pawn-chain and to storm forward with his own King's side Pawns in order to open files for the Rooks.

White actually played 7. P—QR4, with a view to placing the Queen's Bishop on R3. While Black's weakness on black squares is a good argument in favour of this plan, the drawback is that it involves a Pawn-move on the wing on which the opponent is superior, and that it loses a tempo toward the advance on the King's wing. For these reasons the immediate advance of the Pawns on the King's wing was preferable.

7. P—QR4   QKt—B3
8. Kt—B3

More in the spirit of the 7th move would perhaps have been 8. Q—Q2, to follow this up with B—R3. He could not make this Bishop's move immediately on account of P×P; 9. P×P, Q—R4 ch; 10. K—K2, Q—B6. However, after 8. Q—Q2, Q—R4; 9. Kt—B3 he would have succeeded in carrying out his plan. For example: 9. .... Castles; 10. B—R3, P×P; 11. P×P, Q×RP; 12. B—Q3, or 9. .... P—B5; 10. B—R3, Q×RP; 11. B—K2, with excellent attacking chances in both cases.

8. ......   Q—R4
9. B—Q2

This is tantamount to an admission that P—QR4 was a wasted move. Again, Q—Q2 deserved strong consideration, though it may well be that Smyslov did not want to permit the exchange of Queens through P×P, etc., because he felt that with the Queen on the board he could work up a violent King's side attack.

9. ......   P—B5

Depriving White's King's Bishop of his best developing square, Q3, which he might otherwise have chosen to occupy after P×P, at the expense of a broken Pawn position.

10. Kt—Kt5

The provocation of a weakening Pawn-move. The threat is Q—B3, which would force Black to castle right into the attack. However, it was perhaps preferable to play P—KR4 first, in order to keep Black's Knight from Kt3, and also to avoid blocking the Rook's Pawn with the Knight when the latter is chased back. Black's Knights are in each other's way. If White had placed his Pawns on KR5 and Kt4, Black's game would have been very much cramped. White could have continued with Kt—R4, P—B4, Q—B3 and P—B5, with a powerful attack.

| 10. ...... | P—KR3 |
| 11. Kt—R3 | Kt—Kt3 |

Now Black has much more breathing space than he would have had in the line indicated in the note to the 10th move.

12. Q—B3!

Smyslov recognizes that with his Knight on R3 the manœuvre P—B4, P—Kt4, Q—B3, etc., would not have been very promising, because at the crucial moment Black could have stopped the white advance with P—R4. For example: 12. P—B4, QKt—K2; 13. P—Kt4, B—Q2; 14. Q—B3, P—R4, followed by Kt—R5—B4, blocking White completely and leaving Black free to employ most of his forces on the Queen's wing. With his Queen's move he prepares to exchange Black's defending Knight. Though this manœuvre requires two tempi which he could have saved himself, his attack remains formidable, demonstrating the tremendous strength of White's game in this opening.

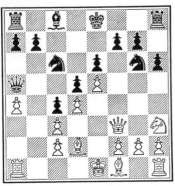

Diagram 182

12.	B—Q2
13. Kt—B4	Kt×Kt
14. Q×Kt	Kt—K2

This move increases the mobility of the Bishop as well as the Knight, and it grooms the latter for defence-duty against the coming onslaught. But now the natural continuation 15.

P—R4, Castles; 16. P—Kt4, P—B3; 17. P×P, R×P would enable White to gain an important tempo with 18. Q—Q6, attacking Bishop and Knight and forcing the black Queen to return home. 14. .... Castles, on the other hand, would have made it quite difficult for White to carry out his plan of attack. For example: 15. P—Kt4, P—B3; 16. P×P, R×P; 17. Q—Q6, R—B2; 18. P—R4, P—K4! and with the Rooks connected and the centre opened, Black would quickly get the upper hand. The only way in which White could have avoided the break in the centre was with a line-up such as 15. Q—Kt3, K—R2; 16. B—K2, P—B3; 17. P×P, R×P; 18. P—B4. But then his attack was greatly slowed down and Black had a good deal of counter-play with QR—KB1, Kt—K2, etc.

15. P—R4   B×P?!

WHEN WINNING PAWNS IS
DANGEROUS

Capturing a Pawn on a wing before completing the development, and thus keeping part of one's forces tied up away from the battle lines which form at a distance, is certainly against the principles of chess strategy. Botvinnik was surely aware of this; but in the heat of battle one is apt to let a tactical mirage blot out a strategic conviction. The exclamation-mark concerns Botvinnik's daring. But after the omission on his last move he almost had to go into this adventure. The alternative, blocking White's advance first with P—KR4 and Kt—B4, may not have seemed desirable to him because it meant creating weak black squares on the King's wing, too, and after a deal of preparations White might have succeeded in driving the Knight from B4 after all.

16. P—R5!

Probably Smyslov considered 16. B—K2, with a view to protecting the Queen's Bishop's Pawn with this Bishop in answer to Black's Q—Kt4, rather than with K—Q1. But with his Pawn-move he definitely prevents Black from blocking the Pawn-storm which he plans, and he feels that he will be able to ward off the threats against his King which Black will surely try to evolve.

| 16. ...... | Q—Kt4! |

The beginning of an ingenious series of moves calculated to disrupt the orderly development of White's forces.

| 17. K—Q1 | R—QB1! |

Threatening R—B3, followed by the sacrifice B×P ch and Q—Kt6 ch, which would lead to mate after R—Kt3.

18. B—B1	R—B3
19. B—K2	R—R3
20. K—Q2	

B×P ch was threatened. B—R3 was not feasible on account of B×P ch; 21. K×B, Q—Kt6 ch and R×B. Thus Black has succeeded in putting White's Queen's Bishop more or less out of commission. The mobility of White's King's Bishop is very limited anyway, due to the control of so many white squares by Black's Pawn chain. Apart from the Pawns, White has therefore really only the Queen and one Rook with which to conduct his attack. Black decides that he can risk castling, with King, Rook and Knight to defend himself. Also, the Rook will soon be ready to become active in the King's Bishop's file, the opening of which White cannot prevent. Still, the fact that the major part of Black's forces is badly tied up on the Queen's side, remains a weakness which White demonstrates most convincingly.

| 20. ...... | Castles |
| 21. P—Kt4 | P—B3 |

| 22. P×P | R×P |
| 23. Q—B7! | |

Regaining the tempo which Black had won through the attack on the Queen. In answer to Q—K3 Black would have had time for Kt—B1—Q3, from where he would have interfered with White's plans through occupation of either K5 or B4.

23.	R—B2
24. Q—Q8 ch	K—R2
25. P—B4	

The march of the Pawns is relentless. White threatens to crush his opponent with 25. P—Kt5.

| 25. ...... | Q—R4!! |

With Q—Q2 Black could have *forced* the exchange of Queens and led into an ending very similar to that which White could now reach by exchanging and continuing as shown in detail below. But the offer of the exchange on R4 gives White the option to leave the Queens on the board and prepares a magnificent combination for this eventuality. Botvinnik, with psychological acumen, assumes that Smyslov will prefer this line if he does not see the hidden threat entailed in the Queen's move. This is actually what happens. Smyslov conceives a series of four moves which apparently leave Black defenceless, only to be struck down by a thunderbolt from a clear sky.

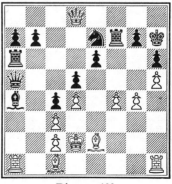

Diagram 183

With 26. Q×Q, R×Q; 27. B—R3, Kt—B1 (apparently best); 28. P—Kt5!!, R×P; 29. P—Kt6 ch, K—Kt1; 30. B—QKt4!, R—R3; 31. KR—KB1, R—KB3; 32. B—Kt4!, B—Q2! (Kt—Q3?; 33. B×Kt, R×R; 34. B×P ch, K—R1; 35. R×R, etc.); 33. R×QR, White could have reached the position of Diagram 184, in which he can keep Black's pieces tied to their posts and decide the issue with his mobile King, while Black's King is shut off in the corner.

The position is full of surprising possibilities which it would be almost impossible to exhaust in a game over the board. Among the fascinating variations, one of which might have come about if Smyslov had bothered looking into the consequences of the Queen-exchange, are some which offer very instructive end-game material and which the student should carefully play through.

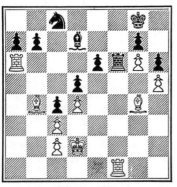

Diagram 184

For example, if Black should continue with 33. .... R×R; 34. B×P ch, K—R; 35. B×B, P×R; 36. B×Kt, R—QR8, he would win one of the Bishops but he would nevertheless lose as follows: 37. B—K6, P—R4; 38. B×QP!, P×B; 39. P×P, P—R4; 40. P×P, R×P; 41. B×P, and White will queen one of his passed Pawns. On 36. .... R—B5, with the intention of capturing the Rook's Pawn, White wins through

37. B—K6 (B—K7?, R—K5!), as the Queen's Pawn runs faster than the Rook's Pawn. White must guard against an attempt by Black to produce a stalemate by sacrificing his Rook's Pawn and then giving up his Rook at a time when White's King's Bishop controls Black's King's Knight's square. The ending might run like this: 36. .... P—R4; 37. B×P, R—KKt8; 38. B—Q8, P—R4. If now 39. B×P, R—QR8; 40. B—B7, R—R1; 41. B—K6, R—K1; 42. B×P?, R—K7 ch; 43. K—B1, R×P ch would draw. One of several ways to force the win would be 40. B—Kt4, R—R1; 41. B—Kt7, R—QKt1; 42. B×P, R×B; 43. K—K3, R—Kt8; 44. B×P, and the Pawns cannot be stopped.

Even if Black chooses the best defence in Diagram 184, i.e. 33. .... P×R, the continuation 34. R—K1 would decide the issue in White's favour. Black cannot move the Knight, because B—K7 would force the Rook to abandon the King's Pawn. After 34. .... Kt—Kt3; 35. B—K7, R—B5; 36. B×P ch, K—R1; 37. B—Q6, R—K5; 38. R×R, P×R; 39. B×B, Kt×B; 40. K—K3, Kt—B3; 41. B—K5, Black is lost, because he cannot permit the exchange of Knight on his B3 which would give White two separate passed Pawns. For example: Kt×P; 42. K×P, P—R4; 43. K—Q5, P—R5; 44. K×P, P—R6; 45. K—Kt3; Kt—B3; 46. B×Kt, P×B; 47. P—Q5, etc.

The Bishop, of course, cannot move because B×P ch would follow. For the same reason the Rook cannot leave B3, and so Black is confined to making moves with the King or the Rook's Pawn. Supposing he plays the King back and forth to the corner and Kt1. Then the White King will go to QR3, and the Bishop to QB5, threatening to capture the Rook's Pawn through K—Kt4—R5, and Black must reply P—R4. With R—QKt1 White then threatens R—Kt7, and after the Bishop moves,

R—QB7, and Black is defenceless.

With the idea of preventing this scheme Black might start with 34. .... P—R4; 35. B—QB5, P—R3, in order to close the Knight's file with B—Kt4 as soon as White plays R—QKt1. But then White replies 36. K—K3—to immobilize Black's Rook—and continues with R—QR1. If Black defends the Pawn by advancing it, he loses control of his QKt5, and after returning with the Rook to K1 the white King goes to QR3—Kt4—R5, captures the Pawn on R6 and wins a piece by proceeding to QB7. If Black permits White to capture the Queen's Rook's Pawn with his Rook, the same situation is produced after the Rook returns to K1. Thus, Black's game would have been lost in every variation after 27. .... Kt—B1. If he played Kt—B3 instead, White would win very quickly through 28. P—Kt5, R × P; 29. P—Kt6 ch, K—Kt1; 30. KR—KB1, R—B3; 31. B—KKt4, P—K4; 32. B—K6 ch, K—R1; 33. R × R, P × R; 34. B—B8, etc. The only move which remains to be considered, therefore, is 27. .... Kt—Kt1, with the idea to reach K5 via B3. In reply White would play 28. B—QKt4, R—R3; 29. K—K3. Then Kt—B3 is not feasible on account of P—Kt5 and P—Kt6, and if Black, instead, continues with B × P, White obtains an overwhelming game with 30. R × R, P × R; 31. P—Kt5, P × P; 32. P × P, K—R1; 33. R—KB1. White is practically a piece ahead.

26. Q—QKt8

Falling into a trap which is indeed beautifully conceived.

26.	Kt—B3
27. Q—K8	R—K2
28. Q—Kt6 ch	K—Kt1
29. B—R3	P—K4!!

This is the move Smyslov had overlooked. Black's Queen's Rook all of a sudden awakes from its long sleep. The threat is to attack the Queen with the Rook through Kt × P,

which deprives her of her only flight square, B5. If White plays 30. B × R, the Knight, in recapturing, again covers that flight square, and the Bishop prevents the Queen's escape to K8. If the Queen tries to escape with 30. Q—B5 P × QP immediately demolishes White's game. Smyslov can get both of Black's Rooks for the Queen, but he can't organize his remaining pieces for a counter-attack and he loses his advanced Pawns so that his resistance collapses within a few moves.

30. BP × P	Kt × QP

If Kt × KP, White's King's position would not be easily assailable, and after 31. Q × R, Q × Q; 32. B × R he would still have good winning chances.

With Black's Knight placed so that he can capture White's King's Bishop, the continuation just sketched is not possible because the white King would be open to too many checks

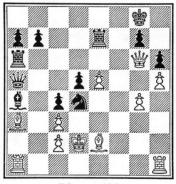

Diagram 185

by Black's Queen. After 31. Q × R, Q × Q; 32. B × R, Kt × B; 33. K × Kt, Black would get his Queen into action with Q—K3! Then White could not play 34. R × B, because he would lose a Rook or Bishop and three Pawns through Q × KtP ch; 35. K—B2, Q—B5 ch; 36. K—Kt2, Q—Q7 ch; 37. K—R3 (K—Kt1?, Q—Q8 ch and Q × BP ch, etc.), Q × P ch;

38. K—Kt4, Q—Q5 ch; 39. K—R3, Q—K6 ch; 40. K—Kt2, Q—K7 ch; 41. K—R3, Q—B6 ch; 42. K—R2, Q—B7 ch; 43. K—R3, Q—B4 ch, and the Queen wins either the Bishop with Q×KP ch or the Queen's Rook with Q×BP ch or the King's Rook with Q—K5 ch. An instructive illustration of the power of the Queen against two disconnected Rooks.

Capturing first the Rook with the Bishop in the position of the Diagram would not have made much difference. After 31. B×R, R×Q; 32. P×R, Kt×B; 33. K×Kt, Q×BP, or 33. B—Kt4, Q—Kt3; 34. K×Kt, Q×P, or 34. R×B, Q—B7, or 34. KR—KB1, Q×P; 35, R×B, P—Q5!; 36. R×P, P×P ch; 37. B×P (K×Kt?, Q—K5 ch, and one of the Rooks is lost), Kt—Kt6; 38. R—B3, Q×KtP, and White must lose at least a Rook for the Knight.

| 31. **B—Kt4** | **Q—Q1** |
| 32. **Q×R** | |

It is quite possible that at this stage White was somewhat short of time and could not analyse the position with sufficient care to see the finesse which Black has at his disposal on the 33rd move. Otherwise he might have tried 32. P×Kt, R×Q; 33. P×R, B—K1; 34. P—Kt5, B×P; 35. P×P, in a last desperate attempt to gather all his men for an attack on Black's King. 34. B×R, Q×B was not feasible, because the threat Q—Kt4, followed by Q—K6 or P—B6, could not have been adequately defended.

32.	**P×Q**
33. **P×Kt**	**R—Kt2!**
34. **R×B**	**Q—Kt4 ch**
35. **K—Q1**	**P—R4**

Winning the Bishop, who cannot move on account of R—Kt8 mate. After 36. B—KB3, R×B; 37. B×P ch, K—B1; 38. R—B1 ch, K—K1; 39. B—B6 ch, K—K2; 40. R×R,

Q×P ch, White resigned. Botvinnik could have forced a mate in seven moves with 35. P—B6! but probably he did not have enough time left to analyse this variation.

An exciting game, rich in material for the student of chess-strategic laws. He will observe how badly a chain of Pawns, locked on squares of one colour, may need the Bishop of the other colour to stem an attack in which the adversary's Bishop of that colour co-operates; he will appreciate how the gain of a Pawn on the Queen's wing may tie up forces which should be readily available for the defence of the King; and he will note how a weakness, produced by a Pawn-move on the King's wing, can make itself felt throughout the middle-game. The adversary will finally be able to lodge a man on the spot which the Pawn no longer protects, and the danger is ever present that the file on which this weak spot is located will be opened for the opposing Rooks.

Modern masters have introduced a number of interesting innovations in the French Defence. In reply to 1. P—K4, P—K3; 2. P—Q4, P—Q4; 3. **Kt—Q2**, a move recommended by Tarrasch with the idea of permitting the support of the centre by P—QB3 without the necessity of moving the Knight again, the continuation 3. .... **Kt—KB3; 4. P—K5, KKt—Q2; 5. B—Q3, P—QB4; 6. P—QB3, P—QKt3!** has been tried, with the object of exchanging the more or less useless Queen's Bishop for White's powerful King's Bishop through B—R3.

In a game I played against Hector Rossetto at Mar del Plata, 1949, I prevented the exchange of the Bishops at the cost of a Pawn: 7. **Q—K2!, Kt—QB3; 8. QKt—B3!!** (Diagram 186).

8. KKt—B3 would not have been feasible, because after P×P; 9. P×P

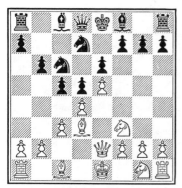

Diagram 186

QKt—Kt5 I could not have moved my Bishop without permitting either B—R3 or Kt—B7 ch.

The game continued: 8. ..... P×P; 9. B—QKt5!, Q—B2; 10. Kt×P!, QKt×P; 11. P—KB4, Kt—B5; 12. KKt—B3, B—K2; 13. Castles, with a strong initiative for White which seems to be well worth a Pawn.

Another interesting try against 3. Kt—Q2 is Kt—QB3 before advancing the Queen's Bishop's Pawn, with the intention of rapidly concentrating all fire on White's King's Pawn as soon as it advances to K5. An example of this method of play is the opening chosen by Carlos Guimard in Game No. 6, page 171.

GAME No. 4

White	Black
A. Gipslis	V. Kortchnoi

Played in the U.S.S.R. Championship Tournament at Moscow, 1963

1. P—K4	P—QB4
2. Kt—KB3	P—Q3
3. P—Q4	P × P
4. Kt × P	Kt—KB3
5. Kt—QB3	P—QR3

This and the next two moves characterize the 'Najdorf Variation' of the Sicilian Defence. It gives Black a more flexible game than either the 'Dragon Variation' mentioned on page 116 or the 'Paulsen Defence' described on page 117, but to a player who believes that general principles of strategy must be valid in any situation which may arise on the chess board, Grandmaster Najdorf's innovation is bound to appear suspicious. The reason is that Black, with only his King's Knight developed, goes on a Pawn-hunting expedition with his Queen, removing her to distant regions, and thus provoking violent onslaughts on his King. If there is any justice up above, Black should not survive such an opening. But despite several years of intensive analysis by the world's leading masters, no conclusive evidence has been adduced so far to show that White has a forced win. As a matter of fact, Black has chalked up an impressive victory here and there, and before venturing to play this opening the ingenious young Soviet master Kortchnoi had no doubt carefully studied it and felt convinced that White does not get enough for the Pawn he sacrifices. Here is what happened:

6. B—KKt5	P—K3
7. P—B4	Q—Kt3

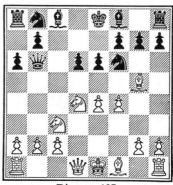

Diagram 187

In reply to 7. .... B—K2, a more solid-looking developing move, White gets a tremendous position with 8. Q—B3, followed by 9. Castles Q. If Black defends with 8. .... Q—B2 and 9. .... QKt—Q2, White can start a 'Pawn-roller' with P—KKt4, which will hardly leave Black enough elbow room for effective resistance.

Black takes the sting out of the threat 8. P—K5, by playing his Queen to Kt3, because after 8. .... P×P; 9. P×P, Q—R4! White's Bishop would be *en prise* if he took the Knight. But 8. Q—Q2 renews the threat as it defends the Bishop. The game continued:

8. Q—Q2   Q×P
9. R—QKt1   Q—R6

and here Master Gipslis surprised Kortchnoi with a new move:

10. P—B5!?

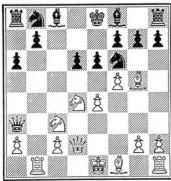

Diagram 188

More logical appears P—K5, which dislodges the only piece Black has developed and increases the likelihood that a direct assault on the black King will be successful. After 10. .... P×P; 11. P×P, KKt—Q2; 12. B—QB4, B—K2; 13. B×P, a sacrifice suggested by the great Soviet master Paul Keres, White's attacking force is so vastly superior to Black's defensive resources that it is surprising how difficult it has been to evolve a line which unquestionably demolishes Black's game. Bobby Fischer defeated the Hungarian master Istvan Bilek in a hair-raising game played at Stockholm in 1962. He continued with 13. .... Castles; 14. Castles, B×B; 15, Q×B, P—R3, and Bilek did not find the right reply. He played 16. Q—R4 instead of Q—R5, against which a satisfactory defence has not yet been discovered.

Most likely Kortchnoi had expected this line and worked out a continuation he considered satisfactory. In the position of Diagram 188 he played

10. ......   Kt—B3
11. P×P   P×P
12. Kt×Kt   P×Kt
13. P—K5!

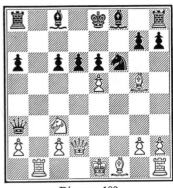

Diagram 189

White sacrifices a second Pawn in order to make the square K4 accessible to his Knight and to bring his Queen's Rook over to the King's wing via QKt3: a finely conceived plan, the danger of which Kortchnoi under-estimates. He should have countered it with Kt—Q2, or, perhaps better still, with Kt—Q4, when 14. Kt×Kt, BP×Kt; 15. P—B4, P×BP; 16. B×P, P—Q4; 17. B—K2, B—B4 would seem to get Black out of trouble, and the sacrifice 17. B×P, P×B; 18. Q×P would fail against B—Kt5 ch.

13.	P×P
14. B×Kt	P×B
15. Kt—K4	B—K2
16. B—K2	Castles
17. R—Kt3	Q—R5
18. P—B4!	

Another fine move. It seals the Queen off from the King's wing and continues to leave Black exposed to a combined onslaught of White's pieces. An exciting situation.

18.	K—R1
19. Castles	R—R2
20. Q—R6	P—KB4

Here Black might have escaped after all through 20. .... Q—R4; 21. Kt×P, Q—B4 ch; 22. K—R1, B×Kt; 23. R×B, R—KKt2; 24. R×R ch, Q×R, though 25. R—Kt8 would still have posed a serious problem for him to solve.

21. R—Kt3	B—Kt5
22. Kt—B6	

Black resigned. The threat is Q×R ch, followed by R—Kt8 mate. QR—KB2 does not help, as 23. Q—Kt5 would force mate in two moves.

GAME No. 5

White	Black
EDWARD LASKER	N. ROSSOLIMO

Played in the International Masters' Tournament of Havana, 1952

1. P—K4	P—QB4
2. Kt—KB3	P—Q3
3. P—Q4	P×P
4. Kt×P	Kt—KB3
5. Kt—QB3	P—QR3
6. P—B4	Q—B2

More aggressive, and probably stronger, is 6. .... P—K4, occupying the centre rather than preventing

White's advance to it. After 7. Kt—B3, QKt—Q2; 8. B—Q3, B—K2, followed by Castles, P—QKt4, and B—Kt2, Black secures a satisfactory development. Grandmaster Rossolimo plans the same deployment of his minor pieces, but prefers to keep his King's Pawn at K3, contesting White's control of the white centre squares (Q5 and KB5).

7. B—Q3	QKt—Q2
8. Kt—B3	P—K3
9. Castles	P—QKt4
10. Q—K1	B—Kt2
11. K—R1	

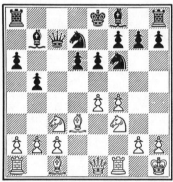

Diagram 190

There was no need to avoid a check in the open diagonal at this point. Simply P—QR3 was indicated, in order to prevent the dislodging of my Knight through P—Kt5.

11.	Kt—B4

Again P—QR3 was the right continuation. I tried to force the opening of the King's file at the cost of my King's Pawn, but the wild procedure I undertook for the purpose was hardly justified by a pronounced superiority of development.

12. P—K5!?	KKt—Q2
13. P—B5	Kt×P
14. Kt×Kt	P×Kt
15. P×P	Kt×P

16. **B—B5**	**Kt—Q5**
17. **B—K4**	**P—B3**

Black had to protect his King's Pawn, which I threatened to win by exchanging Bishops. He could not have defended the Pawn with the natural-looking move B—Q3 because of 18. Kt—Q5!, in answer to which his Queen had no satisfactory flight square: Q—B3 would have failed against Kt—B6 ch. On any other white square she would have been attacked with Kt—Kt6, and Kt×R would then have won the exchange. This left only Q—Q1 or Q—Kt1, as Q—B4 would have been answered by P—QKt4. 18. .... B×Kt, of course, would have permitted the double attack on the Rook and the Bishop's Pawn and lost the game very quickly. On 18. .... Q—Q1, finally, 19. P—B3, Kt—K3; 20. Kt—B6 ch would again have won the exchange, as after 20. .... P×Kt; 21. B×B Black could prevent the murderous Bishop check on his B3 only with R—QB1. But Black's 17th move dispelled all these nice dreams. It actually consolidated Black's extra Pawn and I realized that unless I could get my Queen's Bishop and Queen's Rook into action before Black completed his development, I had little chance to hold my game together. My first thought was 18. B—K3, followed by Q—B2 if he played B—B4. Then, to my delight, I noticed that if he should neglect to develop his Bishop for the sake of winning a second Pawn, with B×B and Kt×BP, he could even get into trouble. A surprise combination offered itself, which I hoped he would not see. This is indeed what developed:

18. **B—K3**	**B×B**
19. **Kt×B**	**Kt×P**
20. **R—B1!**	

In reply to Q—Kt2 I was of course going to play 21. Kt×P ch before capturing the Knight, while Q—B5 would have been met by 21. Q—R4

(Q—K7; 22. Kt×P ch, P×Kt; 23. Q×P, Kt×B?; 24. Q×P ch, etc.).

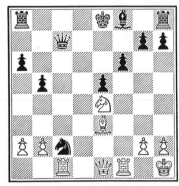

Diagram 191

20.	**Kt×Q**
21. **R×Q**	**Kt—Q6**

The only move, and now the surprise I had prepared gives me at least a draw:

22. **R×BP!!**	**P×R**
23. **Kt×P ch**	**K—Q1**
24. **B—Kt6**	**B—B4?**

With R—QKt1 Rossolimo could have forced me to draw with perpetual check on Kt7 and B7. As happens so frequently, trying to win at all costs, he gets a lost game. He remains with two pieces against Rook and two passed Pawns, one on each wing, and the ensuing ending shows how inferior the minor pieces are apt to be in such a situation.

25. **R—Q7 ch**	**K—B1**
26. **R—B7 ch**	

Perhaps he goes to Kt1! One should probably not set such traps for a grandmaster. But gaining two moves against the timing clock is a good excuse.

26.	**K—Q1**
27. **R×RP ch**	**B×B**
28. **R×R ch**	**K—K2**
29. **R×R**	**Kt—B7 ch!**
30. **K—Kt1**	**Kt—Kt5 ch**

31. K—B1	Kt×Kt
32. R×P	B—Q5
33. R—R5	P—Kt5
34. R—Kt5	Kt—Kt5
35. R×KtP	Kt×P ch
36. K—K2	K—Q3
37. P—R4	Kt—Kt5
38. P—R5	Kt—K6
39. P—R6	Kt—Q4
40. R—R4	B—R2
41. K—B3	Kt—B2
42. K—K4	Kt—K3
43. P—QKt4	Kt—B5
44. P—Kt4	Kt—Q4

A devilish Knight. I realized that I had to give my Rook more scope.

45. R—R3!	Kt×P
46. P—Kt5	K—K3
47. R—R3	B—B5
48. R—R6 ch	K—B2
49. K×P	K—Kt2
50. K—B5	Kt—Q4
51. R—K6	K—B1
52. R—K5	Kt—K2 ch
53. K—K6	

R×Kt would not have won the game, because by the time my King could reach KR7 Black's King would have got to QB2, holding my Rook's Pawn. Then the Bishop could sacrifice himself for my Knight's Pawn.

53.	B—Kt8
54. R—QKt5	Kt—B3
55. K—B6	B—Q5 ch
56. K—Kt6	K—Kt1
57. R—Kt7	Kt—K4 ch
58. K—R6	Kt—B3

He can't play Kt—B2 ch, because I would capture the Knight and after K—R7 one of my Pawns would queen.

59. R—QB7	Kt—R2
60. R—Q7	B—K6
61. K—Kt6	K—B1
62. R—B7 ch	

Black resigned, as K—K1; 63. R×Kt or K—Kt1; 63. R—Q7, B—B4; 64. R—Q8 ch, B—B1; R—R8 would be unanswerable.

GAME No. 6

White	Black
EDWARD LASKER	CARLOS GUIMARD

Played in the Mar del Plata Masters' Tournament, 1949

1. P—K4	P—K3
2. P—Q4	P—Q4
3. Kt—Q2	

If Black replies Kt—KB3, the continuation might be 4. P—K5, KKt—Q2; 5. P—QB3, P—QB4; 6. B—Q3, Kt—QB3; 7. Kt—K2, Q—Kt3; 8. Kt—B3.

3.	Kt—QB3
4. Kt—B3	KKt—B3
5. P—K5	Kt—Q2
6. Kt—Kt3	

A feasible alternative is B—K5, so as to be ready to remove Black's Knight when this becomes necessary to maintain the King's Pawn on K5.

6.	P—B3
7. B—QKt5	P—QR3

Forcing the exchange of the Bishop for the Knight and at the same time bringing another Pawn toward the centre for the attack of White's Pawn-skeleton. However, it soon becomes evident that it would have been better first to develop the King's wing, a course our general strategic principles would suggest as most natural.

8. B×Kt	P×B
9. Castles	P×P

If he wanted to forestall 10. P×P and 11. R—K1, he might have done so with 9. .... P—KB4, although 10. B—Kt5 would then have forced the exchange of his best Bishop. But the idea of the opening is the removal of both of White's centre-Pawns, if possible. The best move was therefore probably 9. .... B—K2. The continuation 10. Kt—R5, compelling the retreat Kt—Kt1, was not to be feared, as Black could soon play P—QB4 and thus free his Knight again.

10. P × P   B—K2

No doubt, Black had in mind the continuation just mentioned, in reply to either 11. Kt—R5 or 11. QKt—Q4, and did not seriously consider the move KKt—Q4 which leaves the King's Pawn unprotected. However, White regains the Pawn immediately with a vastly superior game.

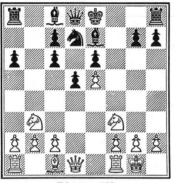

Diagram 192

11. KKt—Q4!!   Kt × P

The retreat to Kt1 would now be very dangerous, as White's Queen stands ready to attack on the King's wing: 11. .... Kt—Kt1; 12. Q—Kt4, Castles; 13. B—R6, R—B2; 14. P—KB4, followed by P—B5.

12. R—K1   Kt—Kt3

He cannot defend the Knight with the Bishop, as R × Kt would win two pieces for the Rook with the Queen-check on R5. 12. .... Q—Q3 would lose a whole piece after 13. B—B4.

13. Kt × BP!   Q—Q3
14. Kt × B   Q × Kt
15. B—K3

The threat B—B5, which prevents Black from castling, practically decides the game.

15. ......   K—B2
16. B—B5   Q—Kt4
17. R—K3   R—Q1
18. R—Kt3   Q—B3

Inviting 19. R—KB3, Kt—B5; 20.

P—Kt3, which would lose because of P—K4; 21. P × Kt, B—Kt5, which wins the Rook.

19. B—K3!

Now, however, R—Kt3 is actually threatened, and Black hasn't time to withdraw his King in view of the second threat, B—Kt5.

19. ......   Q—K4
20. Kt—Q4   Q—Q3

Defending the threat Kt—B6 and threatening in turn to free himself with P—K4.

21. Q—R5   K—Kt1
22. Kt—B3! (Diagram 193)

This prevents P—K4 and gains the square K5 for the Knight. 22. .... P—K4 would be met with 23. Kt—Kt5, Kt—B1; 24. Q—B7 ch, K—R1; 25. Kt × P, winning a piece. 23. .... P—R3; 24. Kt—K4, P × Kt; 25. R × Kt, followed by 26. B × P, also would win easily.

22. ......   R—Q2

Guarding the square KB2. But White now wins the exchange:

23. R—R3   Kt—B1
24. Kt—K5

The Rook has no move. R—K2 would be answered by 25. P—QKt4!!,

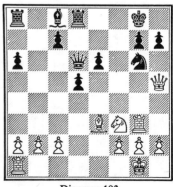

Diagram 193

threatening 26. B—B5, and 25. . . . .
Q×P would fail due to 26. Kt—B6.

24. . . . . . .   P—B4

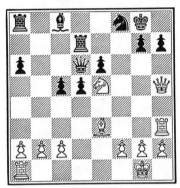

Diagram 194

25. P—QKt4!

This forces access to the square
Q4, from which the Bishop joins the
attack. Black cannot reply P—Q5,
as 26. P×P, Q×P; 27. Kt×R would
win a Pawn in addition to the
exchange. For example: 27. . . . .
Q—B6; 28. B×P, Q×B; 29. R—
Q1, followed by Kt×Kt and Q×P.

25. . . . . . .   P×P
26. Kt×R

Originally I had planned to play
B—Q4 immediately. This would
have led to a beautiful finish if Black
had replied R—K2; 26. B—Q4, R—
K2; 27. Kt—Kt6!!, P×Kt; 28. Q—
R8 ch, K—B2; 29. R—B3 ch, K—
K1; 30. R×Kt ch, etc., or 27. . . . .
Kt×Kt; 28. Q×P ch, K—B2; 29.
Q×P ch, K—K1; 30. Q×Kt ch,
K—Q2; 31. B—B6, etc. But I did
not have enough time to look into
25. . . . . R—QKt2, and apparently
there is no forced win in answer to
that move.

26. . . . . . .   B×Kt
27. B—Q4   R—B1
28. R—K1!   B—K1
He could not play R×P, because
29. R—Kt3 would have followed,

and after Kt—Kt3; 30. R×Kt!,
P×R; 31. Q×KtP, threatening mate
and attacking the Rook, there was
no square for the Rook where it
could defend the mate.

29. Q—K2   B—Kt3
30. P—QB3   P—QR4
31. R—Kt3   R—B5
32. Q—Kt2   Kt—Q2
Black has secured considerable
counter-play. He threatens P—K4
as well as Kt—B4—Q6. Neither 33.
Q—K2 nor R (Kt3)—K3 would prevent the advance of the King's Pawn,
because Black would win the Queen's
Bishop's Pawn in return for it. His
Bishop and the passed Pawn would
then be equivalent to White's Rook.

Under the circumstances, White's
best plan was perhaps 33. P×P,
R×P; 34. Q—R3!, or 33. . . . . P—
K4; 34. B—B5, Kt×B; 35. P×Kt,
R×P; 36. Q—Kt7, followed by R—
Kt3. The actual continuation (Dia-
gram 195) is not without risk.

33. P—B4!?   P×P?
This is what I had hoped for.
Guimard had considered only the
reply 34. B×P, whereupon he would
have obtained even winning chances
with Q—B4 ch; 35. K—R1, P—Q5;
36. Q—Kt7, P×B, etc. Had he seen
that I could recapture with the Rook,
the Bishop being immune because of

Diagram 195

the check on B8, he would have played 33. .... Kt—B4! I would have had nothing better than 34. P×P, Kt—Q6; 35. R×Kt, B×R; 36. P×P (R—B7; 37. Q—Kt6, or 36. .... Q×P; 37. B—K5, Q—B1); a draw was probably unavoidable against best defence.

34.	R×P!	Kt—B4
35.	B—K5	Q—Q1
36.	R×R	P×R
37.	Q—Q4	Q—Q4!

Black's passed Pawn still remains dangerous.

38.	B×P	Kt—Q6
39.	R—Kt1	Q×Q
40.	B×Q	Kt×P
41.	R—Kt8 ch	K—B2
42.	K—B2	Kt—Q6 ch

White's problem is now whether to try holding the Queen's Rook's Pawn and queening it after capturing Black's, or whether to rely on his King's side Pawns finally to force the win. Black's advanced passed Pawn can be kept from queening as the white Bishop controls the colour of the queening square and the Rook can get in back of the Pawn, at the same time keeping Black's King from advancing in the centre. On the other hand, the Knight is a tricky piece in endings of this type and must be watched most carefully. If the King goes to Kt3, the Knight

Diagram 196

can move to B8, attacking the Rook's Pawn and threatening to win the Bishop with the check on K7. This would force the Rook to withdraw to Kt2 instead of playing offensively.

Again, in reply to 43. K—K3, Black wins the Rook's Pawn through Kt—Kt5, because of the simultaneous threat to win the Bishop with Kt—B7 ch. 43. K—K2 would lose the Pawn immediately through Kt—B8 ch, and so 43. K—B3 seems best, which offers Black no opportunities for dangerous double attacks. However, the continuation Kt—Kt5; 44. P—QR3, Kt—Q4, which threatened the advance of the Pawn, did not appear to me very desirable, and so I played:

43.	K—K3	Kt—Kt5
44.	B—B3	Kt×P
45.	R—Kt7 ch	K—K1
46.	B×P	P—B6
47.	R—QB7	P—B7
48.	B—Q2	

Now the Pawn is stopped, the Knight is immobile, and while my Rook and Bishop are partly tied up by the necessity of guarding the square QB1, they remain effective in aiding the advance of the King's side Pawns. For this reason, the ending is indeed won for White.

48.	......	K—Q1
49.	R—B4	K—K2
50.	P—Kt4	K—B3
51.	P—R4	

Threatening P—R5 and R×P.

| 51. | ...... | P—R4 |
| 52. | P—Kt5 ch | |

52. P×P, which did not seem clear to me, would have won without trouble, because after B—B4; 53. R—B7, P—K4; 54. P—R6, B—Kt3; 55. P—R5, B—B4; 56. P—R7, B×P; 57. R×B, P—B8 (Q); 58. B×Q, Kt×B; 59. R—QB7, the Pawn cannot be stopped.

| 53. | ...... | K—K4 |

54. **R—B5 ch!**   **K—Q3**
55. **K—Q4!**
The decisive manœuvre, but—

55. ......   **P—B8 (Q)**
56. **B×Q**   **P—K4 ch**

Diagram 197

57. **K—B4???**
A terrible blunder due to one of those strange cases of complete blindness which befall a player once in a while after hours of concentrated thought. I saw that 57. R×P, Kt×B; 58. R—Kt5 would keep the Knight in captivity, because B—B2 would fail due to 59. P—Kt6!, B—Kt1; 60. R—Kt8 and 61. P—Kt7. But before following up this line in detail, I fell victim of the hallucination that the move of the text, after Kt×B; 58. K—Kt5, would win either the Knight or the Bishop, since 59. R×Kt as well as R—B6 ch was threatened. An awful blow awoke me from my trance:

57. ......   **Kt×B**
58. **K—Kt5**   **B—K1 ch!**
This saves the piece, and the passed King's Pawn then decides the issue. Love's labour lost!

In the position of the Diagram, the continuation 57. R×P, Kt×B; 58. R—Kt5 would indeed have won the game without difficulty. The Bishop had no move to prevent the passed

Pawn from queening. For example: 58. .... B—K1; 59. P—Kt6, K—K2; 60. R—K5 ch, K—B1; 61. P—Kt ch, etc. Or: 58. .... B—B2; 59. P—Kt6, B—K3. 60. P—Kt7, K—K2; 61. R—K5, followed by R×B. Neither could black have saved the game by trying for an ending with the Knight against the Rook: 58. R—Kt5, Kt—K7 ch; 59. K—K3, Kt—Kt6; 60. R—Kt6 ch, K—K4; 61. R×B, Kt—B4 ch; 62. K—B2, Kt×P; 63. R—KB6!, followed by R—B8 and P—Kt6, etc.

GAME No. 7

White	Black
MIKHAIL	MIKHAIL
TAHL	BOTVINNIK

4th match game for the World Championship, played in 1961 at Moscow

1. **P—K4**   **P—QB3**
2. **P—Q4**   **P—Q4**
3. **P—K5**   **P—QB4**
As mentioned on page 113, the customary continuation is 3. .... B—B4. If White likes risky play, he can force the Bishop back with 4. P—KKt4. For Black to answer B—Kt3 would be dangerous because 5. P—KR4, P—KR3; 6. Kt—KR3, followed by Kt—B4, or even the sacrifice, 4. P—K6, P×P; 5. Kt—KR3—B4, would give White good attacking chances.

In reply to 4. .... B—Q2 the continuation might be 5. P—QB3, P—K3; 6. B—Q3, P—QB4; 7. Q—K2, Kt—QB3; 8. B—K3, Q—Kt3; 9. P×P, etc., with an even game.

It is interesting to note that Botvinnik does not hesitate losing a tempo by taking two moves to advance his Pawn to QB4. No doubt he reasoned that White's King's Pawn has also made two moves without advancing the development of his pieces.

4. P × P   P—K3

In the French Defence this position can also come about, but with Black to move.

5. Kt—QB3   Kt—QB3

The Bishop's Pawn does not run away. In reply to 5. .... B × P, White might have played 6. Q—Kt4, but this would not have won a Pawn: 6. .... Kt—K2; 7. Q × KtP, Kt—Kt3; 8. Kt—B3, B—B1; 9. Q—B6, B—K2; 10. Q—Kt7, B—K2, drawing by repetition of moves, or 8. Q—B6, Q × Q; 9. P × Q, Kt—Q2, regaining the Pawn (10. B—QKt5, B—Q5; 11. B—Kt5, P—KR3, etc.).

6. B—KB4   KKt—K2

It is difficult to see why Botvinnik did not take the Pawn at this moment. 7. Q—Kt4, KKt—K2; 8. Q—KtP? would then have failed, because Kt—Kt3 would have threatened to win the Bishop with B—B1, followed by the exchange of Queens, and after 9. B—Kt3 the same continuation would have left White with a very bad end-game prospect. Black could play B—QKt5 and double White's Bishop's Pawn, creating an ideal target for his Rooks. In short, Tahl's strategy would, in this case, have clearly miscarried.

7. Kt—B3   Kt—Kt3
8. B—K3

B—Kt3 would have given White practically no counterplay whatever. Holding the Bishop Pawn at least keeps Black's King's Bishop inactive for a while and opens up possibilities for aggressive action on the Queen's wing.

8.	QKt × P
9. Kt × Kt	Kt × Kt
10. Q—R5	Kt—B3
11. Castles	B—K2
12. P—B4	P—KKt3
13. Q—R6	B—B1
14. Q—Kt5	Q × Q
15. P × Q	

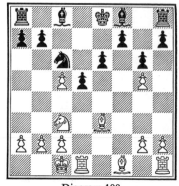

Diagram 198

Black has succeeded in getting a passed Pawn, but how to get him on his way is a problem. White threatens Kt—Kt5—B7 ch—Rook. Black could meet this threat with B—Q2 and R—B1, which in turn would threaten to drive White's Knight back with P—R3, followed by B—Kt2 and Kt—K2. This would protect his Queen's Pawn and permit the King's Pawn to advance. However, meanwhile White would have had time to take counter-measures. These would naturally be directed against the swarm of black Pawns in the centre of the board. Botvinnik very likely pondered the probable consequences of 15. .... B—Q2; 16. Kt—Kt5, R—B1; 17. P—B4! He may have concluded that neither 17. .... P × P; 18. Kt—Q6 ch, B × Kt; 19. R × B nor 17. .... P—QR3; 18. P × P, Kt—Kt5; 19. Kt—B3, B × P; 20. B × B, R × B; 21. K—Kt1, Kt × P; 22. Kt—K4 would give him as much of an advantage as the positional sacrifice of the exchange on which he now embarks and which is indeed beautifully conceived.

15.	P—QR3
16. Kt—R4	B—Q2
17. B—KB4	P—R3!

The subtle point of Black's combination. If White takes the Pawn, his Bishop is pinned after Black recaptures. But he needs the Bishop to win the exchange with Kt—Kt6 and B—B7. Thus he must give up his Knight's Pawn, and with two Bishops and a Pawn against Rook and Knight Black has winning chances due to his great Pawn majority on the King's side. White can obtain counterchances only if he succeeds in opening files for his Rooks. This explains the strategy which he employs from here on.

18.	Kt—Kt6	R—Q1
19.	B—B7	P × P
20.	P—B4	P—Q5
21.	P—QKt4!	B—Kt2

Black can't take the Pawn, for B × R followed by R × P would win a piece. He cannot defend his Queen's Pawn with P—K4 either, as P—Kt5 would drive his Knight away and then B × P, which attacks his King's Rook, would lead to the loss of both of his centre Pawns and still give White time to return with his Bishop to B7 and win the exchange.

22.	B × R	K × B
23.	P—Kt5	Kt—Kt1
24.	B—K2	P—B4
25.	B—B3	

He could not protect his Knight's Pawn first with P—QR4, because Black would have shut off his Bishop with P—K4—K5. Even so, it looks as if he had accomplished his purpose. He gets an open line for his Rooks and a passed Pawn, which offers him counterchances if Black defends his Pawn with B—B1. For in this case White would maintain his Bishop in the long diagonal with P—KR3, and then play K—Q2 to clear the way for the Rooks to the Queen's wing. However, Botvinnik finds a much stronger continuation.

25.	......	P × P!
26.	P × P	B × P
27.	B × P	K—B2!

Diagram 199

All of a sudden White is in mortal danger. If the Bishop goes into the corner, Kt—R3 wins the Bishop's Pawn, White's last hope. His only move would be 29. P—QR4, and after 29. .... Kt × P; 30. P × B, K × Kt; 31. B—B6 the avalanche of black Pawns would bury him.

The same continuation would finish White if in the diagram he withdrew the Bishop to B3, while 28. .... P—Kt5; 29. Kt—R8 ch, K—Q1; 30. B—Kt7 would still give White a few opportunities for 'swindling'.

28. P—QR4!

Evidently Tahl, famed for his ingenious combinations, felt that the complication introduced by this move was more likely to provoke an error than the retreat of the Bishop. Possibly Botvinnik was short of time, or—equally possible—Tahl failed to see the refutation of this move, just as Botvinnik did. Time pressure can induce 'chess-blindness' in the greatest masters.

28.	......	B × P?

B—QR3 was the correct move! If White exchanges Bishops, the all-important Bishop's Pawn falls. And if he plays 29. B—R8, either directly or after 29. B—B3, P—Kt5, then B—KB1! wins the Bishop Pawn, as

R × P would lose a piece. After the move of the text, White retains his Bishop's Pawn and K—Q2 permits both of his Rooks to take part in the attack on the King.

29. Kt × B	K × B
30. K—Q2	Kt—Q2
31. R—Kt1 ch	K—B3
32. KR—QB1	B—K4
33. K—Q3	R—R1

I presume that Botvinnik saw the combination beginning with 34. R—Kt6 which Tahl was threatening. He could not have made it on the preceding move, because Black would have answered K—B2. This threatened B—B5 ch, winning the exchange, as well as Kt × R. One of the points of Tahl's brilliant combination is that when Black captures the Rook, permitting the discovered check 35. P × Kt, the continuation K—Kt2 would be bad, because on 36. Kt—B5 ch the King could not capture the Pawn, in view of 37. Kt—Q7 ch, winning the Bishop. To avoid this contingency, Botvinnik would certainly have thought of answering 33. K—Q3 with B—B5 and after 34. R—B2 continuing with R—Q1! if, with another seven moves to complete before time control, he had not been badly pressed. His terrible threat, Kt—K4 ch, could not have been defended. In reply to his move R—R1, Tahl forces a draw in beautiful style:

34. R—Kt6 ch!	Kt × R
35. P × Kt ch	K—Q2

Not K—Kt4, because 36. R—Kt1 ch would not permit K × Kt (R—R1 ch), and K—R3 would lead to mate in three moves: 37. Kt—B5 ch, 38. K—B4! and R—Kt5 mate.

36. Kt—B5 ch	K—K2
37. R—K1!	R—R6 ch
38. K—B4	R—B6 ch
39. K—Kt5	R—K6

40. R—QR1	B × P
41. R—R7 ch	Drawn

The King can't go to B3, as R—KR7! would attack the Bishop, and at the same time threaten mate with the Knight on Q7. K—Q3 would also lose, because of 42. R—Q7 ch, K—K4; 43. R—KR7!, B—B5; 44. P—Kt7, K—Q4; 45. R—Q7 ch, and the Pawn queens.

But after 41. .... K—K1 White has only a perpetual check: 42. R—KR7, B—B5; 43. Kt—Q7, P—Q6; 44. Kt—B6 ch, Black must go to B1, allowing Kt—Q7 ch, etc., for 44. .... K—Q1 would be answered with P—Kt7 and R—Q7 mate!

What a magnificent game!

GAME No. 8

The position of Diagram 200 was reached after the opening moves 1. P—QB4, Kt—KB3; 2. P—Q4, P—KKt3; 3. Kt—QB3, B—Kt2; 4. P—K4, P—Q3; 5. P—B4, Castles; 6. Kt—B3.

With this advance of the four Pawns Alekhine had obtained winning games in the same tournament against Marshall and Yates. I was convinced, however, that something must be wrong with this opening. The advance of White's King's Bishop's Pawn before castling frequently enables Black to exert pressure in the diagonal QR2—KKt8 with his Queen or Bishop. Besides, opening a game with four Pawn-moves and only one move with a piece violates one of the most important principles of opening-strategy. As I said in the introduction to the chapter on general strategic principles, White can sometimes afford to lose one move during the development stage because he is one move ahead from the start. But in such a case, Black has the right to expect that he will find a way to assume the initiative. In the present

Black: EDWARD LASKER

White: ALEXANDRE ALEKHINE

From a game played in the New York International Tournament, 1924

Diagram 200

position this initiative would naturally be directed against White's Queen's Pawn, because Black's King's Bishop is poised for attack on that Pawn. The two moves to be considered here are therefore P—B4 and P—K4. Subsequent analysis has shown that P—B4, the move with which Black equalizes the game in almost all Queen's Pawn openings, is the best in this case also. If 7. P×P, Q—R4; 8. B—Q2, Q×BP, Black's Queen is commandingly posted, White has difficulties in castling on the King's side, and the open Queen's Bishop's file gives Black the advantage in case White castles on the Queen's side. If 7. P—Q5, Black again obtains pressure in the diagonal QR2—KKt8 through P—K3; 8. B—Q3, P×P; 9. BP×P, Q—Kt3; 10. B—B2, P—B5!

In reply to 6. .... P—K4 White can accept the proffered sacrifice with 7. QP×P, P×P; 8. Kt×P without getting into serious trouble, though Kt—Kt5 poses no easy problem for him.

I played P—K4, because I felt

certain that Alekhine would play 7. BP×P and 8. P—Q5, in view of the success he had had against Yates in a previous round with this strategy which contemplates attacking on the Queen's wing. However, Yates had provoked the advance P—Q5 with Kt—QB3, and as a result he had lost two moves with his Knight. I felt that the provocation of P—Q5, which would relinquish the pressure from my K4 and QB4 and make the latter a strong point for me, would be favourable for me if I did not have to lose time in turn. P—Q5 certainly means loss of time from the point of view of development, as it not only does nothing to increase the mobility of a white piece but adds to Black's mobility by permitting a black Knight to settle on QB4.

The Pawns on QB4 and Q5 secure more territory for White on the Queen's wing, but Black, with his centre-Pawn relieved of pressure, will sooner or later find an opportunity for counteraction on the King's wing (P—KB4).

6. ......   **P—K4**
7. **BP×P**   **P×P**

White cannot continue with 8. Kt×P, because P—QB4 would undermine his centre completely. 9. P—Q5 would be answered with Kt×KP!

8. **P—Q5**   **QKt—Q2**

It is important to prevent White from advancing his Queen's Bishop's Pawn, because he would obtain a great territorial advantage with that advance.

9. **B—Q3**

White cannot attempt preventing Black from occupying QB4 with his Knight by 9. B—K3, because Kt—Kt5 and P—KB4 would follow, with a very strong attack.

9. ......   **Kt—B4**
10. **B—B2**

All play in the early middle-game centres around White's attempt to dislodge the black Knight from B4, and Black's counter-measures. If White had played 10. P—QKt4 immediately, his contemplated attack would have been weakened considerably. Black, after exchanging on Q6, would retain possession of two Bishops and be able to undermine

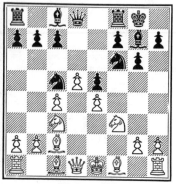

Diagram 201

White's control of QB5 with P—QR4 or even P—QB4 (12. P×P, Q—R4, followed by Kt—Q2).

10. ...... **P—QR4**
Indispensable in order to maintain the Knight on QB4.

11. Castles **Q—Q3**
Possibly Kt—R4 or Kt—Kt5 was here the strongest continuation.

12. Q—K1
Kt—QKt5 would be meaningless on account of Q—K2. The move of the text increases the mobility of White's Queen.

12. ...... **B—Q2**
13. Q—R4 **QR—K1**
Completing the development of the pieces and incidentally defending the square K2, so that after 14. B—Kt5 the Knight can go to R4. 15. P—KKt4, Kt—B5; 16. B×Kt, P×B; 17. P—K5 would then be bad for White because Black would reply Q—Kt3 (not B×P?; 18. Kt—KKt5!).

14. K—R1
14. B—R6, Kt—R4; 15. B×B, K×B would have been in Black's favour because the exchange of the Bishops would have weakened White's KB4 and enabled Black to settle his Knight there. The natural continuation for White is P—QKt3, in order to follow this up with P—QR3 and P—QKt4. He could not play P—QR3 without first posting his Knight's Pawn on Kt3, for otherwise Black would prevent the advance of the Knight's Pawn altogether with P—R5. White's King's move is timely in any case, for if 14. P—QKt3, he could not play P—QR3 without first moving his King away from Kt1, as Black would reply Kt×KtP and regain the piece with Q—Kt3 ch.

14. ...... **P—KR4**
Preparing Kt—R2 and P—KB4. But Kt—R4 would have saved a

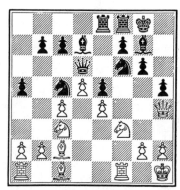

Diagram 202

move and avoided weakening the King's position. 15. P—KKt4 could have been met with either Kt—B5 or Kt—B3. If White exchanges the Knight on his B4, the increased mobility of Black's King's Bishop and Queen's Rook is liable to get White into difficulties. 16. P—Kt5, in reply to Kt—B3, would have simplified Black's problem in opening the King's Bishop's file. The Knight would have gone back to R4 and then P—KB3 would have followed. The move of the text presents White with an extremely valuable tempo, and he would have obtained the superior game had he not gone astray later.

15. P—QKt3	Kt—R2
16. P—QR3	P—B4
17. P—QKt4	Kt—R3

Both Alekhine and myself overlooked that he could satisfactorily protect his Knight's Pawn with 18. R—QKt1. I could not have captured twice on Kt5 because of B—R3. Alekhine felt that now or never was his chance to advance to B5, in view of the counter-action I was threatening on the King's wing. He spent fully fifty-five minutes on his next move, trying to explore all variations entailed in the complicated combination by which he thought to gain his objective on the Queen's side. As happens so often when one works hard to produce 'something out of nothing', he overlooked a simple rejoinder which refutes his combination.

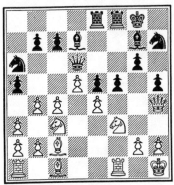

Diagram 203

18. P—B5   Q—KB3

Forcing the exchange of Queens, which is not at all desirable for White as it brings Black's Knight back into play. 19. B—Kt5 cannot be played because Kt×B; 20. Kt×Kt would be followed by B—R3.

| 19. Q×Q | Kt×Q |
| 20. P—B6 | |

The point of White's wrong combination. R—QKt1 still would have been best, though he would have lost the Queen's Pawn through P×KP; 21. B×P, Kt×B; 22. Kt×Kt, B—B4; 23. R—K1, R—Q1, etc.

20.	KtP×P
21. QP×P	B×P!
22. P—Kt5	Kt×P!

This counter-combination secures a winning position.

23. Kt×Kt

He cannot play B×Kt, as P×B; 24. Kt—Q2, P—K6; 25. R×R ch, R×R; 26. Kt—B3, P—K5 would win without difficulty.

23. ......   P×Kt??

With this hasty move I threw the win away. B×P would have left

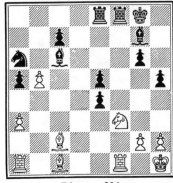

Diagram 204

White with a hopeless position. He could not play 24. Kt (K4)—Q2, because B×R and P—K5 would have followed, winning at' least the exchange. Neither would 24. R—K1 have helped, because after P×Kt; 25. B×P, Kt—B4; 26. B—Q5 ch, K—R1; 27. Kt—Kt5, P—K5; 28. QR—Kt1, B—Q6 or Kt—Q6, winning easily.

24. P×B   P×Kt

Now the weakening effect of the move P—KR4 is apparent. White could probably equalize with 25. B×P, P×P ch; 26. K×P, R×R; 27. K×R, R—KB1 ch; 28. K—K2, R—B3; 29. B×P, R×P when the possession of two Bishops makes up for the Pawn minus. We were both short of time after figuring through the overdose of wild combinations which had to be made practically 'a tempo'.

25. B—K4   P×P ch?

MORE ON THE POWER OF TWO BISHOPS

Much stronger would have been Kt—B4, with a view to pushing the King's Pawn in case White took the Knight's Pawn. After 26. B—Q5 ch, K—R2; 27. B—K3, Kt—K3; 28. B—K4, P×P ch; 29. K×P, B—R3, Black would have had good winning chances.

26. K×P   R×R
27. K×R   K—R2
Here Kt—B4 was obligatory, to get the Knight into play. Now White keeps the Knight shut in and obtains excellent counter-play.

28. B—K3   B—B1
29. R—Q1!
With Black's two minor pieces on the Queen's wing, the attack with the Rook and the two Bishops against the King is bound to be very dangerous. Note how White's Bishops dominate the whole board.

29. ......   B×P
Rather than defending with B—Q3, which would have been answered by 30. R—Q5 and probably have given White a won ending, I submitted to the terrible check on the seventh rank and created a threat of my own on the Queen's Rook's file.

30. R—Q5

Alekhine just barely completed his thirty moves within the time limit. His last move is not the best, because it forces me to unblock my passed Pawn. White's idea was to deprive my Knight of the square Kt5.

30. ......   B—Kt5
In this position the game was adjourned. I remember that Capablanca asked me during the dinner intermission whether I was not lost, and that he was surprised when I expressed my confidence that I could at least draw.

31. R—Q7 ch   K—R1!
The only move. R—K2 was not playable on account of 32. B—Kt5! R—Kt2; 33. B—B6, etc. And on 31. .... K—Kt1 White had 32. B—R6!, with the threat B—Q5 ch and B—Kt7 ch, etc.

32. B—Kt5   R—B1 ch

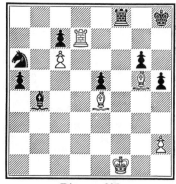

Diagram 205

Defending the mating threat 33. B—B6 ch, 34. B—Q5 ch, etc.

33. K—K2   P—QR5
At last my counter-threat comes to life. Against 34. B—R6 I planned the sacrifice R—KKt1; 35. B—Q5, P—R6!; 36. B×R, K×B; 37. B—B1, P—R7; 38. B—Kt2, B—Q3,

which would have left me with three Pawns for the exchange.

34. B×P   Kt—B4

Not P—R6, because 35. B—R6, P—R7; 36. B—Kt7 ch and 37. B×KP would win.

35. R—K7

He should have played R×P, Kt—K3; 36. R—R7 ch, K—Kt1; 37. B—K3. Then I would have had to draw with Kt—B5 ch, etc. As it is, I am obtaining new winning chances.

35. ......   P—R6!
36. R×BP

If B—R6 instead, I had planned Kt—K3!

36. ......   Kt—K3
37. R—R7 ch   K—Kt1
38. B—B1   P—R7??

Alekhine had 1½ minutes and I had 2½ minutes left to complete the 45th move, and we played in 'rapid transit' style. The last move, which loses the best Pawn without compensation, is a terrible blunder after which the game is drawn. Kt—Q5 ch and Kt×P was the simplest way to win. Against R—R1 White could have defended himself with 39. R—QKt7, P—R7; 40. B—B7 ch, K—R1; 41. B—Kt2.

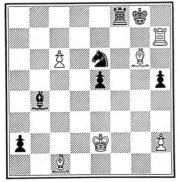

Diagram 206

39. R—QR7   Kt—Q5 ch
40. K—Q3   R—B6 ch
41. K—K4   R—B8
42. B—Kt2   Kt×P
43. R×P   R—B5 ch
44. K—K3   B—B4 ch
45. K—K2   R—B7 ch

Looking over the position after the mad rush of the last seven moves seemed to reveal a slight winning chance for me. White's Bishop is pinned, and I win another Pawn.

46. K—K1   R×P

Perhaps I should have taken the piece for my two Pawns with Kt—Kt5; 47. R—R5, B—Kt3; 48. R×P, R×B; 49. R×P. With the white King tied to the first rank, there was the possibility of mating combinations with my three pieces, commencing with Kt—R7—B6.

As it is, true to the form of the whole game, another wild combination leads to a forced draw.

47. B—K4   Kt—Q5
48. B×Kt   B—Kt5 ch
49. K—B1   R×R
50. B—Q5 ch   K—B1
51. B×R   P×B

and due to the fact that my Bishop is not of the colour of the queening square of my Rook's Pawn, White can sacrifice his Bishop for my Queen's Pawn and block my Rook's Pawn with the King.

In this game the advance of White's Pawns on the Queen's side, led by P—Q5, was particularly dangerous for Black, because due to the preceding exchange of White's King's Bishop's Pawn for Black's King's Pawn Black had no Pawn on Q3 and the advancing white Pawns formed a majority which promised to yield a passed Pawn.

MORE ON P—Q5

Even when no Pawn-exchange has taken place at the time White plays P—Q5, so that White's advance does not threaten to result in a passed

Pawn, the Pawn on Q5, by dint of the fact that it prevents Black from advancing his Queen's Pawn to Q4, often gives White a strong initiative. Black is relegated to defensive manœuvres, unless he can remove the basis K4 of White's Pawn-centre with P—KB4 in such a way that White does not gain control of his K4 with one of his pieces. This is why the advance of Black's Pawn to KB4, unless supported by a Pawn on KKt3 as in the game just discussed, is of doubtful value in positions in which White has his King's Bishop so placed that it supports K4.

The next example furnishes an instructive illustration of this point.

Black: RICHARD RETI

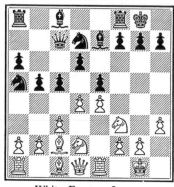

White: EDWARD LASKER

From a game played in the New York International Tournament, 1924

Diagram 207

GAME No. 9

The position of Diagram 207 was brought about by the opening moves 1. P—K4, P—K4; 2. Kt—KB3, Kt—QB3; 3. B—Kt5, P—QR3; 4. B—R4, Kt—B3; 5. Castles, B—K2; 6. R—K1, P—QKt4; 7. B—Kt3, P—Q3; 8. P—B3, Castles; 9. P—KR3, Kt—QR4; 10. B—B2, P—B4; 11. P—Q4, Q—B2; 12. QKt—Q2, Kt—Q2. (Diagram 207)

Black evidently plans to concentrate his efforts on the Queen's wing. He does not fear that in the absence of his King's Knight White will be able to work up a dangerous King's side attack, probably because White's King's Bishop, usually one of the important links in such an attack, is blocked.

13. P—Q5

With the intention to follow this up in the customary manner by Kt—B1, P—KKt4, Kt—Kt3 or K3 and Kt—B5. This is a typical case in which Black should *not* advance his King's Bishop's Pawn. White could not wish for anything better than to have the square K4 available for his

Knight or Bishop or Rook. Strange to say, Reti does make the advance, obviously motivated by the conviction that my Pawn on Q5 is weak and will be lost. But his plan is not a very promising one. As soon as the Pawn on Q5 disappears, Black's Queen's Pawn becomes a target for White's Rooks. Black could have very well continued with Kt—Kt3, Kt—Kt2, P—QR4, P—QKt5, etc., expanding on the Queen's wing and finally opening a file there for his Rooks.

13.	P—B4
14. P×P	Kt—Kt3
15. Kt—K4	

P—KKt4, B—Kt2; 16. Kt—K4 was equally strong. The game almost plays itself.

| 15. ...... | B×P |
| 16. QKt—Kt5 | |

This forces the exchange of the Bishop and a weakening Pawn-move to defend the King's Rook's Pawn.

16.	Q—Q2
17. P—KKt4!	B×B
18. Q×B	P—Kt3

19. Q—K4

Even the Queen has occasion to enjoy the square K4.

19. ......   B×Kt

Probably in order to clear the second rank for defence of KR2, and also to reduce White's attacking forces.

20. Kt×B   Q—QKt2

No doubt Reti expected that I would defend the Pawn with R—Q1, whereupon he could prevent Kt—K6, at least temporarily, with R—B3. But in view of the fact that Black's Knights are tucked away on the Queen's wing, I felt that I should attack on the King's wing with everything I had. For this purpose the move P—KB4 seemed ideally suited. Black had opened the King's file for my Rook, and so his King's Pawn should offer a good target. Naturally, this move had to be carefully calculated, as Black had a variety of alternatives to choose from. In answer to P×P; 22. B×P, QR—K1, I planned to play 23. Q×R, R×Q; 24. R×R ch, K—Kt2; 25. B×P, Kt×P; 26. R—KB1, which would have given me a winning attack. If 21. .... QR—K1, I was going to advance the Pawn to B5. Then Q×P; 23. P×P, Q×Q; 24. Kt×Q, P×P; 25. Kt×QP would have left Black with a very inferior end-game. If 22. .... P×P, White would win through 23. P×P, Q×P; 24. Q—KKt4, K—R1; 25. Kt×RP!, K×Kt; 26. Q—Kt6 ch, K—R1; 27. Q—R6 ch, K—Kt1; 28. K—R2, K—B2; 29. B—Kt5. Reti chose the best continuation (Diagram 208):

21. P—KB4   Q×P
22. P×P   QR—K1

Permitting me a strong passed Pawn. But after P×P; 23. Q×Q ch, Kt×Q; 24. R×P, Kt—B5; 25. B×Kt, R×B; 26. Kt—K6, R—K1; 27. QR—K1, Kt—B5; 28. KR—K2, I would have won the Bishop's Pawn.

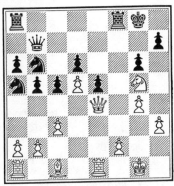

Diagram 208

23. Q×Q ch   Kt×Q
24. P—K6   R—B3

In order to prevent Kt—B7. But now the Queen's Pawn falls.

25. R—Q1   Kt—B2
26. R×P   P—R3?

The only move which prolonged the defence was R—K2. Now the exchange is lost.

27. Kt—K4!   KR×P
28. Kt—B6 ch   R×Kt
29. R×R   K—Kt2
30. R—Q6   R—K2

Two Knights are rather helpless against a Rook in endings.

31. P—Kt3

At last the Bishop gets his chance to go into action.

31. ......   P—B5
32. B—R3!   P×P
33. P×P   Kt×P
34. R—Kt1   Kt—R4
35. R×RP   Kt×R
36. B×R   Resigns.

After Kt—B3; 37. B—Q6, the Knight's Pawn also falls.

ON P—KB5

Our next two examples concern the advance to the fifth rank by the Bishop's Pawns. Quite naturally, the advance P—KB5 portends an attack on the King, while P—QB5 is usually bound up with an attempt to translate a Pawn majority into a passed Pawn.

Normally a Pawn on KB5 is supported by the King's Pawn on K4, and a Pawn on QB5 by the Queen's Pawn on Q4, and the best way to combat the advance of a Bishop's Pawn is almost always a counter-thrust against the supporting centre-Pawns. Thus, when P—KB5 has been played, the opponent will try to attack the King's Pawn with P—Q4, and against P—QB5 he will push his King's Pawn to K4, attacking the Queen's Pawn. If the counter-attack in the centre can be prevented, the advance on the wing is as a rule successful.

GAME No. 10

The following famous game is very instructive in this respect. After the opening moves 1. P—K4, P—K4; 2. Kt—KB3, Kt—QB3; 3. B—Kt5, P—QR3; 4. B×Kt, QP×B; 5. P—Q4, P×P; 6. Q×P, Q×Q; 7. Kt×Q, B—Q3; 8. Kt—QB3, Kt—K2; 9. Castles, Castles; 10. P—B4, R—K1; 11. Kt—Kt3, P—B3 (Diagram 209). Lasker played 12. P—B5, a move few masters would have dared to make, because it creates a backward Pawn on K4. Unless White can decide the game by an attack on the King, he is sure to run into an endgame in which Black has a pronounced advantage due to the pressure he can exert in the open King's file. Evidently Lasker felt certain that he would obtain an overwhelming attack because his Pawn move deprives Black's Queen's Bishop and Knight of almost all mobility. The only black piece the mobility of which is increased by White's Pawn-advance is the King's Bishop. But White plans

Black: José R. Capablanca

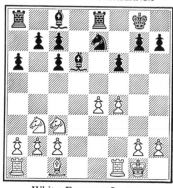

White: Emanuel Lasker

From a game played in the St. Petersburg Tournament, 1914

Diagram 209

to exchange this Bishop immediately. The game proceeded as follows:

12. P—B5   P—QKt3

Black prepares an attack on White's King's Pawn with as many pieces as he can muster for the purpose.

13. B—B4   B—Kt2?

He should have exchanged Bishops and then played P—B4, to keep White's Knight from reaching K6 via Q4. As he plays it, White makes the exchange and thereby creates a weak Pawn on Black's Q3. An interesting example of doubled Pawns becoming weak by getting straightened out.

14. B×B	P×B
15. Kt—Q4	QR—Q1
16. Kt—K6	R—Q2
17. QR—Q1	Kt—B1

He cannot free his game with P—Q4, because 18. R—B2—Q2 would win a Pawn. White doubles his Rooks in the open file in any case, thus forcing Black's Knight to remain at B1. Then he takes precautions to prevent Black from driving his

Queen's Knight away with P—Kt4—Kt5, as this Knight is necessary to protect the only weakness in White's camp, the Pawn on K4. Only after all these preparations have been made does White proceed to storm forward on the King's wing. His superior mobility ensures the success of the operation.

| 18. R—B2 | P—QKt4 |
| 19. KR—Q2 | QR—K2 |

If P—Kt5, White wins the Queen's Pawn through Kt—R4, P—QKt3, Kt—Kt2 and Kt—B4. Black's last move threatens P—B4, which, with the Rook on Q2, would not have been possible on account of 20. Kt×BP. White now prevents P—B4 again, so as to keep Black's Bishop shut in.

| 20. P—QKt4! | K—B2 |

It looks as if Capablanca has made up his mind to sacrifice a Rook for Knight and Pawn in order to escape slow strangulation.

21. P—QR3

White is not in a hurry to start the King's side push. Sooner or later he will have to protect his Pawn at QKt4 in any case, as Black will surely take the first opportunity to play P—QR4.

| 21. ...... | B—R1 |

Preparing the opening of the Queen's Rook's file and its occupation with the Rook. White, however, need take no measures against this manœuvre, as there are no promising invasion-points for Black on the Rook's file. Sacrificing the exchange with R×Kt would have been the only chance for Black to break White's strangle-hold. After protecting the Queen's Pawn with King and Rook, he could then have played the Knight to QB5 or K4. He would probably have lost in the end all the same, but at least he would have gone down fighting.

| 22. K—B2 | R—R2 |

| 23. P—Kt4 | P—R3 |
| 24. R—Q3 |

Diagram 210

Now both of White's Rooks have easy access to the King's wing.

24.	P—QR4
25. P—KR4	P×P
26. P×P	R (2)—K2

Black realizes that there is no future for the Rook on the Queen's Rook's file.

| 27. K—B3 | R—KKt1 |
| 28. K—B4 | P—Kt3 |

A vain attempt at gaining an open file for his Rook. White proceeds unhurriedly but inexorably with his plan.

| 29. R—Kt3 | P—Kt4 ch |
| 30. K—B3! |

An instructive illustration of a fight for an open file. If White captured the Pawn, Black would recapture with check and then occupy the Rook's file. Capturing White's Pawn now would be of no avail. White would regain the Pawn with R—R3 and then win the Pawn on R6 to boot, after doubling Rooks in the Rook's file.

| 30. ...... | Kt—Kt3! |

At last the Knight has a chance to move. It would not do for White to capture the Queen's Pawn, as Kt—B5 and Kt—K4 ch would follow, winning White's King's Knight's Pawn after P×RP.

31. P×P	RP×P
32. R—R3	

White has accomplished his aim. He is in control of the file he has opened, and he threatens to enter the seventh rank with deadly effect. Black can no longer permit R×P, because Kt—B5 would then be answered with R—R7 ch and R—Q8 mate.

32.	R—Q2
33. K—Kt3	

Diagram 211

Preparing a beautiful combination. White wants to sacrifice his King's Pawn in order to gain the square K4 for his Knight, and he does not want to be disturbed by the discovered check P—B4 with which Black could get his Bishop into play.

33.	B—Kt2
34. R (1)—KR1	K—K1
35. P—K5!	

The *coup de grâce*. If Black takes with the Bishop's Pawn, 36. Kt—K4, Kt—Q4; 37. P—B6 decides within a few moves.

35.	QP×P
36. Kt—K4!	Kt—Q4

37. Kt (6)—B5	B—B1

He cannot move the Rook, because Kt×B and Kt—Q6 ch would win a Rook.

38. Kt×R	B×Kt
39. R—R7	

The invasion of the seventh rank. There is no defence.

39.	R—B1
40. R—R1	K—Q1
41. R—R8 ch	B—B1
42. Kt—B5	

and Black resigns, as the mate threatened with Kt—Kt7 ch and R×B can only be defended by Kt—K2, whereupon Kt—K6 ch followed by Kt×R and R—R8 ch leaves White with a whole Rook ahead.

One of the noteworthy features of this game is the masterly fashion in which Lasker manœuvres with his Knights. He utilizes them in the centre of the board, where their mobility is greatest and where they threaten in the direction of both wings. Capablanca's Bishop was almost useless because its mobility remained insignificant throughout the game. Due to this lack of mobility Capablanca had no opportunity whatever for effective counter-action, and Lasker could leisurely prepare the assault on the King's wing.

GAME No. 11

White	Black
FRIDRICK OLAFSSON	ROBERT FISCHER

Played in the Interzonal Tournament at Zürich in 1959

1. P—QB4	Kt—KB3
2. Kt—QB3	P—KKt3
3. P—Q4	B—Kt2
4. P—K4	P—Q3
5. Kt—B3	Castles

6. **B—K2**   **P—K4**
7. **P—Q5**

Most modern masters prefer this continuation to the alternative method of meeting the King's Indian Defence with the developing moves, Castles and R—K1, which gives Black the option of exchanging his centre Pawn and affords him more counterplay than he gets after the text move. The advance of the Queen's Pawn reduces Black's living space on the Queen's wing, but there are also arguments against it—mainly that White's chain of white-squared Pawns frequently reduces his King's Bishop to inactivity. Also, with all pressure removed from Black's centre Pawn, he can often obtain good attacking chances on the King's wing by pushing his King's Bishop's Pawn.

7. ......   **QKt—Q2**

This Knight is sometimes developed to R3, so that he can either be played to B4 or—after P—QB4—go to B2 to support the advance, P—QR3 and P—QKt4.

8. **B—Kt5**

The object of this move, which Petrosian introduced, is to hold back the advance of Black's Bishop Pawn and, if the opportunity presents itself, to castle on the Queen's side and storm Black's King's position with the Pawns on his King's wing.

8. ......   **P—KR3**
9. **B—R4**   **P—R3**

Black plans Q—K1, so as to have his Queen ready for action on the King's wing. His move keeps White's Knight from attacking his Bishop's Pawn with Kt—Kt5 after he is no longer defended.

10. **Kt—Q2**

Preparing P—KKt4

10. ......   **Q—K1**
11. **P—KKt4**   **Kt—R2**
12. **Q—B2**

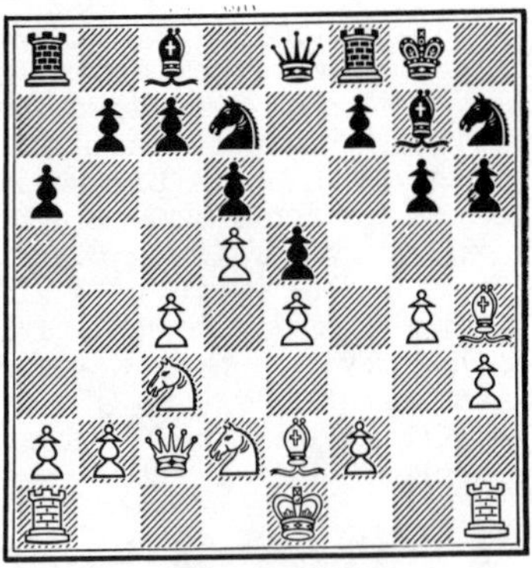

Diagram 212

As White wants to castle on the Queen's side and attack with his Pawns on the King's side, and as Black evidently plans Kt—Kt4, Olafsson might have gained a move for his attack by first playing B—Kt3, so that he could answer Kt—Kt4 with P—KR4.

12. ......   **Kt—Kt4**

Now Fischer threatens Kt—R6—B5. Rather than preventing this passively with P—R3, Olafsson should probably have exchanged pieces on Kt5, and then castled and opened the King's Rook's file with P—KR4.

13. **P—KR3**   **Kt—B4**
14. **Castles Q**

With the centre of the board sealed off, castling was no urgent matter. P—Kt4, followed by Kt—Kt3 and P—B5, would have given White superior operating space on the Queen's wing. Also, B×Kt was still the best way of assuring an open file for the Rooks when opportune. After Kt—Kt3 White could play K—Q2, connecting his Rooks for immediate co-operation on whatever side of the board the disposition of Black's men made this desirable.

14. ......   **B—Q2**
15. **P—B3**   **Kt—R5!**

White's dilatory tactics have given Black an opportunity for aggression. His objective is naturally the advance of the King's Bishop's Pawn, in order to open a file for his Rooks. He proceeds with admirable logic. First he exchanges White's Queen's Knight. This reduces the solidity of White's K4, as well as his fighting force on the Queen's wing. Then he expands his territory there with P—QB4 and P—QKt4, and finally breaks through on the King's Bishop's file.

| 16. Kt × Kt | B × Kt |
| 17. P—Kt3 | B—Q2 |

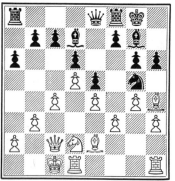

Diagram 213

Here White had his last chance to play B × Kt and open the Rook's file with P—KR4. He might then have continued with Kt—B1—K3. Black's plans of a breakthrough would have been met in that manner much more effectively than by the continuation he actually chooses.

18. B—B2	P—QB4!
19. P—KR4	Kt—R2
20. B—K3	P—QKt4

Black's attack gets going on both wings.

| 21. Kt—Kt1 | P—B4 |
| 22. KtP × P? | |

A serious error. White could expect an opportunity for counterplay only by taking with the King's Pawn and answering P × P with 23. P—Kt5. Then 23. .... P × P; 24. P × P, P—B5 was not possible, on account of Q × Kt ch, and 23. .... P—B5 immediately could have been countered by 24. P × P, B × P; 25. QR—Kt1 ch, K—R1; 26. Q—Kt6!

22.	KKtP × P
23. KP × P	B × P
24. Q—Q2	P—K5
25. QR—Kt1	

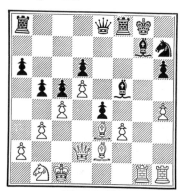

Diagram 214

The crisis is at hand. Olafsson did after all get some counterplay. He threatens not only B × P, but also R × B ch, followed by B × P.

| 25. ...... | KP × P |
| 26. B × RP | |

But here he spoils his chance again. I suspect that this was again one of those desperate races against time in which so many tournament players get involved between the 25th and 40th moves. The ingenious young Icelander could not otherwise have overlooked that he could win a clear tempo by first playing R × B ch and then taking the Bishop's Pawn, likewise with check, in that way regaining the exchange immediately. At the end of this forced exchange he could then have captured the dangerous King's Pawn, which now becomes his downfall.

26.	R—R2!
27. B×B	R×B
28. R×R ch	K×R
29. B—Q3	P×P
30. K—Kt1 ch	K—R1
31. Q—B3 ch	Q—K4
32. Q×Q ch	P×Q

Whether there is anything at all that can be done against these two connected passed Pawns is highly doubtful.

33. B×B	R×B
34. P×P	Kt—B3
35. Kt—Q2	P—B7
36. R—R1	P—K5
37. K—Q1	P—K6

and White resigned the hopeless struggle a few moves later.

The thing to learn from this game is that when countering the King's Indian set-up with P—Q5 White should not delay playing for territorial gain on the Queen's wing. There lie his prospects for successful action.

A King's Indian variation in which this strategic idea is accentuated is the so-called *Saemisch* system, in which White plays P—B3 on the 5th move instead of Kt—KB3. After 5. ...., Castles, he proceeds with 6. B—Kt5, as in the game just discussed. Then, on P—KR3, the Bishop returns to K3, and in reply to P—K4 the push P—Q5 produces a situation in which White can immediately run his King's Rook's Pawn up to R5 if Black prepares the advance of the King's Bishop's Pawn with Kt—R2, the way Fischer did against Olafsson. With the Rook's file opened, White obtains good attacking prospects.

GAME No. 12

The following game is an instructive example showing how a few slight inaccuracies can sufficiently weaken an even game to make it practically untenable.

The diagrammed position arose after the moves 1. P—Q4, P—Q4; 2. P—QB4, P—K3; 3. Kt—KB3, Kt—KB3; 4. Kt—B3, B—K2; 5. P—K3, Castles; 6. B—Q3, P×P; 7. B×BP, P—B4; 8. Castles, P—QR3; 9. Q—K2, P—QKt4; 10. B—Q3.

Black: EMANUEL LASKER

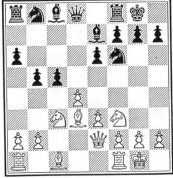

White: REUBEN FINE

From a game played in the Nottingham International Tournament, 1936

Diagram 215

WEAKNESS OF ADVANCED WING-PAWNS

Here Lasker played B—Kt2. More accurate would have been QKt—Q2. After 11. P×P, he could then recapture with the Knight, gaining a developing tempo, as White would have to retreat with his Bishop rather than bringing a new piece into play, unless he was satisfied to give up a Bishop for a Knight. This was most unlikely.

10.	B—Kt2
11. P×P	B×P
12. P—K4	QKt—Q2
13. B—Kt5	P—R3
14. B—R4	P—Kt5

This weakens the Pawn-position and retards the development of the Queen's Rook until it is no longer needed to protect the Queen's Rook's

Pawn. Fine does nothing but complete his development as fast as possible and automatically obtains the better position.

15. Kt—R4	B—K2
16. KR—Q1	Kt—R4
17. B×B	Q×B
18. QR—B1	

White is ready to invade the seventh rank, and Black can prevent this only by moving his Queen's Knight, since he cannot oppose Rooks in the open file as long as his Rook's Pawn is twice attacked. No doubt Lasker first examined the obvious move Kt—B5 which exchanges the useless Knight for a powerful Bishop and removes one of the pieces attacking his Rook's Pawn. Perhaps

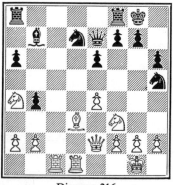

Diagram 216

he did not like the line Kt—B5; 19. Q—K3, Kt×B; 20. R—B7. But after B—B3!; 21. R×B, QKt—K4; 22. Kt×Kt, Kt×Kt; 23. R—B5, KR—Q1, Black had nothing to fear.

| 18. ...... | QKt—B3? |

This third inaccuracy is sufficient to lose the game against the clear, methodical manner in which Fine takes advantage of the awkward position of Black's Knights.

| 19. P—KKt3 | P—R4 |

20. Kt—B5	KR—B1
21. Kt×B	Q×Kt
22. Kt—K5	R×R

The decisive error. He should have kept the Rook to support his Rook's Pawn and played P—Kt4 to be able to move his Knights to the other wing.

| 23. R×R | R—QB1 |

The exchanges would bring the salvation which Black seeks, if the Queen's side Pawns were not so vulnerable. To make matters worse, the black Knight is too far away to reach the Queen's wing for defence.

| 24. R×R ch | Q×R |
| 25. Q—B2! | |

Simplicity itself. If Q×Q; 26. B×Q, Black cannot defend the threat Kt—B6 with P—R5. After 27. P—B3, White remains with a passed Pawn whose march Black cannot halt.

25.	Q—Kt2
26. Q—B6	Q—R2
27. Q—B8 ch	K—R2
28. Kt—B6	Q—B4?

There is no satisfactory defence. The move of the text loses a whole piece. This could have been avoided by Q—Q2, but 29. Q×Q, Kt×Q; 30. Kt×RP, etc., would have left Black again with the hopeless ending alluded to above.

| 29. P—K5 dis ch | P—Kt3 |
| 30. P×Kt | |

and Black resigned after a few more moves.

DANGERS OF SYMMETRY

While discussing the Four Knights Opening, I pointed to the danger which Black runs when imitating White's moves. White is justified in assuming that in symmetrical positions the advantage of the first move will tell sooner or later. But if he tries prematurely to build up threats just because the opponent cannot imitate them without getting a lost game, White is the one who is apt to suffer from the break of the symmetry, rather than Black.

That this may happen even to a player of Grand Mastership calibre is seen in the following game in which Eliskases, playing 'Arturito' Pomar, attempted too soon to profit from the birthright of the first move.

GAME No. 13

Diagram 212 shows the position brought about by the following twelve moves, which it took Eliskases about an hour to conceive, while Pomar, trusting the wisdom of his renowned adversary's thoughts, consumed only seven minutes.

1. Kt—KB3, Kt—KB3; 2. P—KKt3, P—KKt3; 3. B—Kt2, B—Kt2; 4. Castles, Castles; 5. P—Q3, P—Q3; 6. P—K4, P—K4; 7. QKt—Q2, QKt—Q2; 8. Kt—B4, Kt—B4; 9. Kt—K3, Kt—K3; 10. P—B3, P—B3; 11. K—R1, K—R1; 12. Kt—Kt1, Kt—Kt1.

Black: ARTURO POMAR

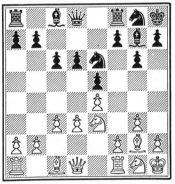

White: ERICH ELISKASES

Played in the International Masters' Tournament of Mar del Plata, 1949

Diagram 217

| 13. Kt—K2 | P—KB4 |

Pomar serves notice that he is ready to go his own way if opportunity beckons.

14. P × P	P × P
15. P—KB4	Kt—K2
16. B—R3	

This threatens to win the Bishop's Pawn after exchanging on K5, and Black cannot imitate the manœuvre with 16. .... P × P; 17. P × P, B—R3, because 18. Kt—Kt3, Kt—Kt3; 19. Kt (K3) × P, Kt (K3) × P; 20. Kt × B, Kt × B; 21. Kt—B7 ch would win the exchange.

However, Tarrasch's maxim, that it is dangerous to win a Pawn before completing the development of the pieces, is still valid to-day. It takes Eliskases three moves to win the Pawn, and meanwhile Pomar gets his Queen's Bishop into play in the long diagonal which White's last move has left unguarded. This gives him such a strong initiative that it takes all of Eliskases's skill to survive.

16.	P × P
17. P × P	P—QKt3!
18. Kt—Kt3	B—Kt2
19. Q—R5	P—B4 ch
20. K—Kt1	R—B3
21. Kt(K3) × P	Kt × Kt
22. B × Kt	

If White had taken with the Knight instead, Black would have replied Q—KKt1!.

| 22. ...... | R—R3 |
| 23. Q—K2 | B—Q5 ch!! |

An ingenious sacrifice which crowns Pomar's masterly positional play. White cannot refuse the gift, because after 24. B—K3, B × B ch; 25. Q × B, Q—R5; 26. Q—K2, R—KKt1; 27. B—K4, Kt × P; 28. R × Kt, R × Kt ch; 29. P × R, Q × P ch; 30. Q—Kt2, Q × R, Black would be a Pawn ahead, in addition to his superior position. 31. B × B, of course, could not be played, as R—KKt3 would follow.

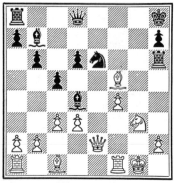

Diagram 218

24. P×B	Kt×QP
25. Q—KB2!	

An invitation to trade three pieces for the Queen with Kt—B6 ch; 26. Q×Kt, etc., of which Pomar naturally does not avail himself. Eliskases avoids the trap 25. Q—Kt4?, Kt×B!; 26. Q×Kt, Q—R5; 27. R—B2, Q×Kt ch!

25.	Q—R5

Pomar was short of time and probably thought that this move was good enough to win so that there was no need to look any further. He might otherwise have played 25. .... Kt×B; 26. Kt×Kt, Q—Kt1 ch!; 27. Kt—Kt3, Q—Q4. Then, neither 28. B—K3 would have saved White's game, because of R—KKt1 and Q—R8, nor 28. Kt—K4, because of R—Kt1 ch; 29. K—R1, Q×Kt ch, etc.

26. R—K1	R—KKt1
27. B—Q2	R×Kt ch!
28. Q×R	Q×Q ch
29. P×Q	R—R8 ch
30. K—B2	R—R7 ch
31. K—B1	

Not K—K3?, Kt—B7 mate.

31.	R—R8 ch

In view of his time pressure, Pomar elects to draw, forgoing the promising try 31. .... Kt×B. Despite the exposed position of White's King, however, 32. R—K8 ch, K—Kt2;

33. B—K1, K—B2; 34. R—K2, Kt×P ch; 35. B×Kt, R—R8 ch; 36. K—B2, R×R; 37. B—R4 would probably have led to a draw in any case.

An exciting game, in which Pomar used up more than two hours for the ten moves beginning with 17. .... P—QKt3.

PRESSURE THROUGH TERRITORIAL ADVANTAGE

For the balance of the illustrative examples I am choosing games with openings which deviate from the standards usually shown in books, in order to point out how the general principles we have discussed indicate the proper procedure. I have tried to select games in which the middle-game and the end-game also offer a good opportunity of recapitualting what I should like the reader to understand when it comes to applying general principles, so that memorization may be restricted to the subordinate role it should play in any field of intellectual endeavour.

GAME No. 14

White	Black
EDWARD LASKER	JOSÉ R. CAPABLANCA

Played in the New York International Masters' Tournament, 1924

1. P—K4   P—KKt3

This move cannot be regarded as adequate, as it does not contest any of the centre-squares.

2. Kt—KB3

But the only way to take advantage of Black's omission on the previous move was to play P—Q4, thus accomplishing the ideal Pawn-formation in the centre. Then the development of the pieces could have been planned so as to maintain the Pawn-centre against whatever manœuvres Black might choose in attacking it. Incidentally, Black would not have very much of a choice. The only reasonable method would be the preparation of P—QB4, as P—Q4 would enable White to close the long diagonal with P—K5, thus rendering Black's first move useless.

2. ......   **B—Kt2**
3. **B—B4**

Again P—Q4 would have been much preferable. The move of the text permits Black to lead the opening into a Sicilian variation in which White's King's Bishop is best placed on K2. My idea was to avoid the method of development customary in the 'Dragon Variation' of the Sicilian and to push the King's Pawn to K5 after preparing this with P—QB3 and P—Q4.

3. ......   **P—QB4**
4. **Castles**   **Kt—QB3**

Black now tries to hold back my Queen's Pawn as long as possible. But he can do that only if he does not develop his King's Knight to B3. In case he tried to get that Knight out with P—K3 and Kt—K2, I planned P—K5, weakening Black's square Q3.

5. **P—B3**   **Q—Kt3**
6. **R—K1**

So as to enable P—Q4 in reply to Kt—B3.

6. ......   **P—Q3**
7. **B—Kt3**

Waiting for Kt—B3. But a more logical waiting move would have been P—KR3, limiting the mobility of Black's Queen's Bishop.

7. ......   **Kt—B3**

Alekhine characterized this move, with which Capablanca justified my opening strategy, as a positional error inexplicable in the world's champion. But, as usual, the player who has not sweated over the game himself does not penetrate the position as deeply as

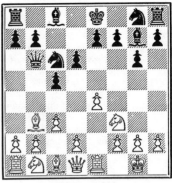

Diagram 219

the contestant himself. Capablanca studied the problem for a long time before finally deciding to permit the advance of my Queen's Pawn. No doubt he considered the alternatives suggested by Alekhine, P—K3 followed by KKt—K2, or P—K4, or B—Q2, very carefully before rejecting them. Had he played P—K3, I should have replied 8. Kt—R3, KKt—K2; 9. Kt—B4, Q—B2; 10. P—Q4, or even 9. P—Q4, P×P; 10. P×P, Kt×P; 11. Kt×Kt, B×Kt; 12. B—K3, with a dangerous advantage in development.

8. **P—Q4**   **P×P**
9. **P×P**   **Castles**
10. **P—KR3**

This move does not lose time and is as valuable as a move which brings up a new piece, because it prevents Black's Queen's Bishop from getting into play. Even B—Q2, which does not really develop Black's Bishop satisfactorily, is not very well possible, on account of 11. P—K5.

10. ......   **Kt—KR4**

Capablanca tries to obtain the advantage of two Bishops to offset his inferior development.

11. **B—K3**   **Kt—R4**
12. **Kt—B3!**   **Kt×B**
13. **P×Kt**

I permitted the exchange of this Bishop rather than that of the Queen's Bishop (12. B—B2, Kt—B5, etc.), because the opening of the Rook's file forces Black to lose another tempo and gives me time to take advantage of the bad placement of Black's Knight. The doubled Pawn is a weakness only if the game turns into an ending. I did not consider this likely to happen in view of the strong attack I was getting.

| 13. ...... | Q—Q1 |
| 14. P—K5! | |

Threatening to win the Knight through P—KKt4. Black cannot exchange Pawns and Queens and then play P—B4, because he would lose the Rook's Pawn.

| 14. ...... | P—B4 |
| 15. B—Kt5! | |

Threatening P×P as well as Kt—Q5, and compelling P—Q4 which solidifies White's centre.

| 15. ...... | P—Q4 |
| 16. Q—B1? | |

The first inexact move. The plan is to play Kt—K2 and then to attack Black's King's Pawn with Q—B5. However, since Black can drive the Queen from the Bishop's file with his Rook, the correct way to execute the plan was 16. Q—Q2, Kt—K2 and Q—Kt4.

16.	B—K3
17. Kt—K2	R—B1
18. Q—Q2	P—QR3

Although Black has gained a move he is still in a bad way. No matter how he plays, he cannot prevent the loss of a Pawn.

| 19. Q—Kt4 | Q—Q2! |

TWO BISHOPS AGAINST BISHOP
AND KNIGHT

With fine judgment Capablanca gives up the Pawn immediately, in order to produce an ending in which

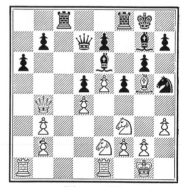

Diagram 220

his two Bishops may tell, rather than laboriously holding on to the Pawn as long as possible and making nothing but defensive moves for the purpose. After 19. .... R—QB2; 20. KR—QB1, R—K1; 21. Kt—K1 and then Kt—Q3—B5, Q—Kt6 and B—Q2—R5 Black would very likely have lost both Pawns on the Queen's wing, without any chance for counterplay.

20. Q×KP	Q×Q
21. B×Q	KR—K1
22. B—Kt4??	

Emanuel Lasker, who had already chalked this game up for me in his mind, told me afterwards he considered this move pathological, from a chess player's viewpoint, because one would do anything rather than invite a Rook to the seventh rank. Naturally, I had also considered B—B5, which my namesake said he would have moved without a moment's hesitation. But I felt that with so many of my pieces at hand I would surely catch the intruder. As a matter of fact, careful analysis seems to show that my feeling was not unjustified. In any case, B—B5 was the correct positional move. Then, if B—R3, I could have continued with 23. Kt—B3—R4—Kt6, with excellent winning chances.

| 22. ...... | R—B7 |

23. B—B3   B—R3!

My plan was, of course, to attack the Rook with my Queen's Knight. I cannot play Kt—B1 immediately, because Kt—B5, with the threat B×Kt and Kt—K7 ch, would be most annoying.

24. P—Kt3   B—Q2!

The two Bishops begin to show their teeth.

25. QR—Q1

To enable Kt—B1—Q3. But to-day, twenty-five years too late, I notice that I should have played Kt—B1 without first making the Rook's move, as the Knight also threatened to go to R2 and Kt4. The consequence might have been 25. Kt—B1, B—QKt4; 26. Kt—R2, B—K7; 27. R×B!, R×R; 28. K—B1, B—K5; 29. Kt—Kt4, R—Q1; 30. R—R5, winning the Queen's Pawn. Black's Rook on K5 has no mobility, and is therefore almost worthless unless Black finds some way of freeing it, which seems well-nigh impossible. I believe the position is untenable for Black.

25. ......   B—QKt4
26. Kt—B1   Kt—Kt2
27. Kt—KR2??

What a horrible move! I planned P—KB4 and saw too late that Black would ruin me with P—Kt4. I should have reasoned that Kt—R2 is probably wrong because it decreases the mobility of the Knight.

27. ......   Kt—K3
28. Kt—Q3

Not Kt—R2, because of P—R4!; 29. B×P, R—R1; 30. Kt—QKt4, R×KtP.

28. ......   B×Kt
29. R×B   B—B8

Both Capablanca and I had to complete our thirtieth move without

Diagram 221

much deliberation. Otherwise he would no doubt have played Kt—Kt4; 30. K—Kt2, Kt—K5; 31. R—B3, R—QB1, which also regains the Pawn but leaves Black with the Bishop of the colour of my vulnerable Queen's Pawn. And I would have answered his last move with 30. K—B1!, Kt—Kt4; 31. R—K2, R×R; 32. K×R, which would have caused Black considerable difficulties. For example: Kt×P; 33. R—Q1, B—R3; 34. Kt—B3, Kt—Kt4; 35. B—Q2!, Kt—B2; 36. B×B, Kt×B; 37. R—QB1, winning the Queen's Pawn after R—Q1; 38. Kt—Kt5!, R—Q2; 39. R—B8 ch, K—Kt2; 40. Kt—K6 ch, K—B2; 41. Kt—B5, R—K2; 42. R—Q8, etc.

30. Kt—B1?   Kt—Kt4

He does not take the Knight's Pawn, because after exchanging Bishops I would occupy the Bishop's file with the King's Rook.

31. K—Kt2   Kt—K5
32. R—B3   K—B2

Capablanca has completely outplayed me in this ending. His Rook on the seventh rank is still a thorn in my flesh. He now threatens R—QB1, and I must give my Knight for his Bishop, whereupon he remains with a powerfully posted Knight against my immobile Bishop.

33. P—KKt4

In order to break open Black's Pawn-chain and thus to obtain some counter-play against his Rook's Pawn.

33.	K—K3
34. Kt—K3	B×Kt
35. R (K)×B	R—QB1
36. K—B1	P—QKt4!

Black can no longer avoid the exchange of his Rook on the seventh rank, but if I should oppose my Rook at this moment, the consequence would be 37. R—K2, R—B8 ch; 38. R—K1, R×R ch; 39. K×R, P—Kt5!; 40. B×P, R—B7. Then my Rook was tied to the defence of the Bishop's Pawn, and despite my material plus I would probably have lost the game.

37. P×P ch	P×P
38. R—B4!	P—KR4
39. R—K2	R—B8 ch
40. R—K1	R×R ch
41. B×R	R×B8
42. R—R4	R—Kt8!
43. R×P	P—B5!

Diagram 222

'A powerful shot', as Capablanca liked to call moves of this type. The threat is P—B6, Kt—Q7 ch, etc. Hard pressed for time—I had to make two more moves before the third hour had elapsed on my clock,

and I had only a few seconds left—I made a blunder, losing my Bishop without compensation. Whether the ending could be saved is doubtful. But I could have made a strong bid with 44. R—R6 ch, K—B4; 45. P—B3, Kt—Kt6 ch; 46. K—Kt2!, R×B?; 47. R—B6 ch, K—Kt4; 48. P—R4 ch!, K—R4; 49. R×BP, Kt—B8; 50. K—B2, Kt—K6!, 51. R—B8, Kt—B7; 52. R—Q8, winning easily. The proper way for Black to play the ending after 46. K—Kt2 would have been R×P ch; 47. B—B2, K—Kt4!; 48. R×P, Kt—B4, when the superior mobility of Black's pieces would have ensured his regaining the two Pawns with the better prospects in the final stage of the game. For example: 49. R—R8, Kt—R5 ch; 50. K—B1, Kt×P; 51. R—Q8, Kt—Q7 ch; 52. K—Kt1, Kt—K5; 53. R—Kt8 ch, K—B4; 54. B—R4, R×P, etc.

44. K—K2??	P—B6 ch
45. K×P	R×B
46. R—R6 ch	K—B4
47. R×P	Kt—Kt4 ch
48. K—Kt2	Kt—K3

and I resigned after a few more moves, as my Pawns are all stopped and readily fall victims to Black's Knight and Rook. This is as fine an example as one can wish for, to demonstrate how much more the mobility of pieces is apt to count in the ending than one or two extra Pawns.

GAME No. 15

White	Black
EDWARD LASKER	FRANK MARSHALL

First game of the match for the United States Championship, played in New York, 1923

1. P—Q4	P—Q4
2. Kt—KB3	Kt—KB3
3. P—B4	P—K3

4. Kt—B3   P—B4

When this game was played, the power of Rubinstein's developing method 5. P×P; 6. P—KKt3, etc., was not yet clearly understood.

5. BP×P   KP×P
6. B×Kt5   B—K3

I was much surprised that Marshall, after considerable deliberation, should play this move, for I remembered that he had himself won a brilliant attack against this defence in the Nuernberg Tournament, 1906, when he continued with 7. P—K4 in his game with Erich Cohn. I also recalled that this opening had occurred in one of the games between Emanuel Lasker and Schlechter in their match for the World Championship in 1910, and that Lasker had chosen 7. P—K3 and told me after the game he could see no advantage in P—K4. Finally it occurred to me that Marshall probably wanted to provoke 7. P—KKt3, a move which I had played against him in a game

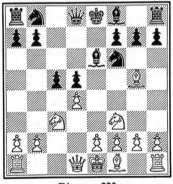

Diagram 223

in Chicago in 1917 and which is not good in this position because of P×P; 8. Kt×P, B—QB4. Then 9. Kt—Kt3 loses through B×P ch followed by Kt—Kt5 ch. Neither is 9. B—Kt2 satisfactory, as Q—Kt3 forces P—K3, a move which does not fit into the Pawn-skeleton characterized by P—KKt3. Although I had

won that game in Chicago, I knew full well that with correct play Marshall should have emerged from the opening with the superior position. For this reason I dropped my misgivings and continued with

7. P—K4   P×KP
8. B—Kt5 ch

At this point Marshall consumed fully a half an hour. I was certain that the move which he finally chose could not be good because it did not further Black's development. I had expected Kt—B3; 9. Kt—K5, Q—Kt3, with hair-raising complications.

8. ......   B—Q2?
9. B×Kt   Q×B
10. Kt×P   Q—QKt3

Now I am two moves ahead in development, and even the simple continuation 11. B×B ch, Kt×B; 12. Castles, P×P; 13. Q×P!, or 12. .... B—K2; 13. P×P, Kt×P; 14. Kt×Kt, Q×Kt; 15. R—B1 would probably win in short order. I chose the more complicated move Q—K2, because B×B ch brings another black piece into play.

11. Q—K2!   B—K2

B×B would be answered by 12. Kt—Q6 dbl ch. Driven into the Queen's file, the black King would then soon succumb to the attack.

12. P×P   Q—R4 ch

I believe it would have been better for Black to play B×B; 13. P×Q, B×Q; 14. K×B, P×P. The open Rook's file and the possession of a Bishop would have been sufficient compensation for the isolated double Pawn.

13. KKt—Q2   Castles
14. B—Q3

Black can hardly take the Pawn, because 15. Castles with the threat Kt—Kt3 or B4 would have been most troublesome.

14. ......   P—B4

Already Marshall thinks of attacking rather than attempting to regain his Pawn. But the hanging position of his King's Bishop gives me an opportunity to win a Pawn through a surprising sacrifice which he cannot accept without submitting to a terrific attack (Diagram 224).

15. Castles   R—K1

P×Kt; 16. Q×P, Q×Kt; 17. Q×P ch, K—B2; 18. Q—R5 ch, K—K3; 19. QR—Q1, etc., or 16. ....

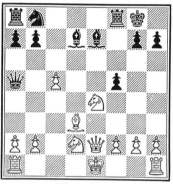

Diagram 224

B—B4; 17. Q—Q5 ch, K—R1; 18. B×B, R×B; 19. Q×R, Q×Kt??; 20. QR—Q1, etc., wins easily.

16. Kt—QKt3   Q—B2
17. Kt—Kt3?

With this bad move I almost threw away the fruits of my labours. On KKt3 the Knight is badly placed because Black can reduce its mobility to almost zero with P—KKt3. The proper move was 17. Kt—B3, in order to answer B×P with 18. Q—B2, winning the Bishop's Pawn or the Queen's Knight's Pawn. For example: Q—K4; 19. Kt×B, Q×Kt (B5); 20. Q—Kt3 ch.

17. ......   P—KKt3
18. Q—B2   B—KB3

The advantage of the two Bishops is beginning to make itself felt.

White has difficulties in contesting the activity of the black Bishop on the long diagonal in which it exerts a most disagreeable pressure on the Knight's Pawn.

19. Kt—K2   Kt—B3
20. Kt—B3

Through this roundabout way of placing the Knight on B3 I lost my advantage in development.

20. ......   Kt—Kt5

Black wants to prevent Kt—Kt5 as well as Kt—Q5. He even gives up one of his Bishops for the purpose, incidentally arriving at a position with Bishops of different colour in which the Pawn plus counts less and less as the pieces are gradually exchanged.

21. B—B4 ch   K—R1
22. Q—Q2   B—B3

QR—Q1 would seem the better move from the viewpoint of general principles, unless Black wanted to avoid the exchange of Queens which White could force with 23. Q—Q6. But the fact that Black would be ready to act with his Rooks in the centre would have been enough to win back the Pawn: Q×Q; 24. P×Q, B—B3 or R—QB1 with a good game.

23. Kt—Kt5   B×Kt
24. B×B   R—K5

Should White answer this with 25. P—B3, Black would play QR—Q1 and then move the King's Rook.

25. Q—Q6   Q—Kt2

This not only attacks the Knight's Pawn again, so that it appears impossible to avoid his loss, but it also threatens to occupy the Queen's file with the Queen's Rook, and to corner the Bishop with P—QR3. In such a situation the thing to do is to search for counter-threats, and these can usually be developed by bringing additional forces into play.

26. QR—Q1!

This develops the Rook and secures control of the open file, as R—Q1 would fail on account of 27. Q×R ch, etc. 26. .... Kt×P would be met with 27. P—B6, B×P?; 28. Q—Q8 ch!, followed by P—B7.

26. ......   **P—QR3**

In order to play Kt×P in reply to B—R4 (B—Q3?, R—Q1), whereupon P—B6 would be met with P—QKt4.

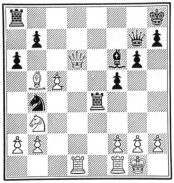

Diagram 225

27. P—B6!

Now the Bishop cannot be taken, because 28. P×P, Q×P; 29. Q×B ch, Q—Kt2; 30. Q×Q ch, K×Q; 31. P—QR3 and 32. P—B3 would leave White with an extra Pawn for which Black would have no compensation.

27.	P×P
28. B×BP	Kt×B
29. Q×Kt	Q—B1
30. R—Q2	

Thus White has succeeded in holding the Pawn, though Black has a Bishop for the Knight, which is an advantage in endings of this type, where Pawns are left on both wings. With Rooks on the board, however, which can develop their full force in the open lines on the Queen's side, White's Queen's Knight's Pawn does not have a very bright future.

30.	P—QR4
31. R—B2	

Keeping control of the Bishop's file and making room for the Knight.

31.	P—R5
32. Kt—Q2	R—K7
33. Kt—B3	R (7)—K1

One would have expected R×R; 34. Q×R, Q—B1, which promised an opportunity of invading the seventh rank. But the move of the text lays a trap. Had I made the natural-looking move 34. KR—B1, Black would have regained his Pawn through B×P!; 35. R×B?, R—QB1, etc.

34. Q—B4   R—K5

The great mobility of Black's Rooks makes it difficult for my Queen to reach an effective square without being driven away from it.

35. Q—B6	R (5)—K1
36. Q—Kt5	KR—Kt1
37. Q—K2	R—K1
38. Q—Q1	QR—Q1
39. Q—B1	

At last the Queen has reached a haven. At the same time she now supports an invasion of the seventh rank by the Rook.

39.	Q—B2
40. P—QR3	R—QKt1

Black has secured an almost ideal position for his task of keeping White's Queen's side Pawns from advancing (Diagram 226).

White must seek a way of reducing the mobility of the Bishop and of exchanging Rooks through threats in the seventh rank.

41. P—R4!

This move accomplishes several things. It provides an escape for the King and thereby relieves the Rooks from the necessity of guarding the first rank. Also, it prevents an attack which Black might initiate with P—Kt4—Kt5, etc. And finally it threatens an occasional Kt—Kt5 which

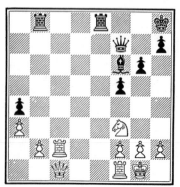

Diagram 226

might force the exchange of the Bishop.

41. ......   Q—KKt2
42. R—B7!!

Now Black cannot reply B×P; 43. Q—B5, B×P; 44. Q—R7, B—K2, because 45. R—K1, R—R1; 46. Q×R!!, R×Q; 47. KR×B, Q—R8 ch; 48. K—R2, K—Kt1; 49. Kt—K5 threatens mate within a few moves and Black has no valid reply.

42. ......   R—K2
43. R—B8 ch   R (2)—K1
44. R×KR ch   R×R
45. Q—B6   Q—B1

Effectively defending the Rook's Pawn, as Q×P would be refuted with B×P, followed by B×RP.

46. R—Kt1

If this move were made merely to defend the Pawn, it would be inexcusable. In endings, Rooks should be used aggressively rather than defensively, whenever possible. The intention of the move in the text is, of course, to advance the Knight's Pawn.

46. ......   R—K7
47. P—QKt4   P×P e.p.
48. R×P   Q—Q1
49. R—Kt1?

A miscalculation. I thought I would win the Rook if Black took

the Pawn. I overlooked that on the 53rd move Black can interpose his Rook, protected by the Queen. 49. R—Kt7 would have won in a few moves. There was no defence against the threat R—Q7. For example: B—K2; 50. R—Q7, Q—QKt1; 51. Q—B3 ch and 52. Q—B4 ch, winning the Rook. Or: 50. .... Q—KB1; 51. Kt—Kt5, threatening Kt—K6 and R×B.

49. ......   B×P
50. Kt×B   Q×Kt
51. Q—B3 ch   K—Kt1
52. R—Kt8 ch   K—B2
53. R—Kt7 ch   R—K2
54. Q—Kt3 ch   K—Kt2

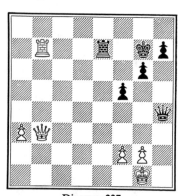

Diagram 227

THE POWER OF A DISTANT PASSED PAWN

In an ending of this type it is much more promising to play with Queen and Pawn against Queen than with Rook and Pawn against Rook, because the passed Pawn can be blocked by the Rook, whilst the Queen can clear the way in front of the Pawn by offering the exchange of Queens, protected by the Pawn. The method employed by White in attempting to force a win is typical and should therefore be carefully followed by the student.

Black must try to expose the white King to the danger of perpetual check by removing the protecting wall of Pawns in front of him. Hence, he must storm forward with his own Pawns as quickly as possible.

The following repetition of moves on my part was due to the approaching time-control at the end of sixty moves.

55. Q—B3 ch	K—B2
56. Q—Kt3 ch	K—Kt2
57. Q—B3 ch	K—B2
58. R×R ch	Q×R
59. P—R4	Q—K7
60. Q—B1	P—Kt4!
61. P—R5	

If Q×P, Black regains the Pawn with P—K8 ch and White's King is much more exposed to checks than he is now.

61.	P—B5
62. Q—KB1	Q—R7
63. Q—Kt5!	

Much better than P—R6, which Black could answer with Q—R4.

63.	K—Kt3
64. Q—Kt6 ch	K—R4
65. P—R6	P—Kt5
66. P—R7	P—Kt6

Diagram 228

In this position White need only play so as to be able to occupy KB3 with a check. Then he can queen his Pawn because in reply to Q—Kt8 ch, the Queen can interpose on B1.

67. P×P	P×P
68. Q—B5 ch	K—Kt3
69. Q—Q6 ch	K—B2
70. Q—B4 ch	K—K2
71. Q—K3 ch	K—Q2
72. K—B1!	

This threatens Q×P. Black could then not capture the passed Pawn because he would lose the Queen through Q—Kt7 ch. White would lose his Pawn with check if he took the Knight's Pawn before moving his King.

72.	Q—R3 ch
73. K—K1	K—B2

Or: Q—QB3; 74. Q—Q3, K—B1; 75. Q—B5 ch, K—Q1; 76. P—R8 (Q)!, Q×Q; 77. Q—B8 ch, etc. He could not have saved the Knight's Pawn.

74. Q×P ch	K—Q2

K—B3 would lose the Queen through P—R8 (Q) followed by Q—B3 ch. 74. .... K—Kt2 permits 75. Q—Kt8 ch, etc.

75. Q—Kt7 ch	K—B1
76. Q—Kt8 ch	Resigns.

GAME No. 16

White	Black
ALEXANDRE ALEKHINE	SAMUEL RESHEVSKY

Played in the Nottingham International Tournament, 1936

1. Kt—KB3	P—Q4
2. P—Q4	Kt—KB3
3. P—K3	

It is strange to see an enterprising player like Alekhine voluntarily assume a defensive role. The Colle System, which this and White's next move characterize, gives the first player a strong attack only against indifferent play on the part of Black. If Black draws the logical conclusion from the fact that White has unnecessarily shut in his Queen's Bishop and brings out his own, either to B4 or to Kt5, he should—and does—obtain at least an even game.

3.	**P—B4**
4. **P—B3**	**QKt—Q2**
5. **QKt—Q2**	**Q—B2**

This move has a premature appearance. Obviously Black plans P—K4, which White promptly prevents. 5. .... P—KKt3 seems best. Black's Queen should not commit herself to a post so early.

6. **Q—R4!**	**P—KKt3**
7. **P—B4**	

At first sight it looks like a waste of time to move this Pawn again; but the position of Black's Queen makes the opening of the Queen's Bishop's file desirable for White. He will regain the development tempo when Black's Queen is obliged to get out of the Bishop's file.

7.	**B—Kt2**
8. **BP×P**	**Kt×P**
9. **Q—Kt3**	

This move is adroitly refuted by Black. White could have obtained the better game with 9. P—K4, KKt—Kt3; 10. Q—B2, Q—Q3; 11. P—QR4!, threatening to win the Knight with P—R5, as played by Colle in a game against Rubinstein.

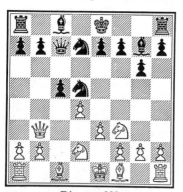

Diagram 229

9.	**KKt—Kt3**
10. **P—QR4**	**P×P!**

Now 11. P—R5 would be met with P×P; 12. P×P, Kt—B4 and KKt—Q2.

11. **P×P**	**P—QR4**
12. **B—Kt5**	**Castles**
13. **Castles**	**Kt—B3**
14. **R—K1!**	

Preventing B—K3, which would be answered by R×B! and Kt—Kt5.

14.	**B—B4**
15. **Kt—B1**	**Q—Q3**

Black has emerged from the opening with an advantage in development and White has an isolated Pawn on which Black is beginning to train his guns. But White makes the most of his compensation, the open King's file.

16. **Q—R3!**	**Q×Q**
17. **R×Q**	**Kt (B)—Q4**

This 'eternal Knight' gives Black the preferable position. To turn it into a win, however, offers a considerable problem.

18. **Kt—Kt3**	**B—Q2**
19. **R—Kt3**	**KR—Q1**

Threatening Kt×P. In turn, White attacks Black's Rook's Pawn.

20. **B—Q2**	**Kt×P**
21. **R—R1**	**Kt (5)—Kt3**
22. **R×P**	**B×B**
23. **R (3)×B**	**P—K3**

Now Kt—QB5 is threatened.

24. **P—Kt3**	**R—Q2**
25. **Kt—K4**	**R×R**
26. **B×R**	**Kt—B1**
27. **Kt—K5**	**B×Kt**

Worthy of consideration was R—K2, threatening to put White's Rook out of business with P—Kt3. With 28. B—Q8, R—K1; 29. R×P, R×B; 30. Kt×BP, R—B1, White would not have obtained sufficient compensation for the piece sacrificed. And if 28. R—B5, Kt—R2; 29. B—Q2, P—Kt 3; 30. R—B1, R—B2, etc. White remained with his weak Pawn on Q4. Apparently Reshevsky felt that after the following forced exchanges he still had enough of an advantage to justify this line of play.

28. P×B   Kt—B2!

White would have answered P—Kt3 with 29. R×Kt! Then R×R; 30. Kt—B6 ch, K—Kt2; 31. Kt×R,

Diagram 230

P×B was bound to end in a draw. 31. .... P×Kt might possibly even have resulted in an advantage for White, because in an ending with mobile Pawns on both sides of the board, the Bishop is usually stronger than the Knight.

29. Kt—B6 ch	K—Kt2
30. Kt×R	Kt×R
31. B—Q2	Kt—K2
32. K—B1	Kt—Q5
33. P—QKt4	Kt—Q4
34. Kt—B5	P—QKt4

TWO KNIGHTS AGAINST BISHOP AND KNIGHT

Due to his centralized Knights, Black has the better of it. White's King has difficulties in approaching.

35. Kt—Q3   P—B3!

Reshevsky plays the ending with admirable accuracy. Both 36. P×P ch and P—B4 would have left White

with plenty of difficulties on his hands. After 36. P×P ch, K×P Black threatened to dislodge White's Knight with P—K4—5. For example: 38. P—B3, K—B4; 39. P—Kt4 ch (otherwise P—R4), K—K3; 40. K—B2, Kt—KB3 and K—Q4. If 36. P—B4, Black's King marches to the Queen's side and gains access to Q4 and QB5. The white Pawn on Kt4 is then likely to fall sooner or later: P—B4; 37. K—B2, K—B2; 38. B—K3, Kt—B7; 39. B—B5, Kt—B6!; 40. B—Q6, Kt—K5 ch; 41. K—K2, K—K1; 42. B—B5, K—Q2; 43. K—Q1, Kt—R6, followed by K—B3 and K—Q4.

Diagram 231

36. B—B1

A wrong combination. But, as said before, it is dubious whether White could have held the game, in view of the greater mobility of Black's King and White's weakness on white squares.

36.	P×P
37. Kt×P	Kt—B7

Alekhine had expected Kt×P, when 38. B—K2, Kt (Q)—B7; 39. K—K2 and 40. K—Q2 would have rendered Black's Knights immobile, turning the ending in White's favour in spite of the Pawn minus.

38. B—Kt2   Kt (7)×P

39. K—K2   K—Kt1

K—B1 would have been answered by 40. Kt—B3!, threatening Kt—K5 as well as Kt—Q4.

40. P—Kt3

White has excellent drawing chances, because—after exchanging Pawns on the King's wing—he is bound to find an opportunity of sacrificing one or even both of his pieces for the remaining black Pawn. We saw in Chapter 2 that an ending with King and two Knights against the lone King cannot be won.

40. ......   Kt—K2
41. Kt—B3   Kt (2)—Q4
42. Kt—Kt5

Kt—K5 would have left Black's Knight on Kt5 with less mobility, and was thus probably preferable.

42. ......   Kt—B2
43. K—K3   Kt—B3
44. P—B4   P—R3
45. Kt—B3   K—B2
46. K—Q3   Kt—Q4

Black cannot advance his passed Pawn as long as his King is not close enough to defend it when attacked by White's King. In order to enable his King to occupy a square in the centre, so as to be ready to swing him to either wing, Reshevsky tries to advance his King's Pawn.

47. B—B1   Kt—B3
48. B—Kt2   Kt—Q2
49. B—R3?

He wants to prevent Kt—B4, after which the Knight's Pawn would threaten to run, supported by Kt—R5. But he should have stopped the approach of the Knight with 49. B—Q4, which at the same time put obstacles in the way of P—K4. Then the manœuvre K—K2—Q3 was not feasible on account of 50. B—Kt7 and Kt—R4. But Black might have tried the sacrifice P—K4! Then 50. B × P, Kt (Q) × B; 51. Kt × Kt ch, Kt × Kt would have lost for White,

on account of Black's outside passed Pawn. 51. P × Kt, K—K3; 52. K—K4, P—Kt5 was also hardly tenable for White. Even so 50. P × P, K—K3; 51. K—K4 was probably lost for White. P—Kt5; 52. B—Kt2 would have permitted Kt—B4 ch followed by Kt—R5 and P—Kt6. And 52. B—K3 would have lost on account of P—Kt6!; 53. K—Q3, Kt × P ch; 54. Kt × Kt, Kt × Kt ch; 55. K—B3, P—Kt7! The only drawing chance lay in 52. Kt—Q2 or B—R1, but the necessity for White's King to wander over to the Queen's wing would always have allowed Black access to the King's side Pawns, which, in the end, was likely to decide the game in his favour.

49. ......   P—K4!
50. K—K3   K—K3
51. B—Kt2   K—Q4!
52. Kt—R4   Kt—Kt3!

Note how the Knights co-operate.

53. B—B1   Kt—B5 ch
54. K—B2   Kt—Kt5!
55. K—K2   Kt—R7
56. B—Q2   P—Kt5

Now White cannot give up his Bishop for two Pawns, because Black remains with two Pawns as long as he is careful to prevent the exchange of his Rook's Pawn: 57. B × P, Kt × B; 58. Kt × P, P—K5, etc.

57. P × P   P—Kt6
58. K—Q1   Kt × P!

Not P—Kt7; 59. K—B2, Kt × B; 60. K × P, Kt—Kt5; 61. K—B3, etc.

59. Kt—Kt2

Kt × P, Kt × Kt; 60. B × P fails to draw, because Kt—K4; 61. B—B1, Kt × B; 62. K × Kt, Kt—B5 leads to mate through K—Q5—B6, etc., before one of the white Pawns queens.

59. ......   K—K5
60. P—R4   Kt—Q6
61. B—R5   Kt—Kt7 ch
62. Resigns.

GAME No. 17

White	Black
MIGUEL NAJDORF	REUBEN FINE

Fourth game of the match played at New York, 1949

1. P—Q4	Kt—KB3
2. P—QB4	P—K3
3. QKt—B3	B—Kt5
4. P—K3	P—QKt3
5. Kt—K2	B—Kt2
6. P—QR3	B—K2

With White's King's Knight on KB3 instead of K2, this would be the normal position of the Queen's Indian Defence, except that White here has his Pawn on QR3.

7. P—Q5

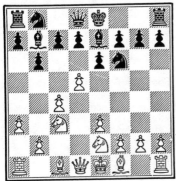

Diagram 232

The cramping effect of this move is so great that Najdorf considers it worth a developing tempo. The following six moves are taken up with Black's efforts at dislodging the advanced Pawn, and White's counter-measures designed to maintain it.

7.	Castles
8. Kt—Kt3	P—Q3
9. B—K2	P—B3
10. P—K4	Kt—R3
11. Castles	Kt—B2
12. R—K1!	

The Pawn is five times attacked and only four times defended, but

after 12. .... BP×P; 13. KP×P, P×P, White would regain the Pawn through B—B3, transposing into the position actually reached in the game.

12.	Q—Q2
13. B—B3	BP×P
14. KP×P	P×P
15. P×P	KR—K1
16. B—Kt5!	

To provoke the weakening move P—KR3. Black's position is bad. His Bishops are blocked, and attempts at exchanging pieces are difficult to realize.

16.	P—KR3
17. B—K3	B—KB1
18. Q—Q4	

Diagram 233

Black must now keep guarding against the threat B×P. After 19. B×P, KKt×P; 20. Kt—R5!, White would win at least a Pawn, apart from the fact that the Pawn-wall protecting Black's King would be broken.

18.	Kt—Kt4
19. Kt×Kt	Q×Kt
20. P—QR4!	Q—B4

The Queen cannot go back to Q2, because White would make the combination just indicated.

21. Q—Q2	Q—B2

22. KR—QB1!
Removing the Rook from the King's file, where it might be subject to exchange, without losing a tempo.

| 22. ...... | Q—Q1 |

23. P—R5
White first cleans up the Queen's wing, always carefully avoiding the exchange of Rooks, with the idea of throwing all his forces over to the King's wing, without leaving any Pawns on the other side which Black might counter-attack. The following skirmish is full of finesse:

23.	P × P
24. R × P	P—R3
25. P—Kt4	R—B1
26. KR—QR1	Q—B2
27. P—Kt5	P × P
28. R × P	R—R1
29. R—QB1	Q—Q2
30. KR—Kt1	B—R3
31. QR—Kt4	Q—Q1
32. B—Kt6	Q—Q2
33. B—Q4	Q—Q1

34. R—R1!
Pinning Black's Queen's Bishop and Rook to their places. To relieve the pin, Black brings his Knight over to the Queen's wing. This, however, weakens his defences on the King's side, and White attacks there with superior forces.

Diagram 234

| 34. ...... | Kt—Q2 |

35. P—R3 | **Kt—B4**
36. Kt—R5
Threatening 37. B × P, B × B; 38. R—KKt4.

| 36. ...... | P—B4 |
| 37. Kt—B4 | Q—Kt4 |

38. P—R4!
The final combination which wins perforce.

| 38. ...... | Q × P |

39. Kt—K6
Fine had forty minutes left in which to make the two moves to be completed within the time-limit. He used all but two seconds of his time, but, worn out by the strain, failed to see his only chance for a possible draw and sealed a move which lost a piece, after studying the position for fifty-six minutes.

39.	Q—K2
40. B × Kt	P × B
41. P—Q6	Q × P??
42. Q × Q	Resigns.

For after B × Q, 43. R—Kt6 wins a piece. Had he played 41. .... Q × Kt, Najdorf could have obtained hardly more than a draw by winning the Queen with 42. B—Q5, because of the rejoinder B—B5!! But his analysis during the adjournment period proved that 42. B × R! would have won: R × B; 43. R—Kt6, B—Kt2; 44. R × R, B × R; 45. P—Q7, Q × R; 46. P—Q8 (Q), Q × Q; 47. Q × Q, B—B3! (only move); 48. P—B3!, and Black cannot defend his Bishops' Pawns. A very exciting game.

GAME No. 18

| White | Black |
| MACHGIELIS EUWE | PAUL KERES |

Played in Rotterdam, 1940

1. P—Q4	Kt—KB3
2. P—QB4	P—K3
3. Kt—KB3	P—QKt3

4. P—KKt3	B—Kt2
5. B—Kt2	B—K2
6. Castles	Castles
7. Kt—B3	Kt—K5

If White arrived at playing P—K4, he would obtain control of so much more territory than Black that the latter would have a hard fight to equalize the position. That is why Black takes measures immediately against the threat 8. Q—B2 which would prepare P—K4. P—Q4 would then be answered by 9. Kt—K5, with advantage for White.

8. Q—B2	Kt × Kt
9. Q × Kt	P—Q3
10. Q—B2	P—KB4

Again preventing P—K4.

11. Kt—K1

White finally enforces the advance of the King's Pawn, but now it no longer increases his control of territory because Black can exchange the Pawn and open the Bishop's file for his Rook. At the same time White's Knight remains *déplacé* for quite some time.

11.	Q—B1
12. P—K4	Kt—Q2
13. P—Q5	

Diagram 235

If White wanted to demonstrate a weakness on Black's K3, he could have done this more effectively by first exchanging on B5: 13. P × P, P × P (R × P?, B—R3); 14. P—Q5, followed by an attempt at lodging the Knight at K6. The way White plays, he permits Black's Knight to occupy QB4 with a tempo and also to open his King's Bishop's file.

| 13. ...... | BP × P! |
| 14. Q × P | |

If B × P, Black wins a Pawn through Kt—B3 (15. B—Kt5?, Kt × P).

| 14. ...... | Kt—B4 |
| 15. Q—K2 | B—KB3! |

Preventing P—QKt4, increasing his Bishop's mobility, and preparing a beautifully exact combination to save his King's Pawn which White tries to win through B—R3.

16. B—R3	R—K1
17. B—K3	Q—Q1
18. B × Kt	P × P
19. B—K6 ch	K—R1
20. R—Q1	QP × B

MOBILE ROOK AND BISHOPS OUTCLASS
QUEEN AND KNIGHT

Everything clicks. White cannot play 21. P × P, because B × QP would follow. Thus Black remains with a passed Pawn, two powerful Bishops, and incidentally in possession of the open King's file in which White's Bishop is in danger unless he immediately proceeds with prophylactic measures. Strategically the game is already won for Keres. The tactical method in which he turns his positional advantage into a win illustrates the tremendous force of two Bishops most beautifully and instructively.

| 21. Kt—Kt2 | P—Q5 |
| 22. P—B4 (Diagram 236) | |

Attempting to anchor his Bishop on K6. But the advance of this Pawn gives Black an unexpected opportunity to attack White's King in the diagonal on which he is posted.

White's best defence would have been Kt—B4 followed by Q—Kt4.

| 22. | ...... | P—Q6!! |
| 23. | R × P | Q × R!! |

Diagram 236

A truly wonderful combination. Black's two Bishops and two Rooks prove far superior to White's Queen, Rook and Knight.

| 24. | Q × Q | B—Q5 ch |
| 25. | R—B2 | |

After K—R1 White would be defenceless against R × B, QR—K1 and R—K7.

| 25. | ...... | R × B |
| 26. | K—B1 | QR—K1! |

This is much stronger than winning back the exchange. White's Rook has hardly any mobility. It is therefore worth less than Black's Bishop, an important member of the force which now makes a mating assault.

| 27. | P—B5 | R—K4 |
| 28. | P—B6 | |

He intends to withdraw the Rook. But if he played R—Q2 immediately, Black could open the Knight's file through P—Kt3, with deadly effect.

| 28. | ...... | P × P |
| 29. | R—Q2 | B—B1!! |

Threatening to pin the Knight with B—R6 and to mate on K8.

30.	Kt—B4	R—K6
31.	Q—Kt1	R—B6 ch
32.	K—Kt2	R × Kt!

Keres opens the Knight's file in any case. The rest is silence.

33.	P × R	R—Kt1 ch
34.	K—B3	B—Kt5 ch
35.	K—K4	R—K1 ch
36.	K—Q5	B—B6 ch

and mate on the next move.

The assertion that two Bishops are preferable to Bishop and Knight must, of course, not be accepted categorically. The consideration of mobility must always remain uppermost in the mind of the player. The following game is one of the many examples which could be cited to illustrate this point.

GAME No. 19

White	Black
HERMAN STEINER	REUBEN FINE

Played in a match of four games, Washington, D.C., 1944

1.	P—Q4	Kt—KB3
2.	Kt—KB3	P—K3
3.	B—Kt5	

This move brings out the Bishop, but it is no doubt premature, because it gives Black the choice of a development in which the white Bishop is of no particular use on Kt5. At this stage White cannot know whether he may not later prefer the Bishop on B4 or Kt2 or K3, depending upon what course the opening takes.

| 3. | ...... | P—KR3 |

P—B4, which leaves the Pawn-formation in front of the King undisturbed, seems stronger.

| 4. | B × Kt | |

This exchange has arguments in favour and against it. In favour of it is the fact that Black's Queen will soon be driven back again either by White's King's Pawn or by his Queen's Knight, so that White will secure an appreciable advantage in development. Against it is the likelihood that the Bishop may come in handy in later operations against the weakened Rook's Pawn, in conjunction with an advance of White's Knight's Pawn to Kt5.

4.	Q×B
5. P—K4	P—B4
6. Kt—B3	P×P

Opening the Bishop's file and avoiding 7. P—K5 followed by 8. P—Q5.

| 7. P—K5 | Q—Q1 |
| 8. Q×P | |

White's advantage in development is impressive.

| 8. ...... | Kt—B3 |
| 9. Q—K3 | P—Q4 |

Otherwise R—Q1 would keep the Pawn backward.

10. P×P e.p.	B×P
11. Castles QR	Q—K2
12. K—Kt1	

KINGS ON OPPOSITE WINGS

A move which may turn out to be desirable in order not to have King and Queen in a diagonal in which the opponent can place a Bishop. But the move should only be made when actually necessary.

After all, the only compensation which White has for Black's two Bishops is his faster development. For this reason he should get his Bishop out, probably to Kt5. If then Castles, he could start his attack with P—KKt4. And if 12. B—Q2, he could have continued with 13. Kt—K4, B—B2; 14. Q—B3, to follow this up with Kt—B5.

12. Kt—K4, B—B2 and 13. P—KKt4 immediately was also to be considered.

| 12. ...... | B—B4 |
| 13. Q—K4 | B×P |

For White to offer the Pawn was courageous, but it seemed justified in view of the fact that Black was still in the developing stage. For Black to take the Pawn, on the other hand, was somewhat venturesome, if not reckless.

| 14. B—Kt5 | Castles |

Naturally, Black would like nothing better than to have White capture twice on B6, opening files on the Queen's side for Black's Rooks. But White initiates an energetic attack on the King's wing.

| 15. P—KKt4! | Q—B4 |

If P—B4, the free play which White obtains for his pieces with 16. P×P, P×P; 17. B—B4 ch, K—R2; 18. Q×Q, Kt×Q; 19. KR—B and Kt—K5 is well worth the Pawn.

| 16. KR—B1 | Q—K6 |

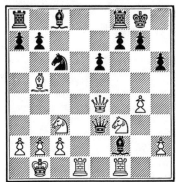

Diagram 237

17. R×B!!

An ingenious way of maintaining the attack.

| 17. ...... | Q×R |
| 18. P—Kt5 | P×P |

19. Kt×P   P—B4
Q—KB4; 20. Q—KR4, P—B3; 21. KKt—K4, Kt—K4; 22. P—KR3 or 21. .... Q—R2; 22. Q—Kt3, Kt—K2; 23. Q—B7 does not look promising for Black.

20. Q—QB4   Q×RP
No doubt Fine was waiting for an opportunity of returning his advantage in material when he could exchange pieces at the same time, for his Pawns on the King's side were apt to decide the ending in his favour. A number of fantastic variations might have occurred had White now continued with 21. Kt—Q5! Black could not have replied B—Q2 on account of 22. B×Kt, B×B; 23. Kt—K7 ch, K—R1; 24. Kt—Kt6 ch and Q×P ch, etc. If 21. .... Q—R4; 22. R—Kt1, B—Q2, White would again have won with 23. B×Kt, B×B; 24. Kt—K7 ch, for after K—R1; 25. Q—B1, the threat Kt×B and R—R1 could not be defended. 21. .... P×Kt; 22. Q×P ch, B—K3; 23. Q×B ch, K—R1; 24. Kt—B7 ch, R×Kt; 25. Q×R would still have been dangerous for Black, due to the exposed position of his King.

21. B×Kt   P×B
22. Q×BP
This looks murderous, as R—R1 is threatened, followed by R—R8 ch, K×R; Q—R1 ch and mate on R7. But here Fine sees his opportunity of simplifying matters by giving back the exchange.

22. ......   Q—R3!
23. Q×R
If R—Kt1, then R—Kt1; 24. Kt—Q5, R—Kt2 defends everything.

23. ......   Q—Kt
24. Q×P

RACING PASSED PAWNS

In this ending Black has the better prospects, because he has a more advanced Pawn than White. Also, the Bishop has greater defensive power than the Knight.

24. ......   P—B5
25. Kt—K4   Q—K4
26. R—Kt1   P—B6
27. P—R4

Later it becomes apparent that here P—Kt3 would have been better. But to foresee this over the board is almost impossible. The move of the text looks logical as it advances the Pawn on his queening mission.

27. ......   R—B2
28. Q—R8   Q—B2
29. Kt—Kt5

Threatening Q—K4. But Fine has a beautiful rejoinder.

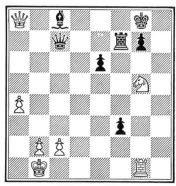

Diagram 238

29. ......   P—B7
30. R—KB1   Q—QB5
Had White played P—Kt3 on his 27th move, the following combination would not have been possible:

31. Q—R1   Q×R ch!!
32. Q×Q   B—R3
33. Q×B   P—B8 (Q) ch
34. Q×Q   R×Q ch
35. K—R2   R—B4!
Black must prevent P—R5. If 35. .... R—K8?, White wins with his connected passed Pawns: 36. P—R5,

R—K4; 37. P—Kt4, R×Kt; 38. P—R6, etc.

36. Kt × P	P—Kt4
37. Kt × P	

White aims at a 'book draw' with three Pawns against the Rook. He could have played 37. P—Kt4, P—Kt5; 38. P—R5, P—Kt6; 39. P—R6, etc., and drawn with Queen, Knight and Pawns against Queen and Rook.

37.	R × Kt
38. P—Kt4	K—B2
39. P—R5	R—Kt6
40. P—R6	K—K3
41. P—R7??	

Too bad to lose such a beautiful and exciting game through a blunder. P—Kt5 or P—B4 first and then P—Kt5 would have drawn, as the black King can never take the Bishop's Pawn and at the same time be in a position to stop the other Pawns from reaching the seventh rank. The result would be the odd draw discussed on p. 31.

41.	R—Kt1
42. P—Kt5	K—Q3
43. P—B4	K—B4
44. Resigns.	

GAME No. 20

White	Black
SAMUEL	EDWARD
RESHEVSKY	LASKER

Played at the International Masters' Tournament of Havana, 1952

1. P—Q4	P—Q4
2. P—QB4	P × P
3. Kt—KB3	Kt—KB3
4. P—K3	P—K3
5. B × P	P—B4
6. Castles	P—QR3
7. Q—K2	P—QKt4
8. B—Kt3	B—Kt2

Perhaps Kt—B3 offers Black better prospects. 9. R—Q1 might then be answered by P—B5; 10. B—B2, Kt—QKt5 and the exchange of the Knight against the Bishop. Without the latter, an attack initiated by the advance of White's King's Pawn would be less dangerous, and Black would have the better endgame with three against two Pawns on the Queen's wing. The argument in favour of 8. .... B—Kt2 is that in reply to 9. P—QR4 Black need not play P—Kt5, making White's QKt4 accessible to his Knight. Instead, he could answer 9. .... QKt—Q2, as upon 10. P×KtP, P×KtP; 11. R×R, Q×R; 12. Q×P he would regain the Pawn by capturing twice on KB6, which would at the same time weaken the stronghold of White's King.

9. Kt—B3	QKt—Q2

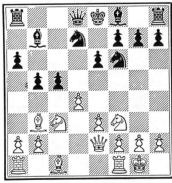

Diagram 239

9. .... Kt—B3 would provoke a violent attack at this early stage: 10. R—Q1, Q—B2; 11. P—Q5!, P×P; 12. P—K4! Then neither 12. .... P—Q5; 13. Kt—Q5, Kt×Kt; 14. P×Kt ch, Kt—K2; 15. Kt—K5, P—B5; 16. B—B4, P×B; 17. QR—B1, Q—Q3; 18. R×P, nor 12. .... Castles; 13. P×P, Kt—QKt5; 14. P—QR4, P—B5; 15. P×P, P×B; 16. P×P would lead to a position anyone would like to defend.

10. R—Q1	Q—B2

Reshevsky studied this position for fully forty minutes, probably analysing the consequences of 11. P—K4, P—Kt5; 12. P—K5. He finally chose calm development instead:

11. **B—Q2**	**B—K2**
12. **QR—B1**	**Q—Kt3**
13. **B—B2**	

Planning P×P and P—K4 without getting his Bishop exchanged.

| 13. ...... | **Castles** |
| 14. **P—QR3** | |

He had to guard against P—Kt5 before pushing his King's Pawn.

I considered 14. .... P×P, naturally not with the idea of winning a Pawn, in reply to 15. P×P, by exchanging my excellently placed Bishop for White's King's Knight and then exposing my Queen to attack in the Queen's file, but in order to produce an isolated Pawn, a most desirable target *if* I could survive the attack which White could launch with almost all of his pieces co-operating, since even one or both of his Rooks could be brought over to the King's wing via the third rank. I concluded that this was much too dangerous and continued development:

| 14. ...... | **KR—Q1** |
| 15. **P×P** | **Q×P!** |

Kt×P Reshevsky could have answered favourably with P—K4, which would have been equally strong after first playing P—QKt4, in case I recaptured with my Bishop. Reshevsky had evidently considered only these two alternatives, for he thought again a long time before replying. My Queen can now get to the King's wing faster than his, and, with my minor pieces developed as well as his, I felt certain that I could work up an attack.

16. **Kt—K4**	**Q—R4**
17. **Kt—Kt3**	**B×Kt**
18. **P×B**	**Q—R6**

Diagram 240

White has two Bishops and an open Knight's file in which to deploy his Rooks. On the other hand, his King is under close observation by the black Queen, and her minor pieces can come to her aid rather quickly. The decisive question is who will come first.

19. **K—R1**	**Kt—K4**
20. **B—B3**	**Kt—Kt3**
21. **P—B4**	**Kt—R5**
22. **R—KKt1**	**R—QB1!**

Diagram 241

I am threatening 22. .... R×B!; 23. P×R, R—Q7!! for if 24. Q×R, the mate threat Kt—B6 wins the Queen, and if 24. Q—B1, the mate threat Kt—Kt5 can be defended only by 25. R—Kt2, as Q×Q would allow

mate by Kt×BP! After 25. ....
Kt×R; 26. Q×R, Q×Q ch; 27.
K×Q, Kt×P ch!, followed by
R×B, I would then have emerged
with a piece and a Pawn ahead!
Of course, it was Reshevsky's turn,
and although R—B1 looked like an
innocent developing move, I assumed
when I decided upon making it, that
he would see all the vicious threats
which it implied, although he had
used so much time during the opening that he had only four minutes
left for the eighteen moves he had to
complete before time control. I
still had sixteen minutes, but after
more than four and a half hours of
exhausting concentration I found
myself compelled to calculate
through combinations very slowly to
avoid gross blunders, and I abstained
from trying to analyse a tempting
alternative which I saw just when I
reached for my Queen's Rook. This
was 22. .... Kt—Kt5, which I
thought would force P—B3, permitting Kt×BP. But I would have
been lost immediately, as 23. Kt—B1
would have defended the mate
threat, attacked my Knight, and
threatened to win my Queen with
24. R—Kt3!

23. P—B3   Kt—Q4
This holds back P—K4, threatens
to exchange one of White's powerful
Bishops, and prepares B—B3.

24. B—R5   R—K1
Not R—Q2, because of B×P ch!

25. B—Q2
Again Reshevsky had prepared the
push of his King's Pawn. He had
made the last three moves rapidly,
glancing at his clock, not without
apprehension, and I was wondering
whether he had considered the reply
25. .... B—B3, which, now that his
Bishop had relinquished the long
diagonal, looked very strong. I calculated: 25. .... B—B3, 26. P—K4,

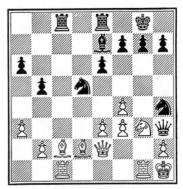

Diagram 242

B×P; 27. P×Kt, B×R; 28. B×B,
P×P. His Queen is then attacked,
and, as she must keep his Bishop
defended, his Bishop's Pawn must
fall. 29. Q—Q3, threatening Q×P
ch, would not help, as after Kt×P
my Rook's Pawn is defended and
Q×P mate as well as Kt×R is
threatened. Meeting both threats
with 30. R—Kt2 would lose a whole
Rook through Q×R! ch; 31. K×Q,
Kt—K8 ch.

If White recaptured on the 28th
move with R×B instead of B×B and
answered P×P with 29. Q—B2, the
advance of the Queen's Pawn would
quickly win: 29. .... P—Q5; 30.
B—Q3, for example, would not be
possible because of R×R ch, followed by R—K8 ch!, etc.

I was elated and wanted to go over
these variations once more, when I
saw to my horror that I had also used
all but four minutes of my time. I
quickly grabbed my Bishop and
moved him—to Q3 instead of B3, a
square that I had not even remotely
considered! Such a thing had never
happened to me, even though in the
fifth playing hour Bishops had on
occasion moved in my mind like
Knights, and vice versa, when the
excitement of time pressure para-
lysed reasoning power.

The beautiful game was lost,
probably even without the blunders

I continued making in the mad race with the clock, while Reshevsky never faltered:

26. Kt—K4!   Kt—B4

Otherwise R—Kt3 or Kt—Kt5 ends all.

27. Kt×B   Kt×Kt
28. P—K4   Kt—K2
29. R—Kt3   Q—R4??

Q—R5 and Kt—Kt3 was the only way out.

30. Q—Kt2   P—Kt3
31. B—Kt4!   Kt—B5
32. R—R3   Resigns

Well, after calming down, I consoled myself with the thought that of all the games I had ever lost this was probably the best, and that the relentless ticking of the clock had found victims even among the greatest masters of the game.

INDEX